Study Guide

Networking Fundamentals

Second Edition

JoAnne Keltner

SO-ACM-375

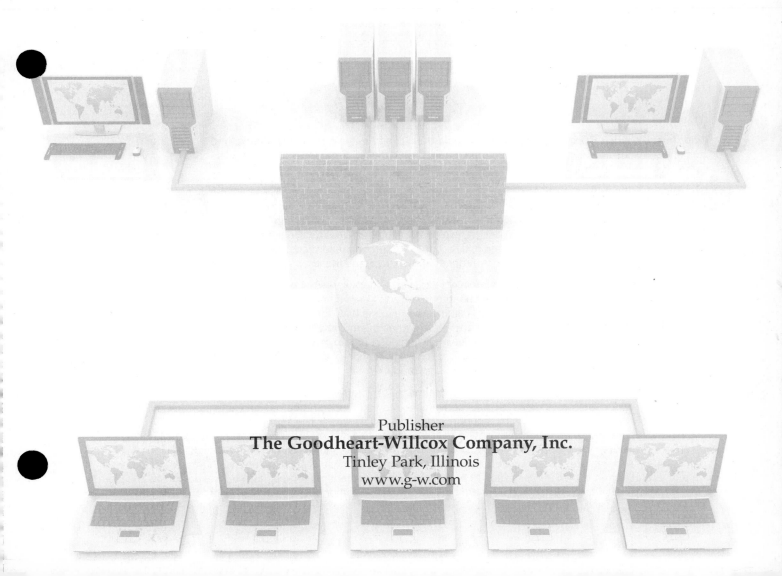

Publisher
The Goodheart-Willcox Company, Inc.
Tinley Park, Illinois
www.g-w.com

Copyright © 2012

by

The Goodheart-Willcox Company, Inc.

Previous edition copyright 2005

All rights reserved. No part of this work may be reproduced, stored, or transmitted in any form
or by any electronic or mechanical means, including information storage and retrieval systems,
without the prior written permission of The Goodheart-Willcox Company, Inc.

Manufactured in the United States of America.

ISBN 978-1-60525-357-2

1 2 3 4 5 6 7 8 9–12–16 15 14 13 12 11

The Goodheart-Willcox Company, Inc. Brand Disclaimer: Brand names, company names, and illustrations for
products and services included in this text are provided for educational purposes only and do not represent or imply
endorsement or recommendation by the author or the publisher.

The Goodheart-Willcox Company, Inc. Safety Notice: The reader is expressly advised to carefully read, understand,
and apply all safety precautions and warnings described in this book or that might also be indicated in undertaking the
activities and exercises described herein to minimize risk of personal injury or injury to others. Common sense and good
judgment should also be exercised and applied to help avoid all potential hazards. The reader should always refer to the
appropriate manufacturer's technical information, directions, and recommendations; then proceed with care to follow
specific equipment operating instructions. The reader should understand these notices and cautions are not exhaustive.

The publisher makes no warranty or representation whatsoever, either expressed or implied, including but not limited
to equipment, procedures, and applications described or referred to herein, their quality, performance, merchantability,
or fitness for a particular purpose. The publisher assumes no responsibility for any changes, errors, or omissions
in this book. The publisher specifically disclaims any liability whatsoever, including any direct, indirect, incidental,
consequential, special, or exemplary damages resulting, in whole or in part, from the reader's use or reliance upon
the information, instructions, procedures, warnings, cautions, applications, or other matter contained in this book. The
publisher assumes no responsibility for the activities of the reader.

The Goodheart-Willcox Company, Inc. Internet Disclaimer: The Internet resources and listings in this Goodheart-
Willcox Publisher product are provided solely as a convenience to you. These resources and listings were reviewed
at the time of publication to provide you with accurate, safe, and appropriate information. Goodheart-Willcox Publisher
has no control over the referenced Web sites and, due to the dynamic nature of the Internet, is not responsible or liable
for the content, products, or performance of links to other Web sites or resources. Goodheart-Willcox Publisher makes
no representation, either expressed or implied, regarding the content of these Web sites, and such references do not
constitute an endorsement or recommendation of the information or content presented. It is your responsibility to take all
protective measures to guard against inappropriate content, viruses, or other destructive elements.

Table of Contents

Copyright by Goodheart-Willcox Co., Inc.

Copyright by Goodheart-Willcox Co., Inc.

Introduction

This *Study Guide* is designed to help you review the terminology and concepts presented in *Networking Fundamentals* by Richard M. Roberts. It will also help prepare you for the CompTIA Network+ Certification exam. It is divided into two sections: Chapter Review and CompTIA Network+ Reference.

The first half of this *Study Guide*, Chapter Review, serves as a review of the key terminology and concepts presented in the *Networking Fundamentals* textbook and those you will encounter on the CompTIA Network+ Certification exam. The introduction of each Chapter Review lists the tasks you should be able to do and the concepts you should be familiar with to successfully complete the CompTIA Network+ Certification exam. The practice exercises are grouped according to related terms and concepts found in the corresponding chapter. They consist of filling in the blank, matching, and labeling. Some practice exercises ask that you derive an answer from the information given, such as converting a given decimal number to a binary number, dividing an assigned IP address into subnets, or determining a distinguished name from a directory map.

The second half of this *Study Guide*, CompTIA Network+ Reference, presents one topic related to a specific CompTIA Network+ Certification exam objective per page. At the top of each page, the featured topic is described, followed by an illustration or a table that will better enable you to remember the key points related to the topic. Also, a list of related topics is presented to help you draw associations between them and the featured topic. At the bottom of the page is the related CompTIA Network+ Objective.

This *Study Guide*, when used as a supplement to the *Networking Fundamentals* textbook, will help you successfully complete a course in networking fundamentals and will increase your ability to pass the CompTIA Network+ Certification exam.

Copyright by Goodheart-Willcox Co., Inc.

Name _____ Date _____ Period _____

Introduction to Networking

Introduction

For the Network+ Certification exam, you should be able to identify the major network topologies, differentiate between common network devices, recall the function of common network protocols, and recall the function of each OSI model layer. You should also be familiar with network models and related terminology.

Practice 1.1

Label the network topologies.

bus	hierarchical star	hybrid	mesh
ring	star	tree	

a. _____   e. _____   f. _____

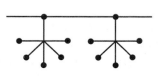

b. _____

c. _____

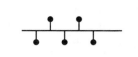

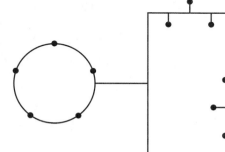

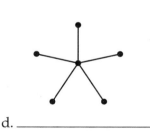

d. _____   g. _____

Practice 1.2

Fill in the blanks for the statements about the network topologies.

access port	backbone	cells	hub
network topology	node	terminating resistor	wireless topology

1. The physical arrangement of computers, computer-related devices, communications devices, and cabling in a network is referred to as _____.

2. A(n) _____ is any device attached to the network that is capable of processing and forwarding data.

3. The bus topology is often used as a(n) _____ to link other topologies.

4. A bus topology requires a(n) _____ at each cable end to absorb the signals when they reach the end of the bus.

5. In a star topology, cables connect each node to a(n) _____ on a hub or switch.

6. The _____ does not use cables to communicate between nodes.

7. In wireless communications, towers are configured throughout an area and divide the area into zones called _____.

8. The star topology uses a(n) _____ as a common electrical connection to all nodes in the topology.

1. _____

2. _____

3. _____

4. _____

5. _____

6. _____

7. _____

8. _____

Practice 1.3

Match the network classification to its definition.

1. _____ LAN

2. _____ MAN

3. _____ WAN

a. A network that consists of two or more LANs connected with private or public communications lines within the same geographic area, such as a city or a university campus. It is managed by a single entity.

b. A network that is usually confined to a single building and is managed by a single entity such as a company.

c. A network that consists of a large number of networks and PCs connected with private and public communications lines throughout many geographic areas.

Copyright by Goodheart-Willcox Co., Inc.

Practice 1.4

Fill in the blanks for the statements about the network models in illustrations *A* and *B*.

centralized	client/server	database server	decentralized
dedicated server	file server	peer-to-peer	print server

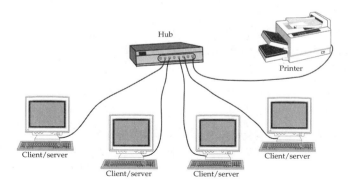

A

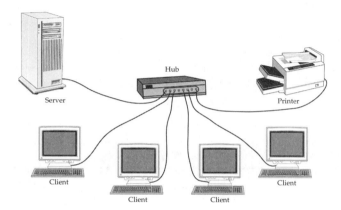

B

1. The network in illustration *A* is an example of a(n) _____ network.

2. The network in illustration *B* is an example of a(n) _____ network.

3. The methodology used to administer a client/server network is called _____ administration.

4. The methodology used to administer a peer-to-peer network is called _____ administration.

5. A(n) _____ is used to store data files that can be accessed by a client.

6. A(n) _____ coordinates printing activities between clients and printers.

7. A(n) _____ contains data files and software programs that query the data.

8. A server that serves a single function is referred to as a(n) _____.

1. _____

2. _____

3. _____

4. _____

5. _____

6. _____

7. _____

8. _____

Copyright by Goodheart-Willcox Co., Inc.

Practice 1.5

Fill in the blanks for the statements about network communications.

connectionless-oriented	connection-oriented	driver	logical identification
MAC address	operating system	protocol	

1. Microsoft Windows Server 2008 is an example of a(n) _____.

   1. _____

2. A direct connection between a source and destination computer is referred to as _____.

   2. _____

3. A connection between a source and destination computer that is not a direct connection is referred to as _____.

   3. _____

4. A(n) _____ is a group of software programs that handle packet formatting and control data transmission.

   4. _____

5. A(n) _____ is a software program that allows a computer to communicate with and transfer data to and from computer hardware.

   5. _____

6. The physical ID of a network card is called a(n) _____.

   6. _____

7. A name used to uniquely identify a computer on a network is called _____.

   7. _____

Practice 1.6

Fill in the blanks for the statements about network protocols.

ATM	FIR	NetBIOS	TCP/IP	LLDP

1. One of the specifications of the _____ protocol is limiting network device names to 15 characters.

   1. _____

2. The _____ protocol was developed for DARPA to communicate over the Internet.

   2. _____

3. The _____ protocol is a wireless protocol that uses Infrared technology to transmit data.

   3. _____

4. The _____ allows network devices to automatically exchange information.

   4. _____

5. The _____ protocol was designed for transmitting data, voice, and video.

   5. _____

Copyright by Goodheart-Willcox Co., Inc.

Practice 1.7

Match the name of the network device to its definition.

1. _____ active hub
2. _____ bridge
3. _____ brouter
4. _____ gateway
5. _____ media converter
6. _____ multilayer switch
7. _____ multistation access unit
8. _____ network interface card
9. _____ passive hub
10. _____ repeater
11. _____ router
12. _____ switch

a. Allows for the quick connection and disconnection of Token Ring cables while maintaining the logic of the ring topology.
b. Contains the electronic components needed to send and receive a digital signal.
c. Makes decisions about routing a packet based on packet content.
d. Amplifies or reshapes a weak signal into its original strength and form.
e. Acts only as a central connection point for network cables.
f. Acts as a central connection point for network cables and regenerates digital signals like a repeater.
g. Connects the local area network to the Internet.
h. Changes one type of electrical signal into another or interfaces one cable type to another.
i. Divides the network into smaller segments, reducing the chance of collisions.
j. Filters network traffic or creates subnetworks from a larger network.
k. Navigates packets across large networks, such as the Internet, using the most efficient route.
l. Combines router and bridge functions.

Practice 1.8

Match the standard or organization to its definition.

1. _____ ANSI
2. _____ CERN
3. _____ EIA
4. _____ IEEE
5. _____ ISO
6. _____ TIA
7. _____ UL
8. _____ W3C

a. A standards maintenance organization mainly concerned with fiber optics, user equipment, wireless communications, and satellite communications.
b. Developed the OSI model and is interested in the standardization of computer equipment.
c. Provides recommendations for Web page language standards.
d. Responsible for the original development of the World Wide Web.
e. Prompts voluntary conformity and standardization.
f. Tests products and materials for safety standards.
g. Concerned with radio communications.
h. Continually develops standards for the networking and communications industry.

Practice 1.9

Match the network device layer to its definition.

1. _____ layer 1 device
2. _____ layer 2 device
3. _____ layer 3 device

a. Makes decisions about where a packet is sent based on a MAC address or a logical name.
b. Makes no decision about where a packet is sent.
c. Makes a decision about where a packet is sent based on a protocol such as the Internet Protocol.

Practice 1.10

Label the layers of the OSI model. Beside each layer, write a brief description.

application	data link	network	physical
presentation	session	transport	

Layer 7	
a. _____	_____
Layer 6	
b. _____	_____
Layer 5	
c. _____	_____
Layer 4	
d. _____	_____
Layer 3	
e. _____	_____
Layer 2	
f. _____	_____
Layer 1	
g. _____	_____

Copyright by Goodheart-Willcox Co., Inc.

Name _____ Date _____

Period _____

Network Media— Copper Core Cable

Introduction

For the Network+ Certification exam, you should be able to categorize the IEEE 802.3 classifications and recall their characteristics. Also, be prepared to categorize network cables, identify network connectors, and differentiate between wiring standards.

Practice 2.1

Label the electrical signals. The following terms can be used more than once.

amplitude	cycle	time	voltage

b. _____

a. _____

c. _____

d. One _____

e. _____

f. One _____

Practice 2.2

Determine the frequency and amplitude of the following analog and digital signals.

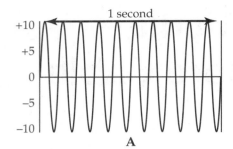

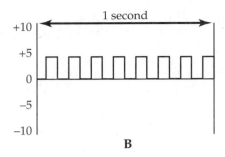

1. The frequency of the analog signal in illustration *A* is _____ Hz.

2. The frequency of the digital signal in illustration *B* is _____ Hz.

3. The amplitude of the analog signal in illustration *A* is _____ volts.

4. The amplitude of the digital signal in illustration *B* is _____ volts.

1. _____

2. _____

3. _____

4. _____

Practice 2.3

Fill in the blanks for the statements about electrical characteristics.

attenuation	crosstalk	interference	latency
noise	Time to Live		

1. A loss of signal strength is referred to as _____.

2. An undesired electromagnetic signal imposed on a desired signal is called _____.

3. Interference that comes from neighboring conductors inside a wire's insulating jacket is called _____.

4. The amount of time it takes a signal to travel from its source to its destination is called _____.

5. If a signal exceeds the allocated _____, it is removed from the network to prevent it from circulating forever.

6. Another name for electromagnetic interference is _____.

1. _____

2. _____

3. _____

4. _____

5. _____

6. _____

Copyright by Goodheart-Willcox Co., Inc.

Practice 2.4

Fill in the blanks for the statements about data transmission. The following terms can be used more than once.

bandwidth	Baseband	Broadband	simplex
full-duplex	half-duplex		

1. The _____ of analog transmission can support several frequencies at once.

2. When a digital signal is transmitted over a cable, it uses the entire _____.

3. The method of transmitting data in the form of several analog signals at the same time is referred to as _____.

4. The method of transmitting data in the form of a digital signal, using the entire bandwidth of a cable is referred to as _____.

5. The bi-directional communication that occurs between two devices simultaneously is _____ communication.

6. Communication that occurs in one direction only is _____ communication.

7. Bi-directional communication that occurs in one direction at a time is _____ communication.

1. _____

2. _____

3. _____

4. _____

5. _____

6. _____

7. _____

Practice 2.5

Fill in the blanks for the statements about electronic terms.

decibel	impedance	magnetic induction
reflected loss	resistance	

1. The opposition to direct current is _____, whereas the opposition to alternating current is _____.

2. The amount of signal reflected from the end of a cable is _____.

3. An electrical phenomenon in which the magnetic field encircling a current-carrying conductor induces current in a conductor of close proximity is _____.

4. A(n) _____ is a unit of measurement that expresses the relationship of power between two electrical forces.

1. _____

2. _____

3. _____

4. _____

Copyright by Goodheart-Willcox Co., Inc.

Practice 2.6

Fill in the blanks for the statements about crosstalk.

Alien Crosstalk	Equal Level Far-End Crosstalk	Far-End Crosstalk	Near-End Crosstalk

1. The measurement of reflected loss at the near end, or input end, of a cable is _____.

2. A measurement of reflective loss at the far end, or output end, of a cable is _____.

3. A measurement calculated by subtracting the effects of attenuation from the FEXT measurement is _____.

4. A measurement of the noise introduced outside the cable jacket, typically caused by other network cables in close proximity is _____.

1. _____

2. _____

3. _____

4. _____

Practice 2.7

Label the parts of each cable.

braided copper shield	copper core	dielectric	foil shield
insulating jacket	insulating outer jacket	plastic spine	twisted pair

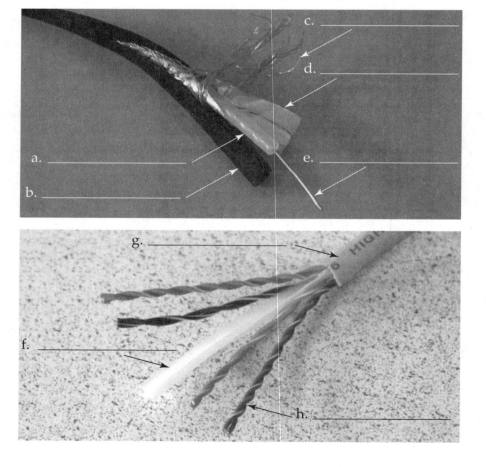

c. _____

d. _____

a. _____

b. _____

e. _____

g. _____

f. _____

h. _____

Copyright by Goodheart-Willcox Co., Inc.

Practice 2.8

Identify the following connector types.

BNC	F-type	RJ-45

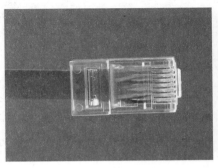  

a. _____ b. _____ c. _____

Practice 2.9

Match the media type to its definition.

1. _____ coaxial cable
2. _____ RG-58
3. _____ RG-6
4. _____ RG-8
5. _____ STP
6. _____ twisted pair
7. _____ UTP

a. Twisted pair cable in which shielding is applied to the entire cable assembly or to individual cable pairs.
b. Twisted pair cable that does not contain shielding.
c. Also known as Thinnet.
d. Also known as Thicknet.
e. Consists of a copper core conductor surrounded by an insulator, shield, and insulating jacket.
f. Standard cable for CATV and satellite systems.
g. Consists of four pairs of twisted conductors.

Practice 2.10

Fill in the chart for the given categories of twisted pair cable.

Category	Maximum Frequency Rating	Data Rate
Category 3	_____ MHz	_____ Mbps
		_____ Mbps
Category 4	_____ MHz	_____ Mbps
Category 5	_____ MHz	_____ Mbps (2 pair)
		_____ Mbps (4 pair)
Category 5e	_____ MHz	_____ Mbps (2 pair)
		_____ Mbps (4 pair)
Category 6	_____ MHz	_____ Gbps (4 pair)
Category 6a	_____ MHz	_____ Gbps (4 pair)
Category 7	_____ MHz	_____ Gbps (4 pair)

Copyright by Goodheart-Willcox Co., Inc.

Practice 2.11

Fill in the data rate and category (10 Mbps, Fast Ethernet, Gigabit Ethernet, and 10 Gigabit Ethernet) of the following 802.3 classifications.

Classification	Data Rate	Category
10BaseT		
100BaseT4		
100BaseTX		
1000BaseCX		
1000BaseT		
10GBaseT		

Practice 2.12

Label the specifications of the network in the illustration.

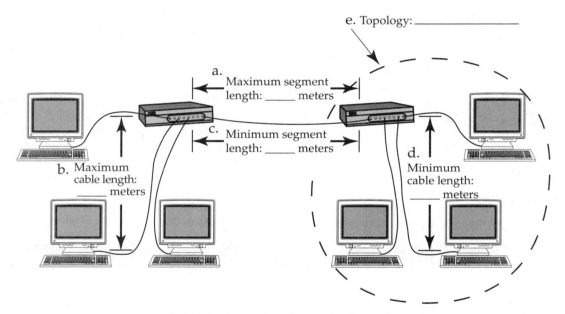

10BaseT, 100BaseTX, 100BaseT4, or 1000BaseT Network

Copyright by Goodheart-Willcox Co., Inc.

Practice 2.13

Fill in the blanks for the statements about 802.3 wiring and connections.

Automatic Medium-Dependent Interface Crossover (Auto-MDIX)		crossover cable
Power over Ethernet (PoE) RJ-45 rollover cable		straight-through cable

1. A(n) _____ is a special cable where the pin order is completely reversed on one end of the cable.

1. _____

2. A(n) _____ allows a transmit signal from one computer to be sent to the receive pins of a network card on the other computer.

2. _____

3. A(n) _____ is constructed with each numbered pin connecting to the matching numbered pin on the opposite end of the cable.

3. _____

4. An electronic chip technology incorporated into Gigabit Ethernet devices to automatically reassign pin functions and eliminate the need for a crossover cable is _____.

4. _____

5. 8P8C is another name for _____.

5. _____

6. The _____ IEEE standard specifies the supply of small amounts of electrical power to network devices such as cameras, IP phones, Wireless Access Points, speakers, and phone or PDA chargers.

6. _____

Practice 2.14

Color the twisted pair conductors according to the indicated color standard.

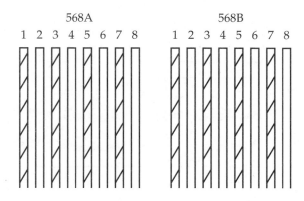

Practice 2.15

Fill in the blanks for the statements about wiring faults.

ground	open	short

1. A(n) _____ occurs in cabling when two conductors are improperly connected, resulting in a shorter circuit path.

2. A(n) _____ occurs when the length of a conductor has an open spot.

3. A(n) _____ occurs when a conductor connects to the earth through a continuous path.

1. _____

2. _____

3. _____

Practice 2.16

Label the common twisted pair wiring errors.

crossed pairs	normal	reversed pair	split pair

a. _____

b. _____

c. _____

d. _____

Copyright by Goodheart-Willcox Co., Inc.

3

Fiber-Optic Cable

Introduction

For the Network+ Certification exam, you should be able to recall the characteristics of fiber-optic cable types, categorize IEEE 802.3 classifications that specify fiber-optic cable and recall their characteristics, and identify fiber-optic connectors.

Practice 3.1

Place a check mark next to each statement that states an advantage of fiber-optic cable.

1. _____ Provides for data security.
2. _____ Resistive to breaks and bends in the fiber-optic core.
3. _____ Immune to electromagnetic interference.
4. _____ Lightweight and small in diameter.
5. _____ Safety.
6. _____ Does not require a high level of expertise to install a connector.
7. _____ Wide bandwidth.
8. _____ Corrosion- and water-resistant.
9. _____ Supports data transmission over longer distances than copper core cable.

Practice 3.2

Match the fiber-optic cable transmission characteristic to its definition.

1. _____ dispersion
2. _____ extrinsic losses
3. _____ Fresenel reflection loss
4. _____ scattering

a. The loss of signal strength due to impurities in the core material.
b. The distortion of a light wave as it reflects off the core cladding.
c. A type of signal loss that commonly occurs at connection points in fiber-optic cabling and is due to refraction property differences in the core material, the connector materials used for sealing the connector, and air.
d. Signal losses caused by physical factors outside the normal core, such as splices, connectors, and bends in the fiber core.

Practice 3.3

Label the fiber-optic cable.

buffer	cladding	glass or plastic core	sheath

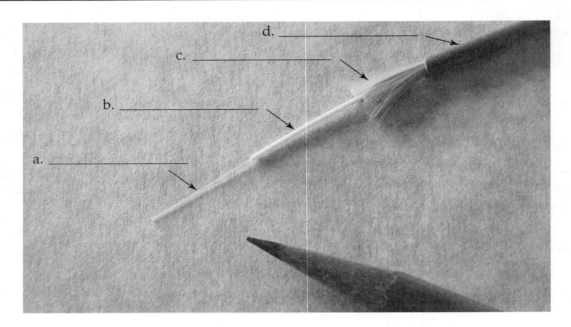

a. _____

b. _____

c. _____

d. _____

Copyright by Goodheart-Willcox Co., Inc.

Practice 3.4

Fill in the blanks for the statements about single-mode and multimode fiber-optic cable. The following terms may be used more than once.

graded-index	multimode	single-mode	step-index

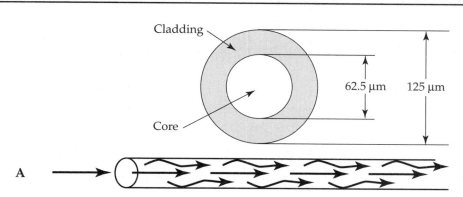

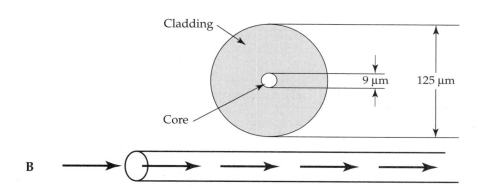

1. The fiber-optic cable in illustration *A* is an example of _____.   1. _____

2. The fiber-optic cable in illustration *B* is an example of _____.   2. _____

3. _____ fiber-optic cable has a large core diameter and is susceptible to attenuation due to dispersion.   3. _____

4. The core of _____ fiber-optic cable is designed to closely match the wavelength of the light signal.   4. _____

5. _____ fiber-optic cable can carry light farther than _____ fiber-optic cable.   5. _____

_____

6. _____ multimode fiber-optic cable is designed with a varying grade of core material.   6. _____

7. _____ multimode fiber-optic cable is a general multimode fiber-optic cable that does not counter dispersion.   7. _____

Practice 3.5

Fill in the chart for the given IEEE 802.3 classifications.

IEEE 802.3 Classification	Single-Mode (S) or Multimode (M)	Core Diameter in Microns	Wavelength	Cable Distance
10BaseFL	_____	_____ _____	_____ nm	_____ m
100BaseFX	_____	_____ _____	_____ nm	_____ m
1000BaseSX	_____	_____ _____	_____ nm	_____ m
1000BaseLX	M	_____ _____	_____ nm	_____ m
1000BaseLX	S	_____ _____	_____ nm	_____ km
10GBaseSR	_____	_____ _____	_____ nm	_____ – _____ m
10GBaseLR	_____	_____	_____ nm	_____ km
10GBaseER	_____	_____	_____ nm	_____ km
10GBaseSW	_____	_____ _____	_____ nm	_____ m _____ m
10GBaseLW	_____	_____	_____ nm	_____ m
10GBaseEW	_____	_____	_____ nm	_____ m

Copyright by Goodheart-Willcox Co., Inc.

Practice 3.6

Record the specifications of the FDDI network in the illustration.

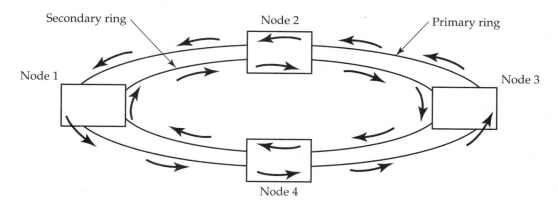

a. Topology: _____

b. Acess Method: _____

c. Data rate: _____

d. FDDI single-mode cable distance: _____

e. FDDI multimode cable distance: _____

f. FDDI single-mode core diameter: _____

g. FDDI multimode core diameter: _____

Practice 3.7

Label the fiber-optic connectors.

FC	LC	MTRJ	SC	ST

a. _____

b. _____

c. _____

d. _____

e. _____

Copyright by Goodheart-Willcox Co., Inc.

4

Wireless Technology

Introduction

For the Network+ Certification exam, you should be able to compare the characteristics of IEEE 802.11, authentication, and encryption wireless standards. You should also be able to implement a basic wireless network.

Practice 4.1

Fill in the blanks for the statements about radio and microwave transmission.

carrier wave	channel	demodulation
modulation	receiver	transmitter

1. A _____ is an electromagnetic wave of a set frequency that is used to carry data.

1. _____

2. The process of mixing a data signal with a carrier wave is _____.

2. _____

3. The process of separating a data signal from a carrier wave is _____.

3. _____

4. A _____ generates a carrier wave and modulates the data signal into the carrier wave.

4. _____

5. A _____ receives the modulated signal and demodulates it.

5. _____

6. The bandwidth of a carrier wave is referred to as a _____.

6. _____

Copyright by Goodheart-Willcox Co., Inc.

Practice 4.2

Label the ISM band with related frequencies and 802.11 wireless standards.

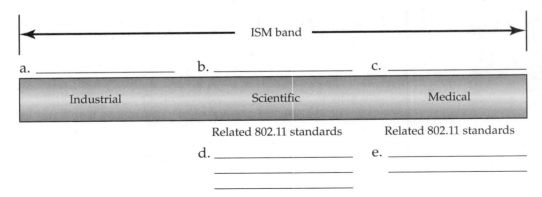

ISM band

a. _____   b. _____   c. _____

Industrial   Scientific   Medical

Related 802.11 standards   Related 802.11 standards

d. _____   e. _____

_____   _____

_____

Practice 4.3

Label the antenna styles.

dipole	flat panel	omni	parabolic	yagi

a. _____

b. _____

c. _____

d. _____

e. _____

Copyright by Goodheart-Willcox Co., Inc.

Practice 4.4

Label the transmission techniques.

direct sequencing spread spectrum (DSSS)   **frequency hopping spread spectrum (FHSS)**

orthogonal frequency-division multiplexing (OFDM)

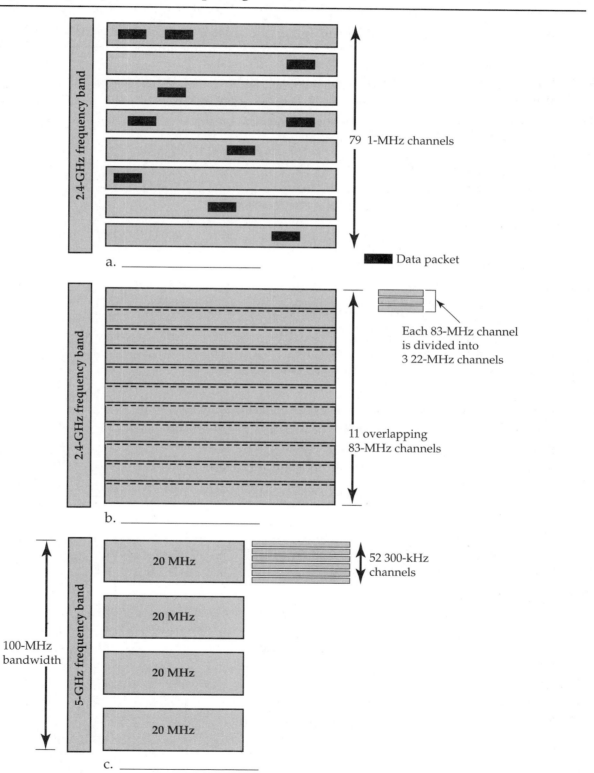

a. _____

b. _____

c. _____

Copyright by Goodheart-Willcox Co., Inc.

Practice 4.5

Fill in the blanks for the statements about data transmission techniques. The following terms may be used more than once.

direct sequencing	direct sequencing spread spectrum (DSSS)	frequency hopping
frequency hopping spread spectrum (FHSS)	Multiple Input Multiple Output (MIMO)	
orthogonal frequency-division multiplexing (OFDM)		spatial multiplexing

1. The spread spectrum technique that transmits data on multiple channels simultaneously is called _____.

2. The spread spectrum technique that transmits data on multiple channels sequentially is called _____.

3. Frequency hopping is also referred to as _____.

4. In the _____ transmission technique, data packets hop from one channel to another in a set pattern determined by a software algorithm.

5. The _____ transmission technique is limited to a maximum of a 2-Mbps data rate.

6. Direct sequencing is also referred to as _____.

7. Most vendors use the _____ transmission technique at 11 Mbps for wireless network systems.

8. The data rates for _____ are 11 Mbps and 33 Mbps. The 33 Mbps is a result of using all three 22-Mbps channels at the same time.

9. The _____ transmission technique uses the 5-GHz frequency and can achieve data rates as high as 54 Mbps.

10. In the _____ transmission technique, each channel is broadcast separately and is referred to as multiplexed.

11. Transmitting two or more streams of data in the same frequency channel is referred to as _____.

12. The networking technology that uses two or more streams of data transmission to increase data throughput and the range of the wireless network is _____.

1. _____

2. _____

3. _____

4. _____

5. _____

6. _____

7. _____

8. _____

9. _____

10. _____

11. _____

12. _____

Copyright by Goodheart-Willcox Co., Inc.

Practice 4.6

Label the wireless network arrangements.

ad hoc mode	infrastructure mode

a. _____

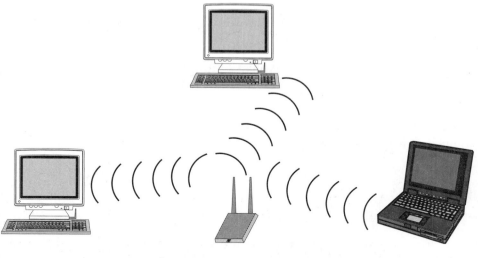

b. _____

Practice 4.7

Fill in the blanks for the statements about wireless networking. Not all of the following terms will be used.

BSS	CSMA/CA	CSMA/CD	dipole
ESSID	IBSS	omni	overlap area
room	security	speed	SSID
Wireless Access Point (WAP)	yagi		

1. All IEEE 802.11 networks use the _____ access method.

2. A Wireless Access Point (WAP) has a(n) _____-type antenna.

3. A(n) _____ is similar to a Windows workgroup name or a domain name.

4. One of the greatest concerns or disadvantages of a wireless network is _____.

5. For computers to communicate with each other in an ad hoc wireless network, all computers must be inside the same _____.

6. A(n) _____ provides a connection between a wireless network and a cable-based network.

7. A(n) _____ is an IEEE term used to describe a group of wireless devices connected as an infrastructure network or an SSID.

8. A network that does not use a Wireless Access Point and usually is a direct connection between two wireless devices is referred to as a(n) _____.

9. A(n) _____ is two or more Wireless Access Points or wireless devices using the same SSID.

1. _____

2. _____

3. _____

4. _____

5. _____

6. _____

7. _____

8. _____

9. _____

Practice 4.8

Fill in the chart for the given IEEE 802.11 classifications.

802.11 Specification	Radio Frequency	Maximum Data Rate	Range (approximate)	Transmission Method
802.11a	_____ GHz	_____ Mbps	_____ m	_____
802.11b	_____ GHz	_____ Mbps	_____ m	_____
802.11g	_____ GHz	_____ Mbps (802.11b mode)	_____ m	_____
	_____ GHz	_____ Mbps (802.11g mode)	_____ m	_____
802.11n	_____ GHz	Up to 300 Mbps. Possibly as high as 600 Mbps	_____ m	_____
	_____ GHz			

Copyright by Goodheart-Willcox Co., Inc.

Practice 4.9

Identify the following statements as relating to infrared, Bluetooth, or satellite. The following terms may be used more than once.

Bluetooth	infrared	satellite

1. _____ is specified in IEEE 802.15 Working Group Wireless Personal Area Networks (PAN).

1. _____

2. _____ is a short-range wireless system designed for 30 meters or less.

2. _____

3. _____ suffers from propagation delay.

3. _____

4. When networking with _____, communicating devices must be in a direct line of sight.

4. _____

5. A(n) _____ travels in a geosynchronous orbit.

5. _____

6. A(n) _____ network is referred to as a piconet or a Personal Area Network (PAN).

6. _____

7. _____ is designed for appliances such as telephones, laptops, palm tops, digital cameras, personal digital assistants, headsets, printers, keyboards, and mice.

7. _____

8. _____ devices do not interfere with 802.11b devices when operated in the same area because they use different formats for configuring data.

8. _____

Practice 4.10

Identify the following characteristics as relating to 802.15, 802.16, USB wireless, or Bluetooth. The following terms may be used more than once.

802.15	802.16	Bluetooth	USB wireless

1. Broadband Wireless Access (BWA): _____

2. Connects devices such as cameras and mobile phones to a PC: _____

3. Data rates as high as 70 Mbps over distances of 30 miles or more: _____

4. Effective range is 30 meters or less: _____

5. Small Ethernet network consisting of personal wireless devices: _____

6. Speeds of up to 480 Mbps at a maximum range of 3 meters: _____

7. Wireless Personal Area Networks (WPAN): _____

Practice 4.11

Fill in the blanks for the statements about wireless networking.

geosynchronous orbit	infrared transmission
microwave transmission	propagation delay

1. When a satellite's speed is synchronized with the earth's rotational speed, the satellite is said to be in _____.

2. The time it takes for data to be transmitted from the earth and satellite is referred to as _____.

3. Point-to-point communications between two devices such as a PDA and PC typically use _____.

4. Communications that use radio wave frequencies between 1 GHz and 300 GHz is referred to as _____.

1. _____

2. _____

3. _____

4. _____

Practice 4.12

Match the authentication or encryption protocol to its definition.

1. _____ 802.1x
2. _____ Extensible Authentication Protocol (EAP)
3. _____ Protected Extensible Authentication Protocol (PEAP)
4. _____ Wireless Application Protocol (WAP)
5. _____ Wired Equivalent Privacy (WEP)
6. _____ Wi-Fi Protected Access (WPA-2)
7. _____ Wi-Fi Protected Access (WPA)
8. _____ Wi-Fi Protected Access-Pre Shared Key (WPA-PSK)

a. A data encryption protocol that makes a wireless network as secure as a wired network.

b. A protocol that ensures authorized access to the network system and network resources on both wireless and wired networks.

c. A protocol that combines the authentication method with encryption.

d. An improved version of EAP.

e. A variation of WPA which can automatically generate a new key after a specified amount of time or number of packets exchanged. It is designed for small-office/home-office (SOHO) networks.

f. A draft standard that provides a means for a client and server to authenticate with each other.

g. Uses the Advanced Encryption Standard (AES) and is backward compatible with WPA devices.

h. Ensures the safe exchange of data between a wireless network and a portable Wi-Fi device. It uses a set of keys to identify a device and to encrypt the data exchanged.

Copyright by Goodheart-Willcox Co., Inc.

Name _____ Date _____

Period _____

Digital Encoding and Data Transmission

Introduction

For the Network+ Certification exam, you should be able to identify a network protocol as connection-oriented or connectionless and a network technology as packet switching or circuit switching; recall the function of unicast, multicast, and broadcast addressing schemes; identify the UDP and TCP default ports, and recall the characteristics of a VLAN. You should be able to recall the function of each OSI model layer and the order in which the data packaging process occurs.

Practice 5.1

Fill in the blanks for the statements about digital signals and encoding.

asynchronous	**bipolar**
Cyclic Redundancy Check (CRC)	**digital encoding**
Manchester encoding	**Non-Return to Zero (NRZ)**
parity check	**synchronous**
time period	**unipolar**

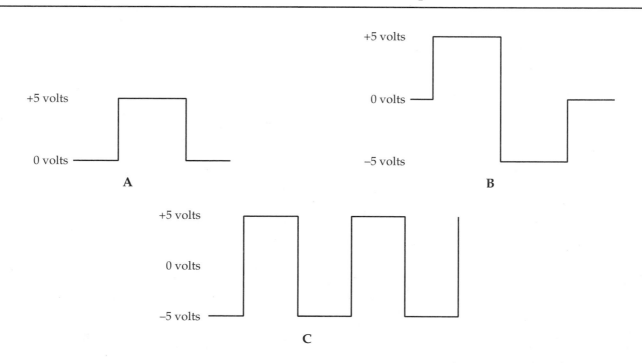

A

B

C

1. Illustration *A* shows an example of a(n) _____ digital signal.

2. Illustration *B* shows an example of a(n) _____ digital signal.

3. When a network interface card converts data into a digital pattern acceptable to the network media, _____ takes place.

4. The rate of recurrence of an expected signal level change is a(n) _____.

5. The digital signal in illustration *C* is an example of the _____ digital encoding scheme.

6. An encoding scheme characterized by a digital pulse transitioning during the midpoint of the time period is _____.

7. No reference signal is used when transmitting data with _____ transmission.

8. A reference signal is used when transmitting data with _____ transmission.

9. A(n) _____ uses complicated mathematical algorithms to determine if one or more bits are corrupt.

10. A(n) _____ is a simple method of verifying the integrity of transmitted data.

1. _____

2. _____

3. _____

4. _____

5. _____

6. _____

7. _____

8. _____

9. _____

10. _____

Practice 5.2

Arrange the data packaging terms in the order of process, from raw data to data transmission.

binary code	digital signal	frame	packet	segments

1. _____

2. _____

3. _____

4. _____

5. _____

Copyright by Goodheart-Willcox Co., Inc.

Practice 5.3

Match the term to its definition.

1. _____ circuit switching

2. _____ connection-oriented communication

3. _____ connectionless communication

4. _____ packet switching

a. A type of communication in which a connection is first established between the source and destination computers before data is transmitted.

b. A type of communication in which data is transmitted to the destination without first establishing a connection.

c. A type of transmission that establishes a permanent connection between two points for the duration of the data transfer period.

d. A type of transmission that does not use a permanent connection between two points for the duration of the data transfer period. Packets may travel different routes to the same destination.

Practice 5.4

Identify the technologies as circuit switching (CS) or packet switching (PS).

1. _____ ATM

2. _____ Ethernet

3. _____ FDDI

4. _____ Frame Relay

5. _____ DSL

6. _____ ISDN

7. _____ T1

Practice 5.5

Fill in the blanks for the statements about data codes.

ASCII	BCD	EBCDIC	HTML	Unicode

1. The number 239 represented as 0010 0011 1001 in binary is an example of _____.

1. _____

2. The _____ character code uses 16 bits to represent individual characters.

2. _____

3. The character code that uses 8 bits to represent alphanumeric characters is _____.

3. _____

4. _____ is an authoring language used to create documents that can be downloaded from the Internet and viewed by a Web browser.

4. _____

5. The IBM character code _____ is similar to ASCII and is used widely on IBM mainframes.

5. _____

Practice 5.6

Match the frame type to its definition.

1. _____ broadcast frame
2. _____ multicast frame
3. _____ unicast frame

a. A frame intended for every computer on the network.
b. A frame intended for one computer on the network.
c. A frame intended for a preselected number of computers.

Practice 5.7

Match the OSI model layer to its function.

1. _____ application
2. _____ presentation
3. _____ session
4. _____ transport
5. _____ network
6. _____ data link
7. _____ physical

a. Converts frames or packets into electronic signals and places them on the network media.
b. Packages data into a universally agreed on form.
c. Ensures accurate delivery.
d. Interfaces to the network system.
e. The network media.
f. Encapsulates packets for routing.
g. Establishes and coordinates communications between two points.

Copyright by Goodheart-Willcox Co., Inc.

6

Name _____ Date _____

Period _____

Network Operating Systems and Network Communications

Introduction

For the Network+ Certification exam, you should be able to identify the protocols that operate at the data link layer. You should also be able to identify and describe the access method used by Ethernet.

Practice 6.1

Fill in the blanks for the statements about user interfaces.

A   B

command prompt	command syntax	graphical user interface (GUI)

1. Illustration *A* is an example of a _____.   1. _____

2. Illustration *B* is an example of a _____.   2. _____

3. The correct manner and arrangement in which a   3. _____
   command is to be typed is called a _____.

Practice 6.2

Label the layers of the OSI model.

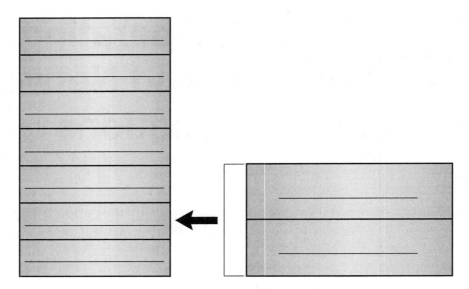

Practice 6.3

Place a check mark next to the protocols that operate at the data link layer.

1. _____ Ethernet

2. _____ SMB

3. _____ Token Ring

4. _____ UDP

5. _____ ATM

6. _____ TCP

7. _____ AFP

8. _____ NFS

9. _____ Token Bus

10. _____ DNS

11. _____ NetBIOS

12. _____ ARCnet

13. _____ IP

Copyright by Goodheart-Willcox Co., Inc.

Practice 6.4

Fill in the blanks for the statements about Ethernet. The following terms may be used more than once.

access method	broadcast storm	collision domain	segmenting

1. A(n) _____ is a method of gaining access to the network media.

1. _____

2. CSMA/CD is an example of a(n) _____ and is used by Ethernet.

2. _____

3. A(n) _____ occurs when a network is flooded with a continuous number of collisions and rebroadcasts.

3. _____

4. The section of a network where collisions occur is referred to as a(n) _____.

4. _____

5. The act of dividing a network into smaller sections to avoid collisions is called _____.

5. _____

Practice 6.5

Match the Token Ring term to its definition.

1. _____ active monitor
2. _____ beaconing
3. _____ loopback test
4. _____ monitor contention
5. _____ ring polling
6. _____ ring purge
7. _____ standby monitor
8. _____ token

a. The process of selecting an active monitor.

b. A computer on a Token Ring network that can become an active monitor if the current active monitor fails or logs off the network.

c. A signal that tests the network interface card to ensure that it is functioning properly.

d. A short binary code that is passed to computers on a ring topology and, in some cases, a bus topology.

e. A ring poll conducted by an active monitor to identify if a computer has logged on or off the ring.

f. Removing a defective token and replacing it with a new one.

g. A computer that is responsible for monitoring the necessary administrative functions associated with Token Ring technology.

h. A recovery process used when a hardware failure occurs on the ring.

Practice 6.6

Record the access method for the following network technologies. The following terms may be used more than once.

CSMA/CA	CSMA/CD	token passing

1. AppleTalk: _____

2. ARCnet: _____

3. Ethernet: _____

4. Token Bus: _____

5. Token Ring: _____

Practice 6.7

Match the network technology to its token passing method.

1. _____ ARCnet

2. _____ Token Bus

3. _____ Token Ring

a. The token is passed around the network to the next downstream neighbor. Before a computer can transmit information on the network, it must seize a token to take control of the network.

b. The token is passed around the network according to a database of sequential MAC addresses. The token can also have a priority code set to allow a specific workstation to have the token before any of the other workstations.

c. Uses a deterministic method of cable access by passing the token to the next highest assigned node number.

Practice 6.8

Fill in the blanks for the statements about NetBIOS.

datagram	de facto standard
dumb terminal	NetBIOS Name Server (NBNS)
session	Universal Naming Convention (UNC)
virtual circuit	

1. Before NetBIOS, the traditional method of networking was connecting a _____ to a mainframe via cabling.

1. _____

2. A _____ is a standard developed because of its widely accepted use in industry.

2. _____

3. A _____ is a short message block that can be sent to a particular computer, sent to a group of computers, or broadcast to all computers connected to the media.

3. _____

Copyright by Goodheart-Willcox Co., Inc.

4. When communication is limited to two particular computers, it is referred to as a _____.

4. _____

5. When computers establish a session, they create a connection-oriented communication known as a _____.

5. _____

6. A _____ resolves NetBIOS computer names to IPv4 addresses.

6. _____

7. NetBIOS uses a standard naming convention called _____.

7. _____

Practice 6.9

Match the discovery protocol to its definition.

1. _____ Address Resolution Protocol (ARP)

2. _____ Cisco Discovery Protocol (CDP)

3. _____ Link-Layer Discovery Protocol (LLDP)

4. _____ Link-Layer Discovery Protocol–Media Endpoint Discovery (LLDP-MED)

5. _____ Link-Layer Topology Discovery (LLTD)

6. _____ Link-Local Multicast Name Resolution (LLMNR)

a. An enhanced version of LLDP used for routers, switches, VoIP devices, and PoE devices.

b. Microsoft's version of LLDP.

c. A service that resolves IP addresses to MAC addresses.

d. A protocol developed as an IEEE specification that identifies devices connected on the LAN.

e. A variation of LLDP designed to support equipment such as Cisco routers, switches, and telephones.

f. A protocol that serves the same function as a DNS server when a DNS server cannot be reached. It resolves names of devices connected collectively on a local network.

Copyright by Goodheart-Willcox Co., Inc.

Name _____ Date _____

Period _____

Microsoft Network Operating Systems

Introduction

For the Network+ Certification exam, you will not need to know specifics about Windows Server operating systems. However, you may be asked general questions about user accounts, user logon, and resource sharing. You will also be asked a question about the Lightweight Directory Access Protocol (LDAP).

Practice 7.1

Fill in the blanks for the statements about the Microsoft network models in illustrations *A* and *B*. The following terms may be used more than once.

domain	**workgroup**

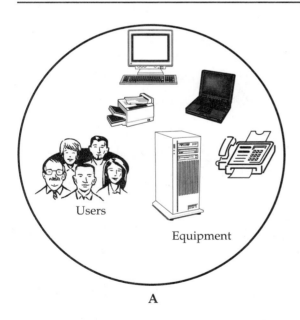

A

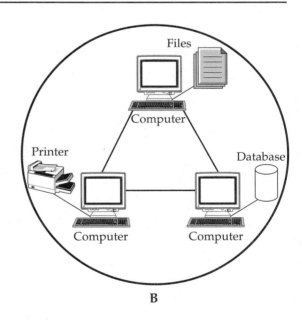

B

1. The Microsoft network model in illustration *A* is an example of a _____, which consists of a collection of users and equipment under one administration.

1. _____

2. The Microsoft network model in illustration *B* is an example of a _____, which is a group of computers that share resources.

2. _____

3. Computers in a peer-to-peer network are grouped together in a _____.

3. _____

4. Computers in a Windows client/server network are grouped together in a _____.

4. _____

5. A _____ is a group of computers that share resources such as files and hardware.

5. _____

6. A _____ is a logical grouping of users and equipment as defined by the network administrator.

6. _____

7. In the _____ model, each computer contains its own database of users.

7. _____

8. In the _____ model, members share a common security database.

8. _____

9. In the _____ model, each user must have a separate account on each computer to use the computer's shared resources.

9. _____

10. The _____ model is limited in scope and is not used for large networks.

10. _____

11. The _____ model makes it easier to manage a large number of users.

11. _____

Practice 7.2

Identify the network characteristics as belonging to a domain (D), workgroup (W), or HomeGroup (HG). Some characteristics have more than one answer.

1. _____ Client/server configuration.

1. _____

2. _____ Peer-to-peer configuration.

2. _____

3. _____ Each computer has a set of user accounts.

3. _____

4. _____ User accounts are stored in a single location.

4. _____

5. _____ Passwords are optional.

5. _____

6. _____ Passwords are required.

6. _____

7. _____ All computers must be on the same LAN or subnet.

7. _____

8. _____ Must be a Windows 7 computer with the network location set to Home.

8. _____

9. _____ Membership is not limited to a subnet or LAN.

9. _____

10. _____ Typically contains 10 to 20 computers.

10. _____

11. _____ Can contain thousands of computers.

11. _____

Copyright by Goodheart-Willcox Co., Inc.

Practice 7.3

Fill in the blanks for the statements about accounts.

auditing	global security policy	group account
local security policy	logon right	network share
permission	security policy	user account

1. The basic requirement for a(n) _____ is a user name and password.

2. A(n) _____ is the ability to log on to the network.

3. A(n) _____ is the ability to access a network share.

4. A(n) _____ is a collection of users who typically share a common job-oriented goal or similar function.

5. A(n) _____ is a blanket policy that secures resources on the network.

6. A(n) _____ is a security policy that affects local users.

7. A(n) _____ is a security policy that affects domain users.

8. A service that tracks the events, use, and access of network resources and writes these actions to a log is called _____.

9. A(n) _____ is a resource on the network that is shared among assigned users.

1. _____

2. _____

3. _____

4. _____

5. _____

6. _____

7. _____

8. _____

9. _____

Practice 7.4

Identify the file sharing protocols as belonging to CIFS, SMB, or NFS.

1. _____ Supports file sharing from a Windows operating system.

2. _____ Supports file sharing from UNIX and Linux operating systems.

3. _____ A dialect of SMB.

4. _____ Mistakenly referred to as CIFS.

5. _____ An attempt by Microsoft to standardize a universal file sharing protocol for the Internet to be used by all operating systems.

1. _____

2. _____

3. _____

4. _____

5. _____

Practice 7.5

Record the maximum partition size for each file system.

1. FAT16

2. FAT32

3. NTFS

1. _____

2. _____

3. _____

Practice 7.6

Identify the network characteristics as belonging to share-level (S) or user-level (U) security.

1. _____ Applies only to shares accessed over the network.

2. _____ Does not secure shares accessed locally.

3. _____ FAT16 and FAT32 allows only for this type of security.

4. _____ Requires a user to authenticate through a security database.

5. _____ Secures shares locally and across the network.

6. _____ Commonly called NTFS permissions.

7. _____ Can be applied to both the directory level and file level.

Practice 7.7

Fill in the blanks for the statements about Active Directory. The following terms may be used more than once.

distinguished name	contiguous namespace	disjointed namespace
forest	namespace	object
organizational unit	tree	

1. A(n) _____ is any physical or logical unit that is defined as part of the network.

1. _____

2. A user, group, printer, volume, directory, or service is an example of a domain _____.

2. _____

3. A(n) _____ is a collection of domains that share a common root domain name and Active Directory database.

3. _____

4. A(n) _____ is a collection of domain trees that share a common Active Directory database.

4. _____

5. The label that identifies a unique location in a structure such as the Internet is called a(n) _____.

5. _____

6. Chicago.XYZcorp.com and Dallas.XYZcorp.com share a(n) _____.

6. _____

7. Chicago.XYZcorp.com and Chicago.DEF.com share a(n) _____ within the same forest.

7. _____

8. A(n) _____ is a container that holds objects or other organizational units and is used to organize a network into manageable units.

8. _____

9. CN=*jsmith*, OU=*Accounting*, DC=Chicago.XYZcorp.com is an example of a(n) _____.

9. _____

Copyright by Goodheart-Willcox Co., Inc.

Practice 7.8

Use the diagram of the Active Directory to write a distinguished name for each of the given names. Use the following attributes within each name: CN, OU, and DC.

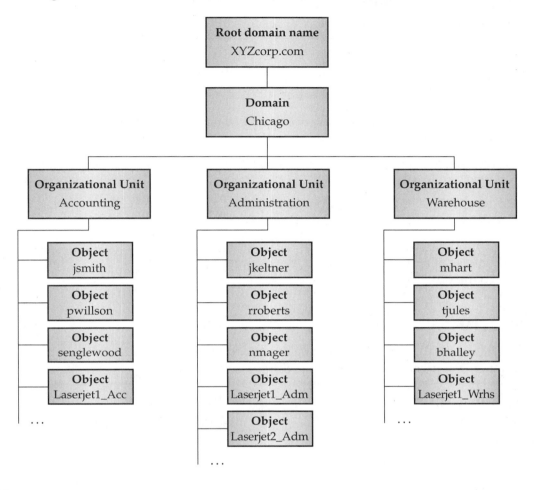

1. jsmith: _____

_____

2. rroberts: _____

_____

3. nmager: _____

_____

3. tjules: _____

_____

4. senglewood: _____

_____

5. bhalley: _____

_____

Copyright by Goodheart-Willcox Co., Inc.

Practice 7.9

Fill in the blanks for the statements about authentication and replication. The following terms may be used more than once.

interactive logon	multimaster replication	network authentication

1. In a Windows 2000/2003/2008 network, authentication occurs during two types of processes: _____ and _____.

2. The authentication process in which the user is verified and given access to the Active Directory is called _____.

3. An authentication process that occurs when a user accesses a resource is called _____.

4. The Windows 2000/2003/2008 environment uses a process called _____ to replicate the security database.

5. In the _____ model, when changes are made to the security database at a domain controller, the changes are replicated to the other domain controllers.

1. _____
   _____

2. _____

3. _____

4. _____

5. _____

Practice 7.10

Identify the server roles that can be used in each version of Windows. The following terms may be used more than once, and each entry may have more than one answer.

backup domain controller (BDC)	**domain controller (DC)**
member server	**primary domain controller (PDC)**
stand-alone server	

1. Windows NT: _____

   _____

   _____

   _____

2. Windows 2000/2003/2008:: _____

   _____

   _____

   _____

Copyright by Goodheart-Willcox Co., Inc.

Practice 7.11

Label the following NT domain trust relationships.

complex trust	one-way trust	two-way trust

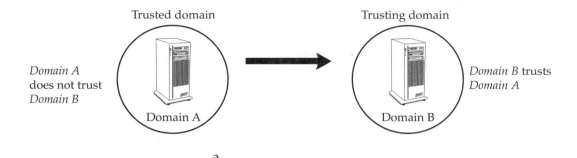

a. _____

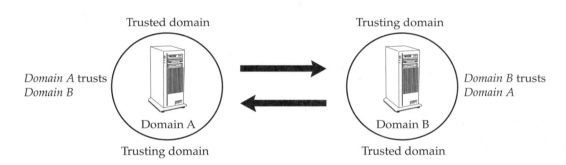

b. _____

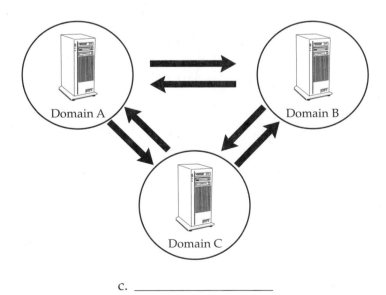

c. _____

Practice 7.12

Match the domain trust relationship term to its definition.

1. _____ complex trust relationship
2. _____ external trust
3. _____ forest trust
4. _____ full-trust relationship
5. _____ one-way trust relationship
6. _____ realm trust
7. _____ trusted domain
8. _____ trusting domain
9. _____ trust relationship
10. _____ two-way trust relationship

a. A relationship between domains that allows users from one domain to access resources on another domain in which they do not have a user account.
b. A trust relationship in which both domains are designated as a trusted domain and a trusting domain.
c. A trust relationship in which more than two domains have a full-trust relationship.
d. Another name for a two-way trust relationship.
e. Allows the trusted domain to access its resources.
f. Allowed to access resources on a trusting domain.
g. A trust relationship in which one domain is the trusted domain and the other is the trusting domain.
h. A trust relationship between a Windows Server 2008 domain and a non-Windows domain.
i. A trust relationship between Windows Server 2008 computer and an older Windows Server operating system or with another Windows Server 2008 that is located in a separate forest.
j. A two-way trust that is designed to share resources between two forests.

Practice 7.13

Match the disk management term to its definition.

1. _____ extended partition
2. _____ free space
3. _____ logical drive
4. _____ partition
5. _____ primary partition
6. _____ volume
7. _____ volume set

a. An area of the hard disk drive that is to be allocated to an operating system.
b. An accessible unit of hard disk drive space as seen through the Windows interface, such as Windows Explorer.
c. A partition that stores a bootable copy of an operating system.
d. The space on a hard disk drive that has not been partitioned.
e. A volume that consists of partitions from two or more hard disk drives.
f. A partition that can contain one or more logical drives. Only one of these can exist on a hard disk drive.
g. A partition on a hard disk drive that is assigned a drive letter.

Copyright by Goodheart-Willcox Co., Inc.

8

UNIX/Linux Operating Systems

Introduction

For the Network+ Certification exam, you do not need to know any specifics about the UNIX/Linux operating system. However, you should be familiar with the ifconfig, mtr, dig, and traceroute commands.

Practice 8.1

Fill in the blanks for the statements about the UNIX/Linux operating system. The following terms may be used more than once.

boot loader	daemon	kernel
module	session	shell

1. A small program called a _____ is used to expand the kernel and to allow for flexibility.

2. The core of an operating system is called a _____.

3. A hardware driver or kernel enhancement is referred to as a _____.

4. A _____ is a program that runs in the background and waits for a client to request its services.

5. The Simple Mail Transfer Protocol is an example of a _____.

6. A _____ is a user interface that interprets and carries out commands from the user.

7. Bash and tcsh are examples of a _____.

8. LILO and GRUB are examples of a _____.

9. A program that starts the operating system load process is called a _____.

10. A _____ is a logical connection with the Linux computer.

1. _____

2. _____

3. _____

4. _____

5. _____

6. _____

7. _____

8. _____

9. _____

10. _____

Practice 8.2

Label the parts of the directory listing.

file or directory owner	**file or directory size**	**file type**
owner's group	**permissions**	

d. _____

c. _____

e. _____

b. _____

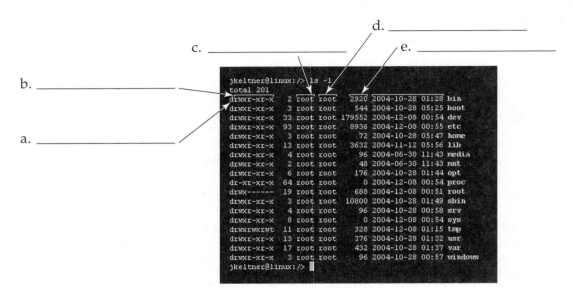

a. _____

```
jkeltner@linux:/> ls -l
total 201
drwxr-xr-x   2 root root    2920 2004-10-28 01:28 bin
drwxr-xr-x   3 root root     544 2004-10-28 05:25 boot
drwxr-xr-x  33 root root  179552 2004-12-08 00:54 dev
drwxr-xr-x  93 root root    8936 2004-12-08 00:55 etc
drwxr-xr-x   3 root root      72 2004-10-28 05:47 home
drwxr-xr-x  13 root root    3632 2004-11-12 05:56 lib
drwxr-xr-x   4 root root      96 2004-06-30 11:43 media
drwxr-xr-x   2 root root      48 2004-06-30 11:43 mnt
drwxr-xr-x   6 root root     176 2004-10-28 01:44 opt
dr-xr-xr-x  64 root root       0 2004-12-08 00:54 proc
drwx------  19 root root     688 2004-12-08 00:51 root
drwxr-xr-x   3 root root   10800 2004-10-28 01:49 sbin
drwxr-xr-x   4 root root      96 2004-10-28 00:58 srv
drwxr-xr-x   8 root root       0 2004-12-08 00:54 sys
drwxrwxrwt  11 root root     328 2004-12-08 01:15 tmp
drwxr-xr-x  13 root root     376 2004-10-28 01:32 usr
drwxr-xr-x  17 root root     432 2004-10-28 01:37 var
drwxr-xr-x   3 root root      96 2004-10-28 00:57 windows
jkeltner@linux:/>
```

Practice 8.3

Match the UNIX/Linux command to its definition.

1. _____ cd <directory>

2. _____ cp <filename> <directory>

3. _____ ls

4. _____ mv <filename> <new filename>

5. _____ pwd

6. _____ rm <filename>

7. _____ rmdir <directory>

a. Renames a file.
b. Changes the directory to the specified directory.
c. Removes (deletes) a file.
d. Displays the path of the current working directory.
e. Removes (deletes) a directory.
f. Lists the contents of the current working directory.
g. Copies a file to a specified directory.

   Copyright by Goodheart-Willcox Co., Inc.

Practice 8.4

Fill in the blanks for the statements about Linux file systems. The following terms may be used more than once.

inode	journaling file system	journal file

1. A(n) _____ ensures file integrity whenever an unexpected system shutdown occurs.

   1. _____

2. Information about each file in a Linux system is stored in a(n) _____.

   2. _____

3. A journaling file system maintains a(n) _____, or a log of all file activity.

   3. _____

4. A(n) _____ is a table entry that contains information such as permissions, file size, and the name of the file owner.

   4. _____

5. Ext3 is an example of a(n) _____.

   5. _____

Practice 8.5

Label the parts of the /etc/fstab file.

device file	file system	mount point	options

c. _____

a. _____   b. _____   d. _____

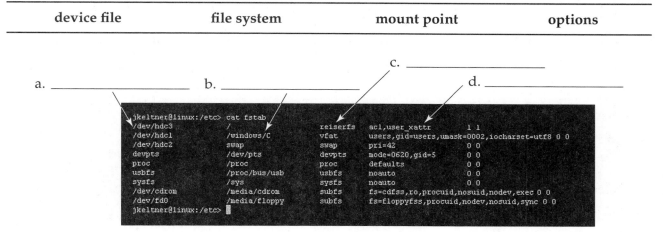

```
jkeltner@linux:/etc> cat fstab
/dev/hdc3        /               reiserfs   acl,user_xattr        1 1
/dev/hdc1        /windows/C      vfat       users,gid=users,umask=0002,iocharset=utf8 0 0
/dev/hdc2        swap            swap       pri=42                0 0
devpts           /dev/pts        devpts     mode=0620,gid=5       0 0
proc             /proc           proc       defaults              0 0
usbfs            /proc/bus/usb   usbfs      noauto                0 0
sysfs            /sys            sysfs      noauto                0 0
/dev/cdrom       /media/cdrom    subfs      fs=cdfss,ro,procuid,nosuid,nodev,exec 0 0
/dev/fd0         /media/floppy   subfs      fs=floppyfss,procuid,nodev,nosuid,sync 0 0
jkeltner@linux:/etc>
```

Practice 8.6

Match the storage device name to its description.

1. _____ sda
2. _____ hdd
3. _____ sdb
4. _____ hdc

   a. Second SCSI drive in a chain.
   b. Slave hard drive on secondary controller.
   c. Master or single hard drive on secondary controller.
   d. First SCSI drive in chain.

Practice 8.7

Label the directory and file rights with the name of the owner of each group of rights.

group	other	user

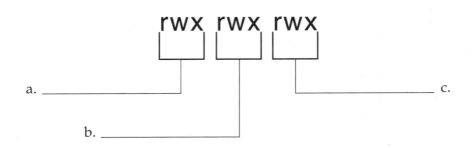

Practice 8.8

Determine (put a check mark by) the permissions for user, group, and other for each set of assigned rights.

1. rw–r—r—

User	Group	Other
read _____	read _____	read _____
write _____	write _____	write _____
execute _____	execute _____	execute _____

2. rwxrwxr—

User	Group	Other
read _____	read _____	read _____
write _____	write _____	write _____
execute _____	execute _____	execute _____

3. rw–rw——

User	Group	Other
read _____	read _____	read _____
write _____	write _____	write _____
execute _____	execute _____	execute _____

4. rwxr–xr—

User	Group	Other
read _____	read _____	read _____
write _____	write _____	write _____
execute _____	execute _____	execute _____

Copyright by Goodheart-Willcox Co., Inc.

5. rw——r—

User	Group	Other
read _____	read _____	read _____
write _____	write _____	write _____
execute _____	execute _____	execute _____

Practice 8.9

Fill in the blanks for the statements about UNIX/Linux authentication.

/	/etc/passwd	/root
password	**root**	**user name**

1. To log on to a UNIX/Linux system, a user must supply a _____ followed by a _____.

1. _____

2. The highest level of administration is the superuser, which has the default user account name of _____.

2. _____

3. The _____ directory is the home directory of the superuser.

3. _____

4. The _____ directory is the highest level of the directory structure.

4. _____

5. When a user is authenticated, the user's user name and password are compared to account information stored in the _____ file.

5. _____

Practice 8.10

Fill in the associated protocol for each UNIX/Linux file and print service.

IPP	lpr	NFS	SMB

1. SAMBA: _____

2. UNIX/Linux file services: _____

3. CUPS: _____

4. lpd: _____

Practice 8.11

Fill in the blanks for the statements about UNIX/Linux file and print services.

Common UNIX Printing System (CUPS)	export
line printer daemon (lpd)	lpr
mount	Network File System (NFS)

1. File sharing is made possible through the _____ protocol.

2. To make files and directories accessible to remote users, the administrator must _____ the files and directories.

3. To view the exported directories, a user at the client computer must _____ the directory.

4. The _____ handles remote and local printing services.

5. The _____ command is used to send print jobs to the line printer daemon (lpd).

6. _____ has been designed to support network printing using the Internet Printing Protocol (IPP).

1. _____

2. _____

3. _____

4. _____

5. _____

6. _____

Copyright by Goodheart-Willcox Co., Inc.

9

Name _____ Date _____

Period _____

Introduction to the Server

Introduction

For the Network+ Certification exam, you should be able to identify the basic characteristics of RAID and storage systems. CompTIA also expects you to have A+ Certification knowledge. Therefore, it is a good idea to review the system resources covered in this chapter.

Practice 9.1

Fill in the blanks for the statements about server types.

blade server	thin client	thin client server	thin server

1. A _____ relies on a thin client server's processing power and memory.

   1. _____

2. A _____ is a powerful server that is extremely thin.

   2. _____

3. A server that has only the hardware and software needed to support and run a specific function is called a _____.

   3. _____

4. A server that provides applications and processing power to a thin client is called a _____.

   4. _____

Practice 9.2

Fill in the blanks for the statements about server hardware.

backplane	firmware
hot swapping	hot-swap technology
logical unit number (LUN)	parallel processing
power-on self-test (POST)	serial attached SCSI (SAS)
Small Computer Systems Interface (SCSI)	

1. A SCSI technology that transfers data in a serial fashion is _____.

   1. _____

2. The computer bus technology that allows you to connect multiple devices to a single controller is _____.

   2. _____

3. The _____ is a numbering scheme used to identify SCSI devices attached to an extender card.

4. A _____ is a simple motherboard that serves as the interface of all major components.

5. Processing a program through more than one CPU simultaneously is referred to as _____.

6. The combination of a BIOS chip and the software program within the chip is called _____.

7. A technology that allows a component to be removed or installed while the system is running is referred to as _____.

8. The _____ is a BIOS routine that performs a series of hardware checks to determine if the computer is in minimal working order.

9. The process of removing components without shutting down the system is called _____.

3. _____

4. _____

5. _____

6. _____

7. _____

8. _____

9. _____

Practice 9.3

Interpret the SCSI binary patterns.

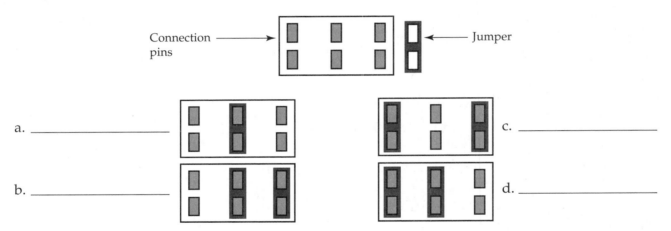

a. _____

b. _____

c. _____

d. _____

Practice 9.4

Fill in the blanks for the statements about system resources. The following terms may be used more than once.

DMA	I/O port	IRQ	memory address assignment

1. A(n) _____ is a circuit that communicates with the CPU.

2. A(n) _____ channel is a circuit that allows devices to communicate and transfer data to and from RAM without the need of CPU intervention.

1. _____

2. _____

Copyright by Goodheart-Willcox Co., Inc.

3. The _____ is a small amount of memory assigned to a device that temporarily holds small amounts of data. It is used to transfer data between two locations.

3. _____

4. A(n) _____ conflict can lead to problems such as an inoperable device, a system crash, and a system lockup.

4. _____

5. A(n) _____ is a large block of memory assigned to a device and is used to transfer data between two locations.

5. _____

6. Large blocks of data that need to be transferred between hardware devices and memory are transferred through a(n) _____ channel that is assigned to the device.

6. _____

7. Hardware devices send an electrical signal to the CPU using an assigned _____ circuit.

7. _____

Practice 9.5

Fill in the blanks for the statements about RAID technology. The following terms may be used more than once.

disk mirroring	disk striping	duplexing
error correction	fault tolerance	parity
Redundant Array of Independent Disks (RAID)		

1. A(n) _____ is a system of disks arranged for speed or fault tolerance, or both.

1. _____

2. A system's ability to recover from a hard disk or hard disk controller failure without the loss of stored data is called _____.

2. _____

3. Dividing data into sections and writing the data across several hard disk drives at the same time is called _____.

3. _____

4. The total data pattern shared between the data storage drives is represented by a binary code known as _____. If any data storage drive fails, the system can use the parity bit to rebuild the missing data.

4. _____

5. The technique of placing each mirrored hard drive on a separate hard disk drive controller is called _____.

5. _____

6. The act of writing the same information to two hard disk drives at the same time is called _____.

6. _____

7. The RAID technique _____ uses traditional error-checking code (ECC) or parity.

7. _____

Practice 9.6

Label the RAID technologies.

RAID 0	**RAID 0/1 or RAID 10**	**RAID 0/5 or RAID 50**
RAID 1	**RAID 1 with duplexing**	**RAID 5**

a. _____

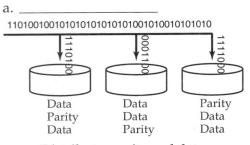

Data   Data   Parity
Parity Data   Data
Data   Parity Data

Distributes parity and data accross all drives

d. _____

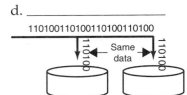

Writes the same information to two hard disk drives at the same time.

b. _____

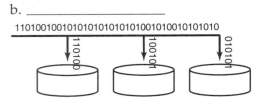

Uses only disk striping accross a group of independant drives.

e. _____

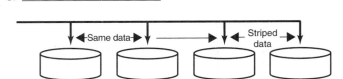

Uses multiple mirrored disk sets and incorporates disk striping.

c. _____

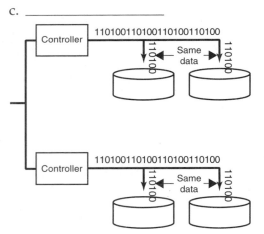

Places each mirrored drive set on a separate hard disk drive controller.

f. _____

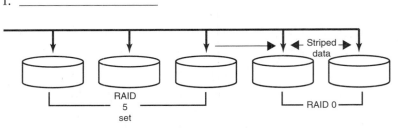

Uses several RAID 5 (block striping with parity) sets and combines them with RAID 0 (disk striping).

Copyright by Goodheart-Willcox Co., Inc.

Practice 9.7

Fill in the blanks for the statements about the storage systems in illustrations *A* and *B*.

network attached storage (NAS)	**storage area network (SAN)**

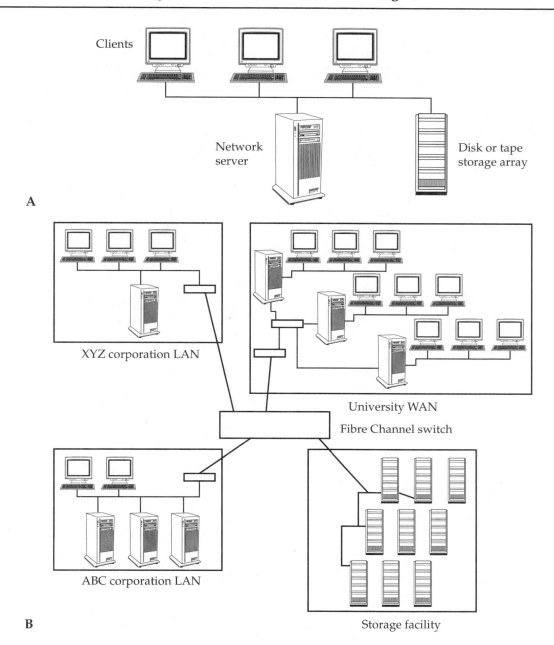

1. The storage system in illustration *A* is an example of _____.

2. The storage system in illustration *B* is an example of _____.

3. A device or collection of devices that provide storage for a single network is called _____.

4. A _____ is a separate, high-speed network that provides a storage facility for one or more networks.

5. A _____ uses a high-speed access media such as Fibre Channel.

1. _____

2. _____

3. _____

4. _____

5. _____

Copyright by Goodheart-Willcox Co., Inc.   *Chapter 9*   Introduction to the Server

Practice 9.8

Fill in the blanks for the statements about the Fibre Channel topologies in illustrations *A*, *B*, and *C*.

arbitrated loop	fabric switched	point-to-point

A   Station1   Channel   Station2

B   Station1   Station2   Station3   Station4

C   Station1   Station2   Station1   Station2

1. The Fibre Channel topology in illustration A is an example of _____.

1. _____

2. The Fibre Channel topology in illustration *B* is an example of _____.

2. _____

3. The Fibre Channel topology in illustration *C* is an example of _____.

3. _____

4. In a(n) _____ Fibre Channel topology, when two points wish to communicate, a private link, or channel, is set up between the two devices.

4. _____

5. In a(n) _____ Fibre Channel topology, two devices set up a direct communication link, or channel, for the duration of the data transfer.

5. _____

6. A Fibre Channel _____ topology is simply a straight connection or channel between two points, such as a mainframe and a server.

6. _____

7. The _____ Fibre Channel topology uses a device known as a fabric switch.

7. _____

8. The _____ Fibre Channel topology is limited to 127 connections.

8. _____

    Copyright by Goodheart-Willcox Co., Inc.

Name _____ Date _____

Period _____

TCP/IP Fundamentals

Introduction

For the Network+ Certification exam, you should be able to identify IPv4 and IPv6 address formats and know the function of the following addressing technologies: DHCP, DNS, and NAT. You should also be able to identify port numbers by their related service and identify the function of common TCP/IP troubleshooting utilities.

Practice 10.1

Record the range and subnet mask of public IP addresses by class.

Public IP Addresses

Class	Range	Subnet Mask
A	_____	_____
B	_____	_____
C	_____	_____

Practice 10.2

Record the class (A, B, or C) and subnet mask of each of the following IP addresses.

1. 27.0.10.253: _____

2. 180.127.43.15: _____

3. 192.169.128.33: _____

4. 50.191.45.200: _____

5. 100.69.45.16: _____

6. 221.90.88.16: _____

7. 190.35.65.50: _____

8. 126.100.59.3: _____

9. 130.49.200.22: _____

10. 168.10.10.5: _____

11. 196.52.60.45: _____

12. 140.223.190.25: _____

13. 222.14.25.65: _____

14. 127.191.65.120: _____

15. 191.16.20.90: _____

Practice 10.3

Record the range and subnet mask of reserved IP addresses by class.

Reserved (Private) IP Addresses

Class	Range	Subnet Mask
A		
B		
C		

Practice 10.4

Identify (place a check mark by) the private IP addresses.

1. _____ 10.25.30.5

2. _____ 11.10.10.2

3. _____ 172.33.16.65

4. _____ 192.168.88.92

5. _____ 192.167.222.13

6. _____ 172.29.45.14

7. _____ 10.33.214.160

8. _____ 10.0.3.15

9. _____ 12.15.82.63

10. _____ 192.168.200.42

11. _____ 172.26.25.20

12. _____ 172.15.92.101

13. _____ 10.127.192.117

14. _____ 192.169.10.25

15. _____ 192.168.50.16

Copyright by Goodheart-Willcox Co., Inc.

Practice 10.5

Record the class, range, and subnet mask of Automatic Private IP Addressing (APIPA) addresses.

APIPA IP Addresses

Range	Subnet Mask
_____	_____

Practice 10.6

Fill in the blanks for the statements about IPv4 addressing.

default gateway address	host	octet
subnet mask	subnetwork	

1. A(n) _____, or node, is a device associated with an IP address on a TCP/IP network.

2. A network within a network is known as a(n) _____.

3. An eight-bit, or one-byte, value is a(n) _____.

4. A(n) _____ is the address of the computer that provides a connection to the Internet.

5. A number similar to an IP address used to determine to which subnetwork a particular IPv4 address belongs is a(n) _____.

1. _____

2. _____

3. _____

4. _____

5. _____

Practice 10.7

Fill in the blanks for the statements about Internet assigned names and numbers.

Integrated Network Information Center (InterNIC)

Internet Corporation for Assigned Names and Numbers (ICANN)   registrar

1. A(n) _____ is a select, private company that is assigned a pool of IP addresses from ICANN and handles domain registration.

2. The _____ is a company that manages domain name registration by allocating domain name registration to select, private companies.

3. The _____ is a branch of the United States government under the direction of the Department of Commerce that was responsible for regulating the Internet, overseeing the issue of domain names, and assigning IP addresses to them.

1. _____

2. _____

3. _____

Practice 10.8

Fill in the blanks for the statements about DNS structure and operation.

| Fully Qualified Domain Name (FDQN) | resolver | second-level domain |
| subdomain | top-level domain | |

1. In a DNS structure, .gov is referred to as a _____.

2. A combination of a host name and a domain name, such as station12.xyzcorp.com, is called a _____.

3. In a DNS structure, faculty.mit.edu would be referred to as a _____.

4. The _____ is a software program located on a host that queries a DNS server to resolve a host name to an IP address.

5. In a DNS structure, mit.edu would be referred to as a _____.

1. _____

2. _____

3. _____

4. _____

5. _____

Practice 10.9

Match the network service to its definition.

1. _____ Address Resolution Protocol (ARP)

2. _____ Bootstrap Protocol (BOOTP)

3. _____ Domain Name System (DNS)

4. _____ Dynamic Host Configuration Protocol (DHCP)

5. _____ Network Address Translation (NAT)

6. _____ Reverse Address Resolution Protocol (RARP)

7. _____ Windows Internet Naming Service (WINS)

a. A protocol that translates private network addresses into an assigned Internet address, and vice versa. In other words, it allows an unregistered private network address to communicate with a legally registered IP address.

b. A service that resolves IP addresses to MAC addresses.

c. A system that associates a host or domain name with an IP address, making it easy to identify and find hosts and networks.

d. A service that resolves NetBIOS names to IP addresses.

e. A service that assigns IP addresses automatically to the hosts on a network.

f. A service that finds the MAC address of a host when the IP address is known.

g. A service that uses a centralized database of the MAC addresses and IP assignments of all devices on the network and assigns the appropriate IP address to a host when it boots.

Copyright by Goodheart-Willcox Co., Inc.

Practice 10.10

Match the IP addressing method to its definition.

1. _____ dynamic addressing
2. _____ dynamic IP assignment
3. _____ static addressing
4. _____ static IP assignment

a. Automatically assigning IP addresses.
b. An IP address that is entered manually for each host on the network.
c. Assigning an IP address manually.
d. An IP address that is issued automatically, typically when the computer boots and joins the network.

Practice 10.11

Fill in the blanks for the statements about TCP/IP ports and sockets.

port number	socket
upper-level port numbers	well-known port numbers

1. Ports 0 through 1023 are referred to as _____.
2. The address 192.168.20.45:80 is an example of a(n) _____.
3. Ports 1024 and higher are referred to as _____.
4. A number associated with the TCP/IP protocol and used to create a virtual connection between two computers running TCP/IP is called a(n) _____.

1. _____
2. _____
3. _____
4. _____

Copyright by Goodheart-Willcox Co., Inc.

Practice 10.12

Record the port number of the commonly used services and protocols.

Service or Protocol	Port Number
FTP	_____
FTP	_____
SSH	_____
Telnet	_____
SMTP	_____
DNS	_____
TFTP	_____
HTTP	_____
POP3	_____
NNTP	_____
NTP	_____
IMPA4	_____
HTTPS	_____
SNMP	_____

Copyright by Goodheart-Willcox Co., Inc.

Practice 10.13

Identify the characteristics as belonging to IPv4 or IPv6.

1. _____ Uses Address Resolution Protocol (ARP).

2. _____ Uses the Neighbor Discovery protocol.

3. _____ IPSec for security is mandatory.

4. _____ IPSec for security is optional.

5. _____ 128-bit addresses.

6. _____ 4-digit hexadecimal numbers divided by colons.

7. _____ 4 octets separated by periods.

8. _____ Uses Type of Services (TOS) field in header plus UDP and TCP packets to deliver time-sensitive data.

9. _____ Improved quality of service.

10. _____ Contains header information that allows routers to immediately identify the packet priority.

Practice 10.14

Identify the characteristics as belonging to a MAC address (MAC) or and EUI-64 identifier (EUI).

1. _____ 24-bit manufacturer's ID and 24-bit unique identifier.

2. _____ 24-bit manufacturer's ID and 40-bit unique ID.

3. _____ Modified to fit inside a 64-bit frame.

4. _____ Randomly generated in Windows Vista and later operating systems.

Practice 10.15

Label the network using IPv6 topography terminology.

global	link-local	unique-local

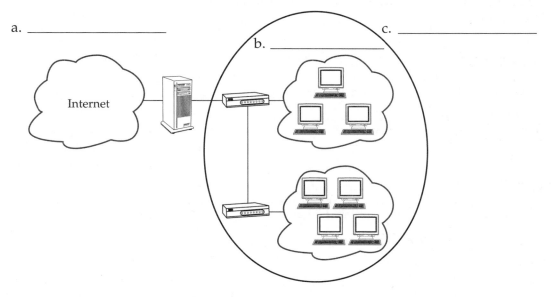

a. _____

b. _____

c. _____

Practice 10.16

Match the IPv6 address classification to its definition.

1. _____ anycast address
2. _____ multicast address
3. _____ unicast address

a. Delivers packets to the nearest interface and is used mainly for supporting router functions.
b. Delivers packets to a single network address.
c. Delivers packets to multiple addresses.

Practice 10.17

Fill in the blanks for the statements about unicast addresses. The following terms may be used more than once.

global unicast	link-local unicast	site-local unicast	unique-local unicast

1. A(n) _____ address is similar to an IPv4 public address.   1. _____
2. The _____ address is a replacement for site-local address.   2. _____
3. The _____ address starts with 2000: or is written as 2000:/3.   3. _____
4. The _____ address starts with FE80 or FE80::/64.   4. _____
5. The _____ address starts with FC00.   5. _____
6. The _____ address serves the same function as an IPv4 APIPA address.   6. _____
7. The _____ address serves the same function as the site-local address.   7. _____
8. The _____ address serves the same function as the IPv4 private address 10.0.0.0, 172.16.0.0, and 192.168.0.0.   8. _____
9. The Network Discovery feature requires the _____ address to function.   9. _____
10. The _____ address can represent the entire local area network or just a portion.   10. _____
11. The scope of a(n) _____ address is the entire Internet as well as the local area network.   11. _____

Practice 10.18

Record the IPv4 and IPv6 loopback addresses.

1. IPv4 loopback address: _____
2. IPv6 loopback address: _____

Practice 10.19

Record the IPv4 and IPv6 unspecified addresses.

1. IPv4 unspecified address: _____
2. IPv6 unspecified address: _____

    Copyright by Goodheart-Willcox Co., Inc.

Practice 10.20

Record the IPv4 and IPv6 multicast destination addresses.

1. IPv4 multicast destination address: _____

2. IPv6 multicast destination address: _____

Practice 10.21

Match the IPv6 transition technology to its definition.

1. _____ 6to4

2. _____ ISATAP

3. _____ Teredo

a. A node-to-node and node-to-router technology used for existing IPv4 network devices to eliminate the need to upgrade network devices.

b. A network address translator that creates a tunnel that allows incoming IPv6 traffic through a firewall designed for IPv4.

c. An IPv6 transition mechanism that provides a means of communicating across the IPv4 Internet while preserving the original IPv6 assigned address of the network device.

Practice 10.22

Match the TCP/IP troubleshooting utility to its function.

1. _____ arp

2. _____ ipconfig

3. _____ nbtstat

4. _____ netstat

5. _____ nlslookup

6. _____ ping

7. _____ traceroute/tracert

8. _____ ifconfig

a. Displays current TCP/IP and port statistics. It can be used to determine network problems such as excessive broadcasts on the network. It also allows the user to monitor network connections.

b. Displays NetBIOS over TCP statistics.

c. Used to send a packet from one host to another on a network and then echo a return reply. It is commonly used to quickly check the connection state of network media between two hosts.

d. Used to troubleshoot a path to a distant destination. This utility displays the approximate hop lapse times between points along the route. The amount of time delay can help analyze network failure or problems caused by excessive time delays.

e. Lists IP addresses resolved to MAC addresses. It can be used to troubleshoot problems with multiple IP assignments and to solve host communication problems.

f. Used to query domain servers when seeking information about domain names and IP addresses. This is a convenient tool when looking for information about a particular domain or IP addresses.

g. Used to verify TCP/IP settings on a Windows XP and later computer.

h. Used to verify TCP/IP settings on a UNIX/Linux computer.

Networking Fundamentals Study Guide

Copyright by Goodheart-Willcox Co., Inc.

Subnetting

Introduction

For the Network+ Certification exam, you should be able to identify common routing protocols. CompTIA requires only that you be able to identify the purpose of subnetting. You will not be asked to perform subnet calculations. However, as a network technician or administrator, you should be able to convert binary to decimal, and vice versa. You should have some minimal practice in subnetting even though you will most likely use a subnet calculator. Working through some subnet exercises will give you a better understanding of the calculations derived from a subnet calculator.

Practice 11.1

Convert the binary numbers to decimal. Use the chart and the space beneath the chart to aid in conversion. The first practice has been completed for you.

1. 11000000: _____ 192 _____

(2⁷) 128	(2⁶) 64	(2⁵) 32	(2⁴) 16	(2³) 8	(2²) 4	(2¹) 2	(2⁰) 1
1	1	0	0	0	0	0	0

$$
\begin{array}{r}
128 \\
+ 64 \\
\hline
192
\end{array}
$$

2. 11111110: _____

(2⁷) 128	(2⁶) 64	(2⁵) 32	(2⁴) 16	(2³) 8	(2²) 4	(2¹) 2	(2⁰) 1

3. 10101000: _____

(2⁷) 128	(2⁶) 64	(2⁵) 32	(2⁴) 16	(2³) 8	(2²) 4	(2¹) 2	(2⁰) 1

4. 10101100: _____

(2⁷) 128	(2⁶) 64	(2⁵) 32	(2⁴) 16	(2³) 8	(2²) 4	(2¹) 2	(2⁰) 1

5. 11111111: _____

(2⁷) 128	(2⁶) 64	(2⁵) 32	(2⁴) 16	(2³) 8	(2²) 4	(2¹) 2	(2⁰) 1

Copyright by Goodheart-Willcox Co., Inc.

6. 01001110: _____

(2^7) 128	(2^6) 64	(2^5) 32	(2^4) 16	(2^3) 8	(2^2) 4	(2^1) 2	(2^0) 1

Practice 11.2

Convert the decimal numbers to binary. Use the chart and the space beneath the chart to aid in conversion. The first practice has been completed for you.

1. 167: _____ 10100111 _____

(2^7) 128	(2^6) 64	(2^5) 32	(2^4) 16	(2^3) 8	(2^2) 4	(2^1) 2	(2^0) 1
1	0	1	0	0	1	1	1

The largest power of two decimal values that can go into 167 is 128. Place a 1 in the 128 position in the chart and then subtract 128 from 167.

$$
\begin{array}{r}
167 \\
- \ 128 \\
\hline
39
\end{array}
$$

The largest power of two decimal values that can go into 39 is 32. Place a 1 in the 32 position in the chart and then subtract 32 from 39.

$$
\begin{array}{r}
39 \\
- \ 32 \\
\hline
7
\end{array}
$$

The largest power of two decimal values that can go into 7 is 4. Place a 1 in the 4 position in the chart and then subtract 4 from 7.

$$
\begin{array}{r}
7 \\
-4 \\
\hline
3
\end{array}
$$

The largest power of two decimal values that can go into 3 is 2. Place a 1 in the 2 position in the chart and then subtract 2 from 3.

$$
\begin{array}{r}
3 \\
-2 \\
\hline
1
\end{array}
$$

The largest power of two decimal values that can go into 1 is 1. Place a 1 in the 1 position in the chart. Place a 0 in the empty positions to derive the complete eight bit binary address.

2. 252: _____

(2^7) 128	(2^6) 64	(2^5) 32	(2^4) 16	(2^3) 8	(2^2) 4	(2^1) 2	(2^0) 1

3. 138: _____

(2^7) 128	(2^6) 64	(2^5) 32	(2^4) 16	(2^3) 8	(2^2) 4	(2^1) 2	(2^0) 1

Copyright by Goodheart-Willcox Co., Inc.

4. 52: _____

(2⁷) 128	(2⁶) 64	(2⁵) 32	(2⁴) 16	(2³) 8	(2²) 4	(2¹) 2	(2⁰) 1

5. 204: _____

(2⁷) 128	(2⁶) 64	(2⁵) 32	(2⁴) 16	(2³) 8	(2²) 4	(2¹) 2	(2⁰) 1

6. 86: _____

(2⁷) 128	(2⁶) 64	(2⁵) 32	(2⁴) 16	(2³) 8	(2²) 4	(2¹) 2	(2⁰) 1

Copyright by Goodheart-Willcox Co., Inc.

Practice 11.3

Record the Class A, Class B, and Class C subnet mask in decimal and binary form.

Class	Decimal	Binary
A		
B		
C		

Practice 11.4

Using an assigned IP address and required number of subnets, determine the new subnet mask, subnet network addresses, host ranges, and broadcast addresses. The first practice has been partially completed for you.

Number of Subnets	Number of Borrowed Bits
2	2
6	3
14	4
30	5
62	6

Table 11-1. Class C network subnet values.

Copyright by Goodheart-Willcox Co., Inc.

1.

Given

Assigned IP address: 192.212.14.35

Number of subnets: 2

Do not allow all 1s and all 0s in the host address.

Answers

Read through the worked practice and then place the answers in this section when prompted.

New subnet mask: _____

1ˢᵗ Subnet

Subnet network address: _____

Broadcast address: _____

Host range: _____

2ⁿᵈ Subnet

Subnet network address: _____

Broadcast address: _____

Host range: _____

Worksheet	
Step 1. Determine the Class of the assigned IP address. *The assigned IP address 192.212.14.35 is a Class C address because the first octet is in the range of 192–223.*	Class C
Step 2. Determine the assigned IP address subnet mask. *Since the assigned IP address is a Class C address, the subnet mask is 255.255.255.0*	Subnet mask: 255.255.255.0
Step 3. Record the subnet mask in binary form for the assigned address.	Subnet mask in binary form: 11111111.11111111.11111111.00000000

Step 4.	Determine the new subnet mask and record it in decimal form. (Refer to **Table 11-1**.) *To determine the new subnet mask, borrow bits from the host portion of the original subnet mask to create the required number of subnets. In this example, two subnets are required. To create two subnets, two bits are borrowed from the host portion of the original subnet mask.*	Original subnet mask: Borrowed bits 11111111.11111111.11111111.**11**000000 Decimal: 255.255.255.192 **New subnet mask:** 255.255.255.192 **(*Record this number in the Answers section.*)**
Step 5.	Record the possible subnets created from the borrowed bits and allow for the reserved values of all ones and all zeros by crossing out the all 0s and all 1s entries. Then, compute the host range for each allowable subnet. *Notice that the 1 bit in the **01** subnet is in the 64 decimal position. Therefore, the host range for that subnet begins with 64. The rest of the bits, those in the host position, are added to this number to derive the end of the host range, 127.* *In the **10** subnet, the 1 bit is in the 128 decimal position. The rest of the bits, those in the host position, are added to 128 to derive the end of the host range, 191.*	Borrowed bits/ Host range possible subnets ~~00~~ 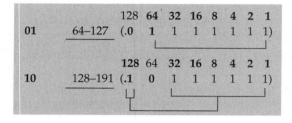 ~~11~~

Step 6.	Record the network address for each subnet.
	
	*The network address is created from the assigned network address and the first number in each host range of allowable subnet patterns (**01** and **10**).*
		Assigned network address:
		192.212.14.0
		
		First number in each host range:
		64
		128
		
		Subnet network address (for subnet 01):
		    192.212.14.64
		
		(*Record this number in the Answers section.*)
		
		Subnet network address (for subnet 10):
		    192.212.14.128
		
		(*Record this number in the Answers section.*)

Copyright by Goodheart-Willcox Co., Inc.

Step 7.	Record a broadcast address for each subnet.
	
	*The broadcast address is created using the assigned network address and the last number in each host range of allowable subnet patterns (**01** and **10**).*
		Assigned network address:
		192.212.14.0
		
		First number in each host range:
		127
		191
		
		Broadcast address (for subnet 01):
		    192.212.14.127
		
		(Record this number in the Answers section.)
		
		Broadcast address (for subnet 10):
		    192.212.14.191
		
		(Record this number in the Answers section.)

Step 8.	Record the final host range for each subnet.
	
	*The host range is created using the assigned network address and the remaining numbers in each host range of allowable subnet patterns (**01** and **10**).*
		Assigned network address:
		192.212.14.0
		
		Remaining numbers for subnet 01:
		65–126
		
		Host range (for subnet 01): 192.212.14.65–
		    192.212.14.126
		
		(Record this number in the Answers section.)
		
		Remaining numbers for subnet 10: 129–190
		
		Host range (for subnet 01): 192.212.14.129–
		    192.212.14.190
		
		(Record this number in the Answers section.)

2.

Given
Assigned IP address: 212.45.67.82
Number of subnets: 2
Do not allow all 1s and all 0s in the host address.

Answers

New subnet mask: _____

1st Subnet

Subnet network address: _____

Broadcast address: _____

Host range: _____

2nd Subnet

Subnet network address: _____

Broadcast address: _____

Host range: _____

Worksheet	
Step 1. Determine the Class of the assigned IP address.	Class:
Step 2. Determine the assigned IP address subnet mask.	Subnet mask:
Step 3. Record the subnet mask in binary form for the assigned address.	Subnet mask in binary form:
Step 4. Determine the new subnet mask and record it in decimal form. (Refer to **Table 11-1**.)	Original subnet mask: Decimal: **New subnet mask:** **(*Record this number in the Answers section.*)**

Copyright by Goodheart-Willcox Co., Inc.

Step 5.	Record the possible subnets created from the borrowed bits and allow for the reserved values of all ones and all zeros by crossing out the all 0s and all 1s entries. Then, compute the host range for each allowable subnet.	Borrowed bits/ possible subnets Host ranges
		01 _____ (.0 1 1 1 1 1 1 1) with 128 64 32 16 8 4 2 1 above; 10 _____ (.1 0 1 1 1 1 1 1) with 128 64 32 16 8 4 2 1 above
Step 6.	Record the network address for each subnet.	Assigned network address: 212.45.67.82 **Subnet network address for 1st subnet (subnet 01):** (*Record this number in the Answers section.*) **Subnet network address for 2nd subnet (subnet 10):** (*Record this number in the Answers section.*)
Step 7.	Record a broadcast address for each subnet.	Assigned network address: 212.45.67.82 **Broadcast address for 1st subnet (subnet 01):** (*Record this number in the Answers section.*) **Broadcast address for 2nd subnet (subnet 10):** (*Record this number in the Answers section.*)
Step 8.	Record the final host range for each subnet.	Assigned network address: 212.45.67.82 Remaining numbers for subnet 01: **Host range for 1st subnet (subnet 01):** (*Record this number in the Answers section.*) Remaining numbers for subnet 10: **Host range for 2nd subnet (subnet 01):** (*Record this number in the Answers section.*)

3.

Given
Assigned IP address: 195.200.86.64
Number of subnets: 6
Do not allow all 1s and all 0s in the host address.

Answers

New subnet mask: _____

1st Subnet

Subnet network address: _____

Broadcast address: _____

Host range: _____

2nd Subnet

Subnet network address: _____

Broadcast address: _____

Host range: _____

3rd Subnet

Subnet network address: _____

Broadcast address: _____

Host range: _____

4th Subnet

Subnet network address: _____

Broadcast address: _____

Host range: _____

5th Subnet

Subnet network address: _____

Broadcast address: _____

Host range: _____

6th Subnet

Subnet network address: _____

Broadcast address: _____

Host range: _____

Copyright by Goodheart-Willcox Co., Inc.

Worksheet	
Step 1. Determine the Class of the assigned IP address.	Class:
Step 2. Determine the assigned IP address subnet mask.	Subnet mask:
Step 3. Record the subnet mask in binary form for the assigned address.	Subnet mask in binary form:
Step 4. Determine the new subnet mask and record it in decimal form. (Refer to **Table 11-1**.)	Original subnet mask: Decimal: **New subnet mask:** (*Record this number in the Answers section.*)
Step 5. Record the possible subnets created from the borrowed bits and allow for the reserved values of all ones and all zeros by crossing out the all 0s and all 1s entries. Then, compute the host range for each allowable subnet.	Borrowed bits/ Host ranges possible subnets

Step 6.	Record the network address for each subnet.	Assigned network address: 195.200.86.64
		Network address for 1st subnet:
		(*Record this number in the Answers section.*)
		Network address for 2nd subnet:
		(*Record this number in the Answers section.*)
		Network address for 3nd subnet:
		(*Record this number in the Answers section.*)
		Network address for 4th subnet:
		(*Record this number in the Answers section.*)
		Network address for 5th subnet:
		(*Record this number in the Answers section.*)
		Network address for 6th subnet:
		(*Record this number in the Answers section.*)
Step 7.	Record a broadcast address for each subnet.	Assigned network address: 195.200.86.64
		Broadcast address for 1st subnet:
		(*Record this number in the Answers section.*)
		Broadcast address for 2nd subnet:
		(*Record this number in the Answers section.*)
		Broadcast address for 3nd subnet:
		(*Record this number in the Answers section.*)
		Broadcast address for 4th subnet:
		(*Record this number in the Answers section.*)
		Broadcast address for 5th subnet:
		(*Record this number in the Answers section.*)
		Broadcast address for 6th subnet:
		(*Record this number in the Answers section.*)

Copyright by Goodheart-Willcox Co., Inc.

Step 8.	Record the final host range for each subnet.	Assigned network address: 195.200.86.64
		Remaining numbers for 1st subnet:
		Host range for 1st subnet :
		(*Record this number in the Answers section.*)
		Remaining numbers for 2nd subnet:
		Host range for 2nd subnet :
		(*Record this number in the Answers section.*)
		Remaining numbers for 3nd subnet:
		Host range for 3nd subnet :
		(*Record this number in the Answers section.*)
		Remaining numbers for 4th subnet:
		Host range for 4th subnet :
		(*Record this number in the Answers section.*)
		Remaining numbers for 5th subnet:
		Host range for 5th subnet :
		(*Record this number in the Answers section.*)
		Remaining numbers for 6th subnet:
		Host range for 6th subnet :
		(*Record this number in the Answers section.*)

Copyright by Goodheart-Willcox Co., Inc.

Practice 11.5

Identify the characteristics as belonging to a bridge (B), switch (S), or router (R). Some characteristics can have more than one answer.

1. _____ Segments the network at layer 2.

2. _____ Segments the network at layer 3.

3. _____ Segments the network at the network layer.

4. _____ Segments the network at the data link layer.

5. _____ Makes decisions based on the source and destination IP addresses.

6. _____ Filters network traffic based on MAC addresses.

7. _____ Used to reduce bandwidth.

8. _____ Used to create a VLAN.

9. _____ Designed with forwarding modes.

10. _____ Forwards broadcast frames.

11. _____ Does not forward broadcasts.

Practice 11.6

Match the switch forwarding mode to its definition.

1. _____ adaptive cut-through

2. _____ cut-through

3. _____ fragment-free

4. _____ store-and-forward

a. A method of switching that checks the first 64 bytes of an Ethernet frame before forwarding it.

b. A method of switching in which a switch operates in cut-through mode by forwarding the frame immediately after receiving it until it detects an unacceptable number of corrupt frames. Then, it operates in the store-and-forward mode or fragment-free mode until the number of corrupt frames is reduced to an acceptable number.

c. A method of switching that forwards the frame immediately after receiving it.

d. A method of switching that reads the entire contents of the frame before forwarding the frame to its destination.

Copyright by Goodheart-Willcox Co., Inc.

Practice 11.7

Fill in the blanks for the statements about basic router terminology.

convergence	dynamic IP address table	hop
router metric	routing	static IP address table

1. The process of selecting the best route to send packets through a network is called _____.

2. A _____ is generated by a software program that communicates with nearby routers.

3. A _____ is a table of addresses that have been manually entered.

4. A measure of how many network devices (such as routers and gateways) a packet must pass through until the packet reaches its destination is referred to as a _____.

5. Steady state, or _____, is the state in which all dynamic routing tables contain the same information.

6. A _____ is the mechanism used to determine or measure the best route.

1. _____

2. _____

3. _____

4. _____

5. _____

6. _____

Practice 11.8

Match the routing protocol classification to its definition.

1. _____ distance vector protocol

2. _____ Exterior Gateway Protocol (EGP)

3. _____ Interior Gateway Protocol (IGP)

4. _____ link state protocol

a. A routing protocol that only transfers information about connections and does not pass its routing table to other devices.

b. A basic routing protocol that is confined to an autonomous network.

c. A basic routing protocol that exchanges information between different autonomous networks.

d. A routing protocol that shares its routing table with other routers.

Practice 11.9

Identify (place a check mark by) the routing protocols that are classified as an Internet Gateway Protocol (IGP).

1. _____ BGP
2. _____ EGP
3. _____ EIGRP
4. _____ IRGP
5. _____ IS-IS
6. _____ OSPF
7. _____ RIP
8. _____ RIPng

Practice 11.10

Identify (place a check mark by) the routing protocols that are classified as an Exterior Gateway Protocol (EGP).

1. _____ BGP
2. _____ EGP
3. _____ EIGRP
4. _____ IRGP
5. _____ IS-IS
6. _____ OSPF
7. _____ RIP
8. _____ RIPng

Practice 11.11

Identify (place a check mark by) the routing protocols that are classified as a link state protocol.

1. _____ BGP
2. _____ EGP
3. _____ EIGRP
4. _____ IRGP
5. _____ IS-IS
6. _____ OSPF
7. _____ RIP
8. _____ RIPng

Copyright by Goodheart-Willcox Co., Inc.

Practice 11.12

Identify (place a check mark by) the routing protocols that are classified as a distance vector protocol.

1. _____ BGP

2. _____ EGP

3. _____ EIGRP

4. _____ IRGP

5. _____ IS-IS

6. _____ OSPF

7. _____ RIP

8. _____ RIPng

Practice 11.13

Match the VLAN term to its definition.

1. _____ dynamic VLAN

2. _____ Spanning Tree Protocol (STP)

3. _____ static VLAN

4. _____ trunking

5. _____ Virtual Local Area Network (VLAN)

6. _____ Virtual Trunking Protocol (VTP)

a. The technique of connecting different VLANs together using a single network link.

b. A layer 2 protocol designed to manage networks based on MAC addresses and to prevent bridge loops.

c. Created when physical ports on a switch are manually assigned to a particular VLAN.

d. A broadcast domain created by one or more switches based on logical (MAC) addresses.

e. Created automatically using software by assigning the device MAC address and the user name to a VLAN.

f. A proprietary protocol developed by Cisco Systems to provide automatic reconfiguration of multiple switches across an entire network.

Practice 11.14

Derive CIDR from the subnet masks.

1. 255.255.254.0: _____

2. 254.0.0.0: _____

3. 255.255.128.0: _____

4. 128.0.0.0: _____

5. 255.192.0.0: _____

6. 255.255.192.0: _____

7. 255.248.0.0: _____

8. 252.0.0.0: _____

9. 255.254.0.0: _____

10. 248.0.0.0: _____

Copyright by Goodheart-Willcox Co., Inc.

12

Name _____ Date _____

Period _____

Multimedia Transmission

Introduction

For the Network+ Certification exam, you should be able to recall the purpose and characteristics of multimedia transmission protocols such as Frame Relay, ATM, VoIP, SIP, and RTP.

Practice 12.1

Match the audio and video signal term to its definition.

1. _____ acoustical echo
2. _____ bit rate
3. _____ codec
4. _____ jitter
5. _____ latency
6. _____ MPEG
7. _____ sampling frequency
8. _____ sampling rate

a. The number of times during a specific period that a sample of a signal's amplitude is taken.
b. The number of bits used to represent the amplitude of an analog signal.
c. The number of times per second that a sample of a signal's amplitude is taken.
d. Small staggers or hesitations in the delivery sequence of audio or video data caused by latency or missing packets.
e. Software, hardware, or a combination of software and hardware that compresses and decompresses video and audio information.
f. A condition that takes place when a microphone and a speaker are in close proximity or the audio is improperly adjusted, causing feedback.
g. An industry standard that ensures compatibility between different cameras, displays, and other multimedia equipment.
h. The delay of data as it travels to its destination.

Practice 12.2

Match the multimedia transmission protocol to its definition.

1. _____ Asynchronous Transfer Mode (ATM)

2. _____ Frame Relay

3. _____ Voice over IP (VoIP)

4. _____ X.25

a. An Internet telephony protocol designed for high-performance data delivery and quality of service. It relies on existing TCP/IP technology and existing TCP/IP networking equipment.

b. A packet switching protocol that typically uses leased lines such as T1 to carry data over long distances.

c. A protocol that uses analog signals to transmit data across long distances.

d. A protocol designed especially for transmitting data, voice, and video.

Practice 12.3

Identify the characteristics of a permanent virtual circuit (PVC) and Committed Information Rate (CIR).

1. _____ Guaranteed bandwidth a commercial carrier will provide a subscriber.

2. _____ Behaves like a hard-wired connection between the destination and source.

3. _____ It can follow many different paths while transmitting data.

Practice 12.4

Fill in the blank for the statements about ATM and VoIP. The following terms can be used more than once.

ATM	VoIP
1. The _____ protocol is especially designed for carrying audio, video, and multimedia.	1. _____
2. The _____ protocol can support a bandwidth of 622 Mbps.	2. _____
3. The _____ protocol can be used by mixing TCP/IP with modern telephone technologies.	3. _____
4. The _____ protocol is designed to divide text and audio/video into cells of 53 bytes each.	4. _____
5. The _____ protocol typically uses a series of UDP packets to send time-sensitive data, such as telephone conversation.	5. _____
6. The _____ protocol can be transmitted at a Constant Bit Rate (CBR), Variable Bit Rate (VBR), Available Bit Rate (ABR), or Unspecified Bit Rate (UBR).	6. _____
7. _____ is an Internet telephony protocol that relies on existing TCP/IP technology and existing TCP/IP networking equipment.	7. _____

Copyright by Goodheart-Willcox Co., Inc.

8. The _____ cells carrying audio and video are given the highest priority so that a constant flow of the time-sensitive data can be maintained.

8. _____

9. The _____ protocol is separate from the TCP/IP stack and uses special equipment designed for the protocol, such as switches and dedicated communication lines.

9. _____

10. _____ uses the TCP protocol for applications such as video or audio streaming because the TCP protocol has a sequence number in the header, which ensures packets are arranged in proper sequence when they arrive at the final destination.

10. _____

Practice 12.5

Match the ATM data transfer classification to its definition.

1. _____ ABR

2. _____ CBR

3. _____ UBR

4. _____ VBR

5. _____ VBR-NRT

6. _____ VBR-RT

a. An ATM data transfer classification in which the cell rate automatically adjusts to support time-sensitive data. It uses multiplexing techniques to provide a minimum CBR for time-sensitive audio and video transmissions while controlling the data rate of non-time-sensitive data, such as text or plain e-mail.

b. An ATM data transfer classification in which a steady stream of ATM cells move at a predictable rate.

c. An ATM data transfer classification that allows cells to move at a variable rate. The rate of movement depends on the type of data contained in each cell.

d. An ATM data transfer classification that allows cells to move at a variable rate depending on the cell's contents to support real-time audio and video transfers.

e. An ATM data transfer classification most appropriate for file transfer. It uses the available bit rate associated with the networking medium. The speed of the file transfer is affected by the amount of traffic on the network system.

f. An ATM data transfer classification that does not guarantee any speed or meet requirements of any special application such as multimedia or telephony. This classification is typically applied inside TCP/IP frames.

Practice 12.6

Fill in the blank for the statements about VoIP transmission technology and protocols. The following terms can be used more than once.

bandwidth shaper	H.323	hard phone
Quality of Service (QoS)	Real-time Transport Protocol (RTP)	Session Initiation Protocol
(SIP)	soft phone	telephone gateway

1. A(n) _____ is a specialized piece of equipment that connects a packet-style network communications system to a telephone system using the _____ protocol.

2. The _____ standard is the telecommunications standard for audio, video, and data communications using IP or packet-type networks defined by the International Telecommunication Union (ITU).

3. A(n) _____ is used to prioritize network packets to ensure quality of service for time-sensitive applications such as VoIP.

4. The standard and protocol for initiating, maintaining, and terminating the exchange of voice, multimedia, gaming, chat, and more is called _____.

5. The _____ does not carry the data, but rather establishes and maintains the session until the session is terminated.

6. A(n) _____ is a physical telephonic device, and a(n)_____ is a virtual telephonic device.

7. The _____ is a standard and a protocol used to stream voice and video in real time.

8. The _____ protocol gives time-sensitive packets, such as those carrying telephone conversations, a higher priority than data packets.

1. _____
_____

2. _____

3. _____

4. _____

5. _____

6. _____
_____

7. _____

8. _____

Copyright by Goodheart-Willcox Co., Inc.

Practice 12.7

Fill in the blank for the statements about VoIP troubleshooting. The following terms can be used more than once.

audio device configuration	connection failure	firewall	impedance mismatch
jitter	latency	protocol analyzer	

1. One of the most common causes of VoIP echo is _____.

    1. _____

2. A common example of _____ is connecting a two-wire local loop telephone circuit to a four-wire telephone circuit.

    2. _____

3. One of the most common sources of VoIP problems is the computer's _____ blocking the packets.

    3. _____

4. Performance problems are typically caused by _____ and _____.

    4. _____
    _____

5. A complete failure of the VoIP system generally relates to a(n) _____ between the destination and source.

    5. _____

6. What may seem to be a complete failure of the VoIP system could be due to the _____.

    6. _____

7. Dropping or losing packets causes _____ and results in a choppy voice transmission.

    7. _____

8. A(n) _____ can be used to verify the exchange of packets needed to support a VoIP service.

    8. _____

Copyright by Goodheart-Willcox Co., Inc.

13

Name _____ Date _____

Period _____

Web Servers and Services

Introduction

For the Network+ Certification exam, you should be familiar with the function of the following protocols: FTP, HTTP, HTTPS, IMAP4, NNTP, POP3, SFTP, SMTP, and TFTP.

Practice 13.1

Identify the characteristics of an Internet (inter), intranet (intra), and extranet (extra).

1. _____ Referred to as the World Wide Web.

1. _____

2. _____ A private network that services a specific group of users within a LAN.

2. _____

3. _____ Allows internal and external access to Web pages by personnel.

3. _____

4. _____ Allows partner companies, employees, and authorized customer access.

4. _____

5. _____ A collection of interconnected networks from all around the world.

5. _____

6. _____ Can be accessed by the general public.

6. _____

Practice 13.2

Label the parts of a URL.

domain name	path	port	protocol	resource

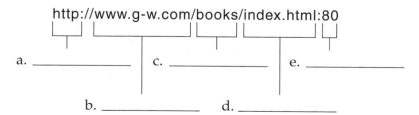

URL

http://www.g-w.com/books/index.html:80

a. _____   c. _____   e. _____

b. _____   d. _____

Practice 13.3

Match the Web communications term to its definition.

1. _____ CSS
2. _____ HTML
3. _____ HTTP
4. _____ JavaScript
5. _____ NNTP
6. _____ SGML
7. _____ SOAP
8. _____ XML

a. A protocol designed for communications between a Web browser and a Web server.
b. A markup language based on the same principles as HTML, with the added ability to create custom tags.
c. An enhancement to HTML tags that can be embedded into a Web page or exist as a separate page to control all pages in a Web site.
d. A set of rules constructed from XML for Web-based messages that allows a client to freely interact with a Web page on the Web server, rather than download it.
e. Programming language used to create Web pages.
f. A TCP/IP protocol that is designed to distribute news messages to NNTP clients and NNTP servers across the Internet.
g. The original standard for both HTML and XML.
h. A programming language that is designed to be embedded into an HTML Web page and allow the user to interact with the Web page.

Practice 13.4

Fill in the blanks for the statements about Web services. The following terms may be used more than once.

HTML tag	hyperlink	Hypertext Markup Language (HTML)
Hypertext Transfer Protocol (HTTP)	newsgroup	search engine
Web browser	Web server	Web site

1. <body> is an example of a(n) _____.

1. _____

2. Apache and IIS are examples of _____ software.

2. _____

3. A(n) _____ is a location on the World Wide Web that contains a collection of Web pages and files that can be accessed through the Internet.

3. _____

4. A(n) _____ permits the user to navigate the World Wide Web and then interprets and displays Web pages.

4. _____

5. Google is an example of a(n) _____.

5. _____

6. Firefox is an example of a(n) _____.

6. _____

Copyright by Goodheart-Willcox Co., Inc.

7. A(n) _____ is an instruction for how the text and graphics should appear when displayed in a Web browser.

7. _____

8. Clicking a(n) _____ on a Web page will take you to another Web page or to an area on the same Web page.

8. _____

9. The _____ is a programming language used to create Web pages.

9. _____

10. The _____ is designed for communication between a Web browser and a Web server.

10. _____

11. News articles arranged in groups or categories on an NNTP server are referred to as a(n) _____.

11. _____

Practice 13.5

Fill in the blanks for the statements about the FTP protocol. The following terms may be used more than once.

anonymous FTP	FTP	SFTP	TFTP

1. The lightweight version of FTP is called _____.

1. _____

2. The _____ protocol uses UDP packets and, therefore, does not establish a connection between the client and server.

2. _____

3. The _____ protocol requires a user name and password but does not encrypt the password or the contents of transferred files.

3. _____

4. The _____ protocol never requires the use of a user name and password because it uses UDP packets for transferring data.

4. _____

5. The _____ protocol uses fewer commands than FTP.

5. _____

6. The _____ protocol is a secure version of FTP.

6. _____

7. The _____ protocol encrypts the user name, password, and data to provide a high level of security.

7. _____

8. With the _____ protocol, the client is allowed to transfer files, but not to view the directory listing at the FTP site.

8. _____

9. A(n) _____ site does not require a password or any other form of authentication to access the site.

9. _____

Practice 13.6

Fill in the blanks for the statements about e-mail service protocols. The following terms may be used more than once.

HTTP	IMAP	MIME	POP	SMTP

1. The mail server uses the _____ or _____ protocol to communicate with and to download e-mail to the client.

1. _____

    _____

2. A protocol that is part of the TCP/IP protocol suite and is designed to transfer plain text e-mail messages from an e-mail client to a mail server and from a mail server to a mail server is called _____.

2. _____

3. A sophisticated mail access protocol that can manipulate e-mail while it is on the server is called _____.

3. _____

4. When setting up an e-mail account, the mail server is designated as a(n) _____ server for sending e-mail and as a(n) _____ or _____ server for retrieving e-mail.

4. _____

    _____

    _____

5. Web-based e-mail is also referred to as _____ e-mail.

5. _____

6. A simple protocol designed to access a mail server and download messages to the e-mail client is called _____.

6. _____

7. The _____ protocol allows e-mail attachments to be transferred as separate files using SMTP as the transport protocol.

7. _____

Practice 13.7

Match the mail communication term to its definition.

1. _____ mail gateway
2. _____ mail filter
3. _____ spam
4. _____ spamming
5. _____ spammer

a. An unwanted or unsolicited e-mail such as advertisement.
b. Blocks unwanted e-mail messages.
c. A person who engages in distributing unsolicited e-mail or sending e-mail with some sort of advertisement as a probe.
d. A special software and device used to connect two normally incompatible e-mail systems.
e. The distribution of unsolicited e-mail.

Copyright by Goodheart-Willcox Co., Inc.

14

Name _____ Date _____

Period _____

Remote Access and Long-Distance Communications

Introduction

For the Network+ Certification exam, you should be able to recall the basic characteristics of Internet access and WAN technologies.

Practice 14.1

Fill in the blanks for the statements about telecommunications systems. The following terms may be used more than once.

Local Central Office	**Local Exchange Carrier (LEC)**	**local loop**
Point of Presence (PoP)	**Public Switched Telephone Network (PSTN)**	**trunk line**

1. A _____ consists of hundreds of pairs of twisted pair cable or fiber-optic cable.

   1. _____

2. The Local Central Office can be tied to another Local Central Office via a _____.

   2. _____

3. The _____ is the section of wiring between customer premises and the Local Central Office.

   3. _____

4. A local carrier is often referred to as a _____ and is made of one or more Local Central Offices.

   4. _____

5. The location where the customer's telephone lines connect to the switchgear is called the _____.

   5. _____

6. The _____ is the point where the telephone company line connects to the subscriber line.

   6. _____

Practice 14.2

Identify the data rate of the Internet access technologies. The following terms may be used more than once.

1.544 Mbps	1.544 Mbps–52 Mbps	27 Mbps–37 Mbps
400 kbps–2 Mbps	44.736 Mbps	56 kbps

1. Cable Internet service (downstream): _____

2. xDSL: _____

3. PRI-ISDN: _____

4. PSTN: _____

5. Satellite Internet service: _____

6. T1: _____

7. T3: _____

Practice 14.3

Write the full name of the ISDN acronyms.

1. BRI-ISDN: _____ ISDN.

2. PRI-ISDN: _____ ISDN.

3. B-ISDN: _____ ISDN.

Practice 14.4

Fill in the blanks for the statements about ISDN. The following terms may be used more than once.

1.544 Mbps	128 kbps	bearer	B-ISDN
BRI-ISDN	delta	PRI-ISDN	

1. BRI-ISDN has a maximum data rate of _____.   1. _____

2. PRI-ISDN has a maximum data rate of _____.   2. _____

3. _____ consists of two B channels and one D channel.   3. _____

4. _____ can carry multiple frequencies.   4. _____

5. The _____ channel carries control signals.   5. _____

6. The _____ channel carries voice, video, or a combination of voice and data.   6. _____

7. The _____ channel has a maximum bandwidth of 16 kbps.   7. _____

8. Each _____ channel has a maximum bandwidth of 64 kbps.   8. _____

9. _____ consists of twenty-three B channels and one D channel.   9. _____

Copyright by Goodheart-Willcox Co., Inc.

Practice 14.5

Match the WAN connection technology to its definition.

1. _____ Basic Rate ISDN (BRI-ISDN)
2. _____ Broadband ISDN (B-ISDN)
3. _____ Cable Internet access
4. _____ Digital Subscriber Line (DSL)
5. _____ FDDI
6. _____ Frame Relay
7. _____ Integrated Services Digital Network (ISDN)
8. _____ Primary Rate ISDN (PRI-ISDN)
9. _____ Satellite Internet service
10. _____ Synchronous Optical Network (SONET)
11. _____ T-carrier
12. _____ X.25

a. A digital, packet switching technology.
b. An analog packet switching network technology developed in the 1970s, which can support a maximum bandwidth of 56 kbps.
c. Similar in design to T-carrier technology except that it bases its technology on fiber-optic cable.
d. A dual ring, fiber-optic arrangement often used in a MAN distribution system because of its reliability and its high bandwidth.
e. Uses the Cable television distribution system to provide Internet access.
f. Consists of a small dish for downloading and a landline, such as a traditional telephone line, for uploading.
g. A long-distance connection technology that provides a means for a fully digital transmission over channels that are capable of speeds of up to 64 kbps.
h. A category of ISDN that consists of three conductors: two B channels, referred to as *bearer channels,* and one D channel, referred to as the *delta channel.*
i. A category of ISDN that consists of twenty-three B channels and one D channel. It has a total data rate of 1.544 Mbps.
j. A category of ISDN that is designed to carry multiple frequencies.
k. A leased line dedicated to networking that uses multiple frequencies as separate channels on the existing telephone local loop. The multiple channels combine to carry more data than the original telephone modem design.
l. A leased line that follows one of the standards known as fractional T1, T1, T2, or T3.

Practice 14.6

Fill in the access method and data rate for the WAN connection technologies.

WAN Connection Technology	Access Method (dial-up, direct connection, or virtual connection)	Data Rate
PSTN	_____	_____
xDSL	_____	_____ to _____
Cable Internet service	_____	Downstream: _____ to _____ Upstream: _____ to _____
PRI-ISDN	_____	_____
Fractional T1	_____	_____
T1	_____	_____
T3	_____	_____
ATM	_____	_____ to _____
FDDI	_____	_____
SONET	_____	_____ to _____
Frame Relay	_____	_____ to _____
X.25	_____	_____

Copyright by Goodheart-Willcox Co., Inc.

Practice 14.7

Match the remote access protocol to its function.

1. _____ Bandwidth Allocation Protocol (BAP)
2. _____ Layer 2 Forwarding (L2F)
3. _____ Layer 2 Tunneling Protocol (L2TP)
4. _____ Multi-Protocol Label Switching (MPLS)
5. _____ Multilink Point-to-Point Protocol (MLPPP)
6. _____ Point-to-Point Protocol (PPP)
7. _____ Point-to-Point Protocol over Ethernet (PPPoE)
8. _____ Point-to-Point Tunneling Protocol (PPTP)
9. _____ Remote Desktop Protocol (RDP)
10. _____ Serial Line Internet Protocol (SLIP)
11. _____ Virtual Private Network (VPN)

a. Creates a simulated, independent network through software over a public network.

b. A remote access protocol that can combine two or more physical links so that they act as one, thus increasing the supported bandwidth. This protocol works with ISDN lines, PSTN lines, and X.25 technology.

c. A routing protocol that allows a label to be attached to an IP packet in order to route the packet to a specific destination.

d. A remote access protocol that allows one or more hosts on an Ethernet network to establish an individual PPP connection with an ISP.

e. A remote access protocol that is an enhanced version of PPP. It is designed to enhance security and to make use of a virtually private network using the public Internet.

f. A remote access protocol, similar to PPTP, designed to enhance security and to make use of a virtually private network using the public Internet.

g. A remote access protocol that enables a PC to connect to a remote network using a serial line connection, typically through a telephone line. It is a synchronous protocol that supports multiple protocols such as IPX and AppleTalk.

h. A communications protocol that can change the number of lines or channels according to current bandwidth.

i. A remote access protocol that enables a PC to connect to a remote network using a serial line connection, typically through a telephone line. It is an asynchronous protocol that supports only IP.

j. A presentation protocol that allows Windows computers to communicate directly with Windows-based clients.

k. A tunneling protocol that uses IPSec to encrypt the contents of the encapsulated PPP protocol.

Networking Fundamentals Study Guide

Copyright by Goodheart-Willcox Co., Inc.

15

Name _____ Date _____

Period _____

Network Security

Introduction

For the Network+ Certification exam, you should be able to recall the function of security devices such as Intrusion Detection Systems (IDSs), Intrusion Prevention Systems (IPSs), and network- and host-based firewalls. You should also be able to identify the basic characteristics of authentication and security protocols, identify common security threats and their characteristics, and explain the common features of a firewall.

Practice 15.1

Fill in the blanks for the statements about hackers, crackers, and intruders. The following terms may be used more than once.

cracker	hacker	intruder

1. The term _____ originally described any computer enthusiast who lacked formal training.

2. The term _____ has been redefined to identify anyone who gains unauthorized access to a computer system.

3. A(n) _____ is defined as anyone who gains access to a computer system without authorization and with the intent to do harm or play pranks.

4. According to the *Networking Fundamentals* textbook, anyone who gains access to a computer system they are not authorized to access is called a(n) _____.

1. _____

2. _____

3. _____

4. _____

Practice 15.2

Match the network security breach to its definition.

1. _____ backdoor
2. _____ Denial of Service (DoS)
3. _____ macro virus
4. _____ man in the middle (MITM)
5. _____ phishing
6. _____ replay attack
7. _____ Smurf attack
8. _____ social engineering
9. _____ spoofing
10. _____ Trojan horse
11. _____ worm

a. A method of using previously copied and stored information, such as an IP or MAC address, to establish an unauthorized connection with the destination.

b. The manipulation of personnel by the use of deceit to gain security information.

c. Fooling the destination by using an IP address other than the true IP address of a source to create a fake identity.

d. A software program that can spread easily and rapidly to many different computers.

e. A program designed to gain access to a computer while pretending to be something else.

f. Denying access to a server by overloading the server with bogus requests.

g. A type of DoS that consists of spoofing the target address and then pinging the target broadcast address.

h. A virus created by storing a series of keystrokes known as a "macro" produced by a word-processing software application.

i. A method of Internet fraud that involves using e-mail to steal a person's identity and other sensitive information, such as financial.

j. A software access port to the computer that a Trojan horse has infected.

k. A method of intercepting a network transmission, reading it, and then placing it back on route to its intended destination.

Practice 15.3

Identify the characteristics as belonging to an Intrusion Detection System (IDS) or an Intrusion Prevention System (IPS). Some characteristics may belong to both IDS and IPS.

1. _____ Only detects unauthorized activity.

1. _____

2. _____ Requires some form of port monitoring.

2. _____

3. _____ A reactive security protection system.

3. _____

4. _____ Detects unauthorized activity and performs some function to stop the activity.

4. _____

5. _____ Microsoft Event Viewer is an example of this type of system.

5. _____

6. _____ An antivirus software program is an example of this type of system.

6. _____

7. _____ Can generate false positives.

7. _____

Copyright by Goodheart-Willcox Co., Inc.

Practice 15.4

Fill in the blanks for the statements about security terminology. The following terms may be used more than once.

asymmetric-key	Certificate Authority (CA)	ciphertext
cryptology	digital certificate	encryption
key	Public Key Infrastructure (PKI)	symmetric-key

1. The method of using an algorithm to encode data is called _____.

1. _____

2. The science of encoding data is called _____.

2. _____

3. Encrypted data is referred to as _____.

3. _____

4. An algorithm used to encode data is called a(n) _____.

4. _____

5. In _____ encryption, both parties use the same key to perform encryption and decryption.

5. _____

6. In _____ encryption, two keys are used: a private key and a public key.

6. _____

7. Typically, a service referred to as the _____ contains the security list of users authorized to access the private key owner's messages, using a public key.

7. _____

8. A(n) _____ is a file that commonly contains data such as the user's name and e-mail address, the public key value assigned to the user, the validity period of the public key, and issuing authority identifier information.

8. _____

9. Secret-key cryptography is also called _____.

9. _____

10. Public-key cryptography is also called _____.

10. _____

11. The use of public keys to create a secure environment for the exchange of data between network devices is called _____.

11. _____

Copyright by Goodheart-Willcox Co., Inc.

Practice 15.5

Match the security protocols to their definitions.

1. _____ Independent Computer Architecture (ICA)
2. _____ IP Security (IPSec)
3. _____ Secure Copy Protocol (SCP)
4. _____ Secure HTTP (S-HTTP)
5. _____ Secure Shell (SSH)
6. _____ Security Sockets Layer (SSL)
7. _____ Transport Layer Security (TLS)

a. A security protocol developed by Netscape to secure transactions between Web servers and individuals using the Internet for such purposes as credit card transactions.

b. An Internet security protocol that secures individual messages between the client and server rather than the connection.

c. A security protocol developed by the Internet Engineering Task Force (IETF) to secure transactions between Web servers and individuals using the Internet for such purposes as credit card transactions.

d. A protocol that provides secure network services over an insecure network medium such as the Internet.

e. A proprietary protocol designed by Citrix Systems to support the exchange of software applications between a server and client.

f. An IETF standard for securing point-to-point connections in an IP-based network using encryption techniques.

g. A protocol that provides a secure way of transferring files between computers.

Practice 15.6

Fill in the blanks for the statements about IPSec. The following terms may be used more than once.

Authentication Header (AH)	Encapsulation Security Payload (ESP)	Kerberos
transport	tunnel	

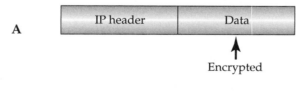

A

Encrypted

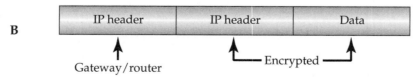

B

Gateway/router — Encrypted

1. The IPSec mode in illustration *A* is an example of _____ mode.   1. _____

2. The IPSec mode in illustration *B* is an example of _____ mode.   2. _____

3. The _____ mode encrypts the payload and the header information.   3. _____

Copyright by Goodheart-Willcox Co., Inc.

4. The _____ mode encrypts only the payload (data) portion of the packet.

4. _____

5. Two common protocols associated with IPSec are _____ and _____.

5. _____

_____

6. When implementing IPSec, authentication can be verified using _____, a preshared key or digital certificate.

6. _____

Practice 15.7

Fill in the blanks for the statements about wireless security.

802.11i	**Media Access Control (MAC) filter**
Remote Authentication Dial-In User Service (RADIUS)	**Wi-Fi Protected Access (WPA)**
Wi-Fi Protected Access 2 (WPA2)	**Wired Equivalent Privacy (WEP)**

1. A(n) _____ allows or restricts Wireless Access Point access based on the MAC address of a wireless network card.

1. _____

2. The first attempt to secure the data transferred across a wireless network was with the _____ protocol.

2. _____

3. The _____ uses a more complex encryption system than WEP and has become the replacement for WEP.

3. _____

4. The _____ protocol is an enhanced version of WPA.

4. _____

5. The _____ standard specifies the use of a 128-bit Advanced Encryption Standard (AES) for data encryption.

5. _____

6. The _____ service allows remote access servers to authenticate to a central server.

6. _____

Practice 15.8

Label the components required by 802.11i.

authentication server	authenticator	RADIUS	supplicant

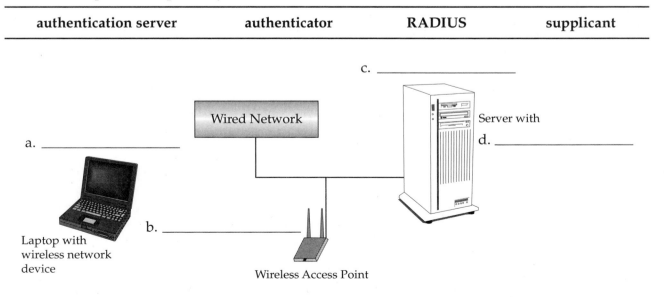

c. _____

Wired Network

a. _____

Server with

d. _____

b. _____

Laptop with wireless network device

Wireless Access Point

Practice 15.9

Fill in the blanks for the statements about wireless security. The following terms may be used more than once.

AAA proxy	accounting	authentication	authorization

1. Triple A is a security standard that consists of three parts: _____, _____, _____.

   1. _____
      _____
      _____

2. The process of identifying which system resources a user may use is called _____.

   2. _____

3. A(n) _____ system tracks what resources a user accesses and keeps a record of user activity.

   3. _____

4. The process of verifying the identity of a user is called _____.

   4. _____

5. Diameter is an IETF standard and _____ protocol designed to secure a connection between two or more devices.

   5. _____

6. The _____ is any network device that acts as an intermediary to exchange security packets between the AAA server and an AAA client.

   6. _____

Practice 15.10

Identify the characteristics as belonging to RADIUS (R) or TACACS+ (T).

1. _____ Uses separate databases for authentication, authorization, and accounting.

2. _____ Encrypts only the password.

3. _____ Uses connectionless UDP.

4. _____ Uses a token-based authentication method.

5. _____ Uses connection-oriented TCP.

6. _____ Uses one database for authentication, authorization, and accounting.

7. _____ Encrypts the entire exchange of logon packets.

Copyright by Goodheart-Willcox Co., Inc.

Practice 15.11

Match the authentication protocol to its definition.

1. _____ Challenge Handshake Authentication Protocol (CHAP)

2. _____ Extensible Authentication Protocol (EAP)

3. _____ Kerberos

4. _____ Lightweight Extensible Authentication Protocol (LEAP)

5. _____ Microsoft Challenge Handshake Authentication Protocol (MS-CHAP)

6. _____ Password Authentication Protocol (PAP)

7. _____ Protected Extensible Authentication Protocol (PEAP)

8. _____ Wi-Fi protected Access (WPA)

a. An authentication protocol that sends a user name and password in plain text format.

b. An authentication protocol that sends an encrypted string of characters that represent the user name and password. It does not send the actual user name and password.

c. An enhanced version of CHAP that encrypts the user name, password, and data and must be used with Microsoft operating systems.

d. An IETF standard that is used for network access and authentication in a client/server environment when IP is not available.

e. A security authentication system that provides both authentication and encryption services and uses a two-way method of authentication.

f. Enhances EAP authentication by encapsulating the EAP protocol inside an encrypted PEAP packet over a wireless network.

g. An authentication system developed by Cisco that periodically re-authenticates the wireless connection.

h. Developed by the Wi-Fi organization as a solution to the vulnerabilities discovered in WEP.

Practice 15.12

Fill in the blanks for the statements about security implementation.

hash	open ports	service pack	Zero Configuration (Zeroconf)

1. A third-party utility or the **netstat** utility should be used to check for _____.

2. If a Wireless Access Point (WAP) is installed with default settings and it uses _____ to configure the clients, anyone using a wireless network card of the same brand as the WAP can access the network.

3. Before the installation of an operating system or software application is considered complete, the latest _____ must be installed.

4. A network administrator must ensure that secure passwords, which an intruder cannot easily crack or _____, are used.

1. _____

2. _____

3. _____

4. _____

Practice 15.13

Fill in the blank for the statements about firewalls and proxy servers.

application gateway	circuit-level gateway	content filter
demilitarized zone (DMZ)	firewall	firewall signature identification
packet filter	proxy server	stateful packet inspection
stateless packet inspection		

1. A(n) _____ is a hardware device or software that passes or blocks packets as they enter or leave a network system.

2. A(n) _____ inspects each packet as it passes through the firewall and then accepts or rejects the packet based on a set of rules.

3. The firewall inspection method called _____ inspects the sequence of packets to detect missing packets or an altered sequence.

4. The firewall inspection method called _____ inspects and filters individual packet attributes such as IP address, port number, and protocols.

5. A(n) _____ is configured to accept traffic based on the exact match of the application permitted.

6. A(n) _____ monitors a connection until it is successfully established between the destination and source host.

1. _____

2. _____

3. _____

4. _____

5. _____

6. _____

Copyright by Goodheart-Willcox Co., Inc.

7. The _____ is a hardware device or software that provides security based on packet contents.

7. _____

8. The _____ is the area of a network that permits access from a host located outside the local area network.

8. _____

9. A hardware device or software that works in similar fashion as antivirus protection is called _____.

9. _____

10. A(n) _____ can cache information such as frequently visited Web sites and their IP addresses.

10. _____

Practice 15.14

Identify the characteristics as belonging to biometrics (B) or smart card (SC).

1. _____ A science.

2. _____ A technology.

3. _____ Uses the unique features of a person to confirm his or her identification.

4. _____ Incorporates a special card into the security system.

5. _____ Often used in conjunction with a personal identification number (PIN).

Practice 15.15

Fill in the blank for the statements about security tools. The following terms may be used more than once.

audit tool	netstat utility	packet sniffer
protocol analyzer	self-hack tool	system backup

1. To check for open ports, use the _____ with the **-a** switch at the command prompt.

1. _____

2. Event Viewer is considered a(n) _____ because it allows network activity or events to be monitored and logged.

2. _____

3. GFI LANguard can be used as a(n) _____ to probe the LAN for open communication ports and general security weaknesses.

3. _____

4. A(n) _____ can reveal information about protocols such as the source and destination IP address, MAC address, port address, time of transmission, and the contents of unencrypted packets.

4. _____

5. A(n) _____ is mainly designed as a tool to capture packet contents and header information and to provide limited information.

5. _____

6. The _____ can be used to restore corrupted data; however, any data that has been modified or saved since the last backup cannot be restored.

6. _____

Practice 15.16

Match the data security compliance requirement to its definition.

1. _____ California SB 1386

2. _____ Health Insurance Portability and Accountability Act (HIPAA)

3. _____ Payment Card Industry Data Security Standard (PCI DSS)

4. _____ Sarbanes-Oxley (SOX)

a. A legislative act that requires all organizations that own or have access to personal information of California residents to notify the person of any breach of security of his or her personal data.

b. A legislative act that imposes standards on financial institutions to secure personal financial records.

c. A set of standards designed to protect health records.

d. A set of credit card security standards designed to protect credit card information.

Copyright by Goodheart-Willcox Co., Inc.

16

Name _____ Date _____

Period _____

A Closer Look at the OSI Model

Introduction

For the Network+ Certification exam, you should be able to identify the function of each OSI model layer. You should also be able to identify the layer at which a network device operates.

Practice 16.1

Match the OSI layer to its definition.

1. _____ application
2. _____ data link
3. _____ network
4. _____ physical
5. _____ presentation
6. _____ session
7. _____ transport

a. Negotiates a common set of symbols that the source and destination hosts can interpret.
b. Establishes, maintains, and terminates the connection with the destination.
c. Converts the data package into electrical pulses and places them on the network media.
d. Interfaces with the networking application.
e. Provides reliable end-to-end data transmissions and error-checking techniques based on sequence packet numbers and software programs.
f. Concerned with navigating the network by using IP addresses.
g. Provides the path for the raw digital pulses that are moved along cables and connectors.

Practice 16.2

Fill in the blank for the statements about the layers of the OSI model. The following terms may be used more than once.

application	data link	network	physical
presentation	session	transport	

1. The _____ layer is where IP addressing is added to the segment and the segment is turned into a packet by including the IP address of the destination and source.

2. The _____ layer establishes, maintains, and terminates a connection with a destination host.

3. The _____ layer is where the user interfaces with the network system using network programs such as a Web browser, FTP, Telnet, and an e-mail client.

4. The _____ layer is concerned with bit sequence and with using an acceptable data format such as ASCII, EBCDIC, and CODEC.

5. The _____ layer provides the path for digital signals and represents the media, connectors, and passive components.

6. The _____ layer is concerned with providing reliable, accurate data in the most efficient manner.

7. The _____ layer is where frames are converted into a serial stream of data and decisions based on MAC addresses are made.

8. Token is the name given to the packet that exchanges _____ information between the source and destination.

9. At the _____ layer, the destination host and source host decide the maximum size of each segment and the amount of segments that will be sent before requiring an acknowledgment. This process is called *windowing*, or *flow control*.

10. At the _____ layer, the size of the packet is determined based on the buffer size (amount of memory to temporarily store data) at the destination and source host.

11. The _____ layer uses Service Access Points (SAPs), or MAC addresses that identify a protocol and its service, to communicate with protocols at various layers of the OSI model.

12. The _____ layer uses the Internet Management Protocol (IGMP) to support multicasting, or sending the same data packet to a group of hosts identified by one IP address.

1. _____

2. _____

3. _____

4. _____

5. _____

6. _____

7. _____

8. _____

9. _____

10. _____

11. _____

12. _____

Copyright by Goodheart-Willcox Co., Inc.

Practice 16.3

Fill in the blanks for the statements about the MAC and LLC sublayers.

LLC	MAC
1. The _____ sublayer converts the frame and its contents into a series of digital pulses to be carried on the media (physical layer).	1. _____
2. The _____ sublayer prepares for half-duplex or full-duplex transmission based on media type.	2. _____
3. The _____ sublayer is concerned with framing the contents of the upper levels, including the MAC addresses of the source and destination.	3. _____
4. The _____ sublayer performs collision avoidance.	4. _____
5. The _____ sublayer deals with physical addresses rather than logical addresses.	5. _____
6. The _____ sublayer ensures the reliability of the physical connection rather than of the data contained within the frame.	6. _____
7. The _____ sublayer negotiates transmission speed.	7. _____
8. The _____ sublayer performs a Cyclic Redundancy Check (CRC).	8. _____

Practice 16.4

Match the network device to the statement about how it handles packet delivery. Statements can be used more than once.

1. _____ bridge
2. _____ hub
3. _____ network interface card
4. _____ repeater
5. _____ router
6. _____ switch (layer 3)
7. _____ transceiver
8. _____ WAP

a. Makes no decision about where a packet is sent.
b. Makes decisions about where a packet is sent based on a MAC address or a logical name.
c. Makes a decision about where a packet is sent based on a protocol such as the Internet protocol.

Practice 16.5

Identify the OSI layer(s) at which the following network devices operate. Some network devices operate at more than one layer.

application	data link	network	physical
presentation	session	transport	

1. bridge: _____

2. gateway: _____

3. hub: _____

4. network interface card: _____

5. repeater: _____

6. router: _____

7. switch (layer 2): _____

8. transceiver: _____

9. switch (layer 3): _____

10. Wireless Access Point: _____

11. switch (layer 4): _____

12. amplifier: _____

Copyright by Goodheart-Willcox Co., Inc.

17

Name _____ Date _____

Period _____

Maintaining the Network

Introduction

For the Network+ Certification exam, you should be able to identify the types of methods used in maintaining a network, such as establishing a baseline, using monitoring tools, documenting and carrying out policies and procedures, and applying patches and updates. You should also be able to recall the characteristics of common security threats.

Practice 17.1

Fill in the blanks for the statements about monitoring the server and network.

average utilization	baseline
frame size average	frame size peak
peak utilization	Simple Network Management Protocol (SNMP)
swap file	

1. When an operating system uses the _____ instead of RAM, data processing slows because the hard disk drive cannot perform at the same high speed as the RAM.

1. _____

2. The only way to objectively determine the performance of a network or server is to establish a(n) _____ immediately after the network or server is installed.

2. _____

3. The highest level of utilization experience by a network is called _____.

3. _____

4. The average amount of utilization or traffic on the network in the time period monitored is called _____.

4. _____

5. The _____ is a record of the largest frame size recorded during the time period monitored.

5. _____

6. The _____ is the average of all frame sizes during the period monitored.

6. _____

7. The _____ was designed by the ITEF to support network management, allowing an administrator to manage and monitor network devices and services from a single location.

7. _____

Practice 17.2

Fill in the blanks for the statements about maintaining the network.

bug	cluster	disaster recovery
fault tolerance	service pack	

1. A software program error is referred to as a _____.

2. Microsoft uses the term _____ to describe a collection of software patches, or fixes.

3. A _____ is a group of servers that share the network demand and allow a server to be taken off-line without disrupting network activities.

4. A system's ability to continue operation during a system hardware or software error is referred to as _____.

5. The restoration of a system to normal operation after a disaster has occurred is referred to as _____.

1. _____

2. _____

3. _____

4. _____

5. _____

Practice 17.3

Identify each of the strategies and devices as either fault tolerance (FT), disaster recovery (DR), or neither (leave blank).

1. _____ a comparable disk drive kept in storage

2. _____ a running system and backup data kept at a storage facility

3. _____ clustered servers

4. _____ cold spare

5. _____ dual ring topology

6. _____ full backup with a differential backup

7. _____ full backup with incremental backups

8. _____ generator

9. _____ hot spare

10. _____ RAID 0

11. _____ RAID 5

12. _____ Uninterruptible Power Supply (UPS)

Copyright by Goodheart-Willcox Co., Inc.

Practice 17.4

Fill in the blanks for the statements about backup and restore strategies. Some of the following terms may be used more than once.

differential	each	full	incremental	the last

1. A(n) _____ backup operation copies all identified data during a single backup period.

2. A(n) _____ backup backs up all data that has been changed since the last full backup.

3. A(n) _____ backup copies only files that have changed since the last backup.

4. The archive bit is reset every time a(n) _____ backup or a(n) _____ backup is performed.

5. The archive bit is not reset when a(n) _____ backup is performed or when a file is copied using commands such as **copy** and **xcopy**.

6. When restoring data from an incremental backup, _____ incremental tape is needed as well as the last full backup.

7. When restoring data from a differential backup, the last full backup and _____ differential backup created are needed.

1. _____

2. _____

3. _____

4. _____

5. _____

6. _____

7. _____

Practice 17.5

Match the disaster recovery technique to its definition.

1. _____ cold site
2. _____ cold spare
3. _____ hot site
4. _____ hot spare
5. _____ warm site

a. A backup component that can automatically replace the failed system component without the intervention of a technician.
b. A data storage facility where backup data is stored.
c. A data storage facility where hardware and data are stored, but the data has not yet been loaded onto the hardware.
d. Any compatible drive that is in storage and used to replace a failed drive.
e. A data storage facility where a backup of data is stored as well as a running system containing the most up-to-date data.

Copyright by Goodheart-Willcox Co., Inc.

Practice 17.6

Match the power device or term to its definition.

1. _____ continuous UPS
2. _____ generator
3. _____ isolation transformer
4. _____ lightning arrestor
5. _____ power conditioning
6. _____ standby UPS
7. _____ Uninterruptible Power Supply (UPS)

a. A special piece of electrical equipment designed to dampen the effects of an electrical surge caused by lightning.
b. A device that ensures constant and consistent network performance by supplying electrical energy in case of a power failure or blackout.
c. A UPS unit that waits until there is a disruption in commercial electricity before it takes over the responsibility of supplying electrical energy.
d. A UPS unit that provides a steady supply of electrical energy at all times, even when there is no electrical problem.
e. A device that uses a transformer to isolate a circuit from other circuits emanating from the same electrical source.
f. The process of eliminating spikes and any type of variation in the desired AC signal pattern.
g. A device that creates and provides electricity.

Practice 17.7

Label the conditions of commercial electrical power.

blackout	brownout	spike	surge

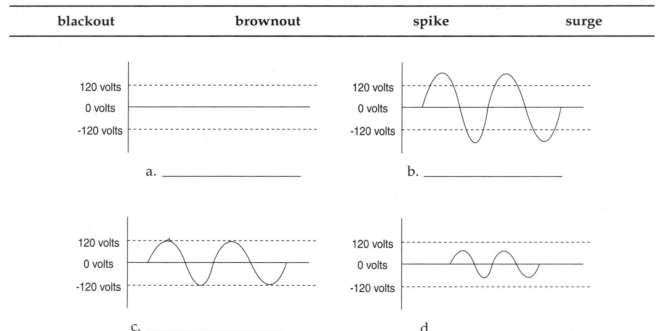

a. _____

b. _____

c. _____

d. _____

Copyright by Goodheart-Willcox Co., Inc.

Practice 17.8

Match the malware and antivirus software term to its definition.

1. _____ antivirus suite
2. _____ backdoor virus
3. _____ hoax
4. _____ joke program
5. _____ logic bomb
6. _____ macro virus
7. _____ malware
8. _____ MBR virus

a. An antivirus software package that includes additional features.
b. A software program designed to perform some type of unauthorized activity on a computer.
c. A type of malware designed with some sort of joke as the payload.
d. A type of malware that attacks the master boot record (MBR) of a hard disk drive.
e. A type of malware that remains dormant until a certain event takes place.
f. A type of malware designed to go undetected and create a backdoor on a computer.
g. A message that is spread about a real or unreal virus.
h. A virus created by the macro feature of a software application program.

Practice 17.9

Match the malware and antivirus software term to its definition.

1. _____ password virus
2. _____ polymorphic virus
3. _____ scan engine
4. _____ stealth virus
5. _____ Trojan horse
6. _____ virus
7. _____ virus pattern file
8. _____ worm

a. A software program that reads each file indicated in the scan configuration and checks it against the virus signatures in the virus pattern file.
b. A type of malware that appears as a gift, a utility, a game, or an e-mail attachment.
c. A database of virus signatures, or codes, unique to each known virus.
d. A type of malware designed to breach security by stealing passwords.
e. A type of malware that infects files on a computer and automatically spreads to other computers.
f. A type of malware that changes its characteristics or profile as it spreads to resist detection.
g. A type of malware that hides from normal detection by incorporating itself into part of a known and usually required program.
h. A type of malware that replicates itself on a computer after infecting it.

Copyright by Goodheart-Willcox Co., Inc.

18

Fundamentals of Troubleshooting the Network

Introduction

For the Network+ Certification exam, you should be able to select the appropriate network utility or tool for a given troubleshooting scenario. You should also be familiar with CompTIA's network troubleshooting methodology.

Practice 18.1

Match the CompTIA Network+ troubleshooting methodology to its example.

1. _____ Information gathering—identify symptoms and problems.

2. _____ Identify the affected areas of the network.

3. _____ Determine if anything has changed.

4. _____ Establish the most probable cause.

5. _____ Determine if escalation is necessary.

6. _____ Create an action plan and solution identifying potential effects.

7. _____ Implement and test the solution.

8. _____ Identify the results and effects of the solution.

9. _____ Document the solution and the entire process.

a. Asking a question such as, "Was a new hardware device recently installed?"

b. Asking a series of simple questions to better understand and isolate the problem.

c. Keeping a history of a system, including problems and solutions.

d. Attempting to duplicate the problem.

e. Conducting an Internet search using key words related to the symptom.

f. Documenting your work as you progress through the process of diagnosing and implementing a possible solution.

g. Determining the scope or area of the problem.

h. Before applying a possible solution, considering the extent of how it will affect the existing system.

i. Determining if the problem should be passed on to a supervisor or someone with more expertise.

Practice 18.2

Identify the stage of computer operation for each computer failure.

POST	OS load and initiation	after a successful logon

1. corrupt driver file: _____

2. corrupt service: _____

3. hardware failure: _____

4. corrupt software application: _____

5. corrupt operating system: _____

Practice 18.3

Arrange the Windows Vista, Windows 7, and Windows Server 2008 boot process phases in the order of occurrence.

initial startup	kernel loading	logon phase
POST	Windows Boot Loader	Windows Boot Manager

1. _____

2. _____

3. _____

4. _____

5. _____

6. _____

Practice 18.4

Match the boot event to the related boot process phase.

1. _____ initial startup

2. _____ kernel loading

3. _____ logon phase

4. _____ POST

5. _____ Windows Boot Loader

6. _____ Windows Boot Manager

a. The winlogon.exe program is executed and the logon dialog box appears.

b. The POST routine looks for the boot device where the MBR is stored.

c. The system firmware performs a quick check of hardware components and verifies that all hardware devices listed in the configuration database are present and appear to be in working order.

d. The winload.exe loads the NT kernel (ntoskrnl.exe) and hardware abstract layer (HAL) into RAM and then executes the kernel.

e. The NT kernel loads the device drivers, initializes the HAL, and initializes the computer settings using stored values in the registry.

f. The BIOS loads bootmgr. The bootmgr program starts winload.exe.

Networking Fundamentals Study Guide

Copyright by Goodheart-Willcox Co., Inc.

Practice 18.5

Match the Windows troubleshooting tool to its function.

1. _____ system repair disc
2. _____ Last Known Good Configuration
3. _____ Recovery Console
4. _____ Roll Back Driver
5. _____ safe mode
6. _____ System Configuration
7. _____ System Restore

a. Allows the technician to select the startup items or services to be loaded.
b. Allows the technician to enter system commands in an attempt to recover the system.
c. Loads only standard video drivers and essential drivers.
d. A disc used to repair or replace items such as the MBR, file allocation tables, system registry files, or system configuration files.
e. Reverts the system to the last driver configured for a specific device.
f. Replaces the system registry with the last copy of the registry made during a successful boot.
g. Restores the operating system to a condition established at a previous time by rolling back the registry and removing executable files that were installed after the rollback date.

Practice 18.6

Match the network troubleshooting tool to its description.

1. _____ loopback
2. _____ network analyzer
3. _____ network cable tester
4. _____ Optical Time Domain Reflectometer (OTDR)
5. _____ protocol analyzer
6. _____ Time Domain Reflectometer (TDR)
7. _____ tone generator and tracer
8. _____ wireless network tester/analyzer

a. Consists of two components: one that produces and transmits an analog or digital signal on a cable and the other that receives the signal. The two components work together to detect a cable fault.
b. A device used when checking a hardware device's ability to transmit and receive signals.
c. A device that performs a series of checks of cable integrity. It can quickly detect opens, shorts, and grounds.
d. Checks signal strength and measures radio and electromagnetic interference.
e. Sends an electronic pulse down copper core cable and then reads signal bounce to locate cable faults.
f. Tests the entire network infrastructure.
g. Sends light energy through a fiber-optic cable to detect defects in the core and connectors.
h. Captures and monitors data frames traveling across the network media.

Practice 18.7

Match the appropriate network utility to a troubleshooting scenario.

1. _____ **arp**

2. _____ **ipconfig/ifconfig/winipcfg**

3. _____ **nbstat**

4. _____ **net**

5. _____ **netstat**

6. _____ **nslookup/dig**

7. _____ **pathping**

8. _____ **ping**

9. _____ **ping localhost**

10. _____ **route**

11. _____ **tracert/traceroute**

a. Verify that a connection exists between the destination and the source.
b. Verify a path to a distant destination.
c. Display information about active TCP/IP connections.
d. Verify that the WINS server is functioning properly or that NetBIOS over TCP has been configured correctly on the network interface card.
e. Display information contained in the local routing table.
f. Verify that the TCP/IP protocol is configured for the network interface card at the host.
g. Verify the physical address of another client or device on the local network.
h. Verify that the DNS server is available and that there is a complete network media path to the DNS server.
i. A Microsoft command-line tool used to investigate the local network.
j. Identify the IP configuration of a computer.
k. Provides statistical analysis of the route to each router or gateway along a path to identify intermittent network bottlenecks.

Practice 18.8

Label each troubleshooting utility display.

arp -a	ipconfig	nbtstat -c	net stats
netstat -e	netstat -r	nslookup	pathping
ping	route print	tracert/traceroute	

```
Ethernet adapter Local Area Connection:

    Connection-specific DNS Suffix  . : gwp.com
    IP Address. . . . . . . . . . . . : 192.0.0.187
    Subnet Mask . . . . . . . . . . . : 255.255.255.0
    Default Gateway . . . . . . . . . : 192.0.0.110
```

a. _____

Copyright by Goodheart-Willcox Co., Inc.

b. _____

c. _____

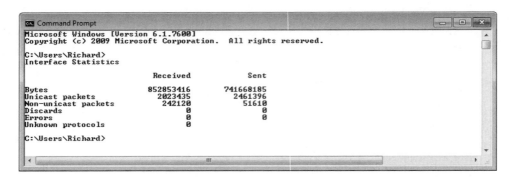

d. _____

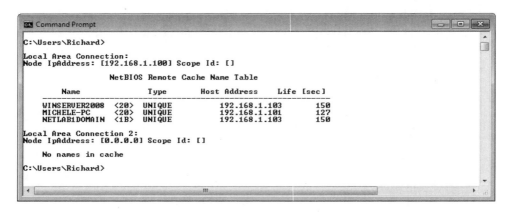

e. _____

```
Command Prompt - nslookup

Microsoft Windows [Version 6.1.7600]
Copyright (c) 2009 Microsoft Corporation.  All rights reserved.

C:\Users\Richard>
Default Server:  cns.bonitasprngs.fl.naples.comcast.net
Address:  68.87.74.166

>
```

f. _____

Copyright by Goodheart-Willcox Co., Inc.

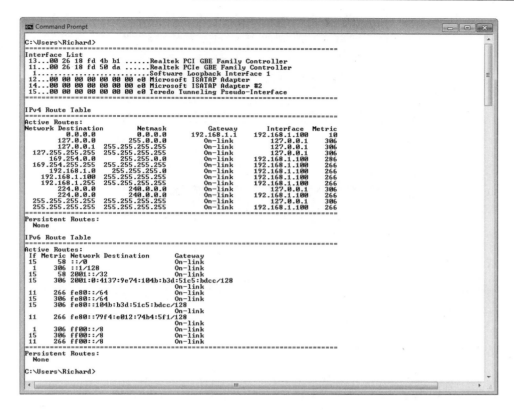

```
C:\Users\Richard>
===========================================================================
Interface List
 13...00 26 18 fd 4b b1 ......Realtek PCI GBE Family Controller
 11...00 26 18 fd 50 da ......Realtek PCIe GBE Family Controller
  1...........................Software Loopback Interface 1
 12...00 00 00 00 00 00 00 e0 Microsoft ISATAP Adapter
 14...00 00 00 00 00 00 00 e0 Microsoft ISATAP Adapter #2
 15...00 00 00 00 00 00 00 e0 Teredo Tunneling Pseudo-Interface
===========================================================================

IPv4 Route Table
===========================================================================
Active Routes:
Network Destination        Netmask          Gateway       Interface  Metric
          0.0.0.0          0.0.0.0      192.168.1.1   192.168.1.100     10
        127.0.0.0        255.0.0.0         On-link         127.0.0.1    306
        127.0.0.1  255.255.255.255         On-link         127.0.0.1    306
  127.255.255.255  255.255.255.255         On-link         127.0.0.1    306
      169.254.0.0      255.255.0.0         On-link     192.168.1.100    286
  169.254.255.255  255.255.255.255         On-link     192.168.1.100    266
      192.168.1.0    255.255.255.0         On-link     192.168.1.100    266
    192.168.1.100  255.255.255.255         On-link     192.168.1.100    266
    192.168.1.255  255.255.255.255         On-link     192.168.1.100    266
        224.0.0.0        240.0.0.0         On-link         127.0.0.1    306
        224.0.0.0        240.0.0.0         On-link     192.168.1.100    266
  255.255.255.255  255.255.255.255         On-link         127.0.0.1    306
  255.255.255.255  255.255.255.255         On-link     192.168.1.100    266
===========================================================================
Persistent Routes:
  None

IPv6 Route Table
===========================================================================
Active Routes:
 If Metric Network Destination      Gateway
 15     58 ::/0                      On-link
  1    306 ::1/128                   On-link
 15     58 2001::/32                 On-link
 15    306 2001:0:4137:9e74:104b:b3d:51c5:bdcc/128
                                     On-link
 11    266 fe80::/64                 On-link
 15    306 fe80::/64                 On-link
 15    306 fe80::104b:b3d:51c5:bdcc/128
                                     On-link
 11    266 fe80::79f4:e012:74b4:5f1/128
                                     On-link
  1    306 ff00::/8                  On-link
 15    306 ff00::/8                  On-link
 11    266 ff00::/8                  On-link
===========================================================================
Persistent Routes:
  None

C:\Users\Richard>
```

g. _____

```
C:\Users\Richard>
===========================================================================
Interface List
 13...00 26 18 fd 4b b1 ......Realtek PCI GBE Family Controller
 11...00 26 18 fd 50 da ......Realtek PCIe GBE Family Controller
  1...........................Software Loopback Interface 1
 12...00 00 00 00 00 00 00 e0 Microsoft ISATAP Adapter
 14...00 00 00 00 00 00 00 e0 Microsoft ISATAP Adapter #2
 15...00 00 00 00 00 00 00 e0 Teredo Tunneling Pseudo-Interface
===========================================================================

IPv4 Route Table
===========================================================================
Active Routes:
Network Destination        Netmask          Gateway       Interface  Metric
          0.0.0.0          0.0.0.0      192.168.1.1   192.168.1.100     10
        127.0.0.0        255.0.0.0         On-link         127.0.0.1    306
        127.0.0.1  255.255.255.255         On-link         127.0.0.1    306
  127.255.255.255  255.255.255.255         On-link         127.0.0.1    306
      169.254.0.0      255.255.0.0         On-link     192.168.1.100    286
  169.254.255.255  255.255.255.255         On-link     192.168.1.100    266
      192.168.1.0    255.255.255.0         On-link     192.168.1.100    266
    192.168.1.100  255.255.255.255         On-link     192.168.1.100    266
    192.168.1.255  255.255.255.255         On-link     192.168.1.100    266
        224.0.0.0        240.0.0.0         On-link         127.0.0.1    306
        224.0.0.0        240.0.0.0         On-link     192.168.1.100    266
  255.255.255.255  255.255.255.255         On-link         127.0.0.1    306
  255.255.255.255  255.255.255.255         On-link     192.168.1.100    266
===========================================================================
Persistent Routes:
  None

IPv6 Route Table
===========================================================================
Active Routes:
 If Metric Network Destination      Gateway
 15     58 ::/0                      On-link
  1    306 ::1/128                   On-link
 15     58 2001::/32                 On-link
 15    306 2001:0:4137:9e74:104b:b3d:51c5:bdcc/128
                                     On-link
 11    266 fe80::/64                 On-link
 15    306 fe80::/64                 On-link
 15    306 fe80::104b:b3d:51c5:bdcc/128
                                     On-link
 11    266 fe80::79f4:e012:74b4:5f1/128
                                     On-link
  1    306 ff00::/8                  On-link
 15    306 ff00::/8                  On-link
 11    266 ff00::/8                  On-link
===========================================================================
Persistent Routes:
  None

C:\Users\Richard>
```

h. _____

i. _____

```
Reply from 192.168.0.1: bytes=32 time<1ms TTL=250
Reply from 192.168.0.1: bytes=32 time<1ms TTL=250
Reply from 192.168.0.1: bytes=32 time<1ms TTL=250
Reply from 192.168.0.1: bytes=32 time<1ms TTL=250
```

j. _____

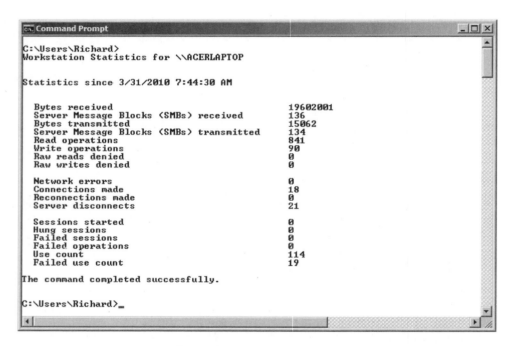

k. _____

Copyright by Goodheart-Willcox Co., Inc.

19

Name _____ Date _____

Period _____

Designing and Installing a New Network

Introduction

For the Network+ Certification exam, you should be familiar with wiring distribution components such as patch panels, smart jacks, and 66 and 110 blocks and be able to recall horizontal cabling distances as defined in the ANSI/TIA/EIA TSB-75 standard.

Practice 19.1

Match the architectural design element to its definition.

1. _____ entrance facility

2. _____ equipment room

3. _____ main entrance room

4. _____ telecommunications closet

5. _____ telecommunications room

6. _____ work area

a. The place where public or private telecommunications enter the building.

b. The room that is used as the entrance location for public or private communication cables.

c. A room that contains the telecommunications equipment for the building such as the Private Branch Exchange (PBX), servers, and telecommunications wiring system terminations.

d. The place where employees perform their normal office duties.

e. A room or enclosed space that houses telecommunications equipment, such as cable termination and cross connect wiring, and serves as a transition point between backbone and horizontal wiring.

f. An enclosed space that houses telecommunications cable termination equipment and is the recognized transition point between the backbone and horizontal wiring.

Practice 19.2

Match the wiring and wiring connection point term to its definition.

1. _____ backbone
2. _____ Consolidation Point (CP)
3. _____ demarcation point
4. _____ horizontal cross connect
5. _____ horizontal wiring
6. _____ Main Distribution Frame (MDF)
7. _____ Multi-User Telecommunication Outlet Assembly (MUTOA)
8. _____ Network Interface Device (NID)
9. _____ Optical Network Terminal (ONT)
10. _____ smart jack

a. A mechanical means of connecting horizontal cabling systems to other cables or equipment.
b. The cable connection point where the private telecommunications cables come into a building and then connect or distribute to other areas in the building. It typically consists of a cable rack and physical cable connections for the individual cable conductors.
c. The section of cable that runs from individual work areas to the telecommunications closet.
d. Any device that connects the commercial carrier local loop to the private customer's premises wiring.
e. A cable that is located between the telecommunications closets, equipment rooms, and main entrance facility.
f. The point where the customer equipment or cable meets the telecommunications provider cable or equipment.
g. An intelligent connection point, which incorporates additional electronics that allow it to perform specific functions.
h. A grouping of outlets that serves up to 12 work areas.
i. A connection to the horizontal wiring system, which in turn feeds to a wall outlet or a MUTOA.
j. A fiber-optic cable termination point between the customer and the service provider. It can provide multiple services such as telephone, television, and Internet access.

Practice 19.3

Match the wiring and wiring connection point term to its definition.

1. _____ insulation-displacement connector (IDC)
2. _____ patch panel
3. _____ punch down block
4. _____ punch down tool

a. A block of connections designed for terminating solid copper wire and typically consisting of insulation-displacement connectors.
b. A type of network and telecommunications cable termination connector designed to remove the insulation of individual conductors while being inserted with a punch down tool.
c. A tool used for pushing individual twisted pair wires into an insulation-displacement connector and automatically trimming conductor excess.
d. A rack-mounted device that has RJ-45 jacks on the front and a matching series of connections on the back.

Copyright by Goodheart-Willcox Co., Inc.

Practice 19.4

Label the maximum allowable cable length, taking into consideration the following rules:

❑ The overall length of the horizontal wiring is limited to 100 meters.
❑ The horizontal run from the telecommunications outlet to the telecommunications room is limited to 90 meters.
❑ The length of a patch panel cable is limited to 7 meters.

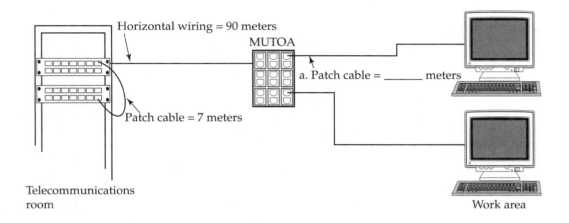

Horizontal wiring = 90 meters
MUTOA
a. Patch cable = _____ meters
Patch cable = 7 meters
Telecommunications room
Work area

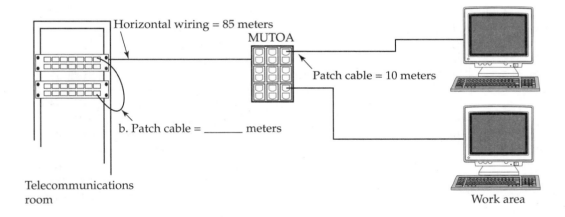

Horizontal wiring = 85 meters
MUTOA
Patch cable = 10 meters
b. Patch cable = _____ meters
Telecommunications room
Work area

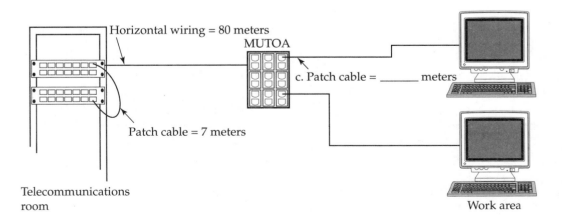

Horizontal wiring = 80 meters
MUTOA
c. Patch cable = _____ meters
Patch cable = 7 meters
Telecommunications room
Work area

Copyright by Goodheart-Willcox Co., Inc.   *Chapter 19* Designing and Installing a New Network   **143**

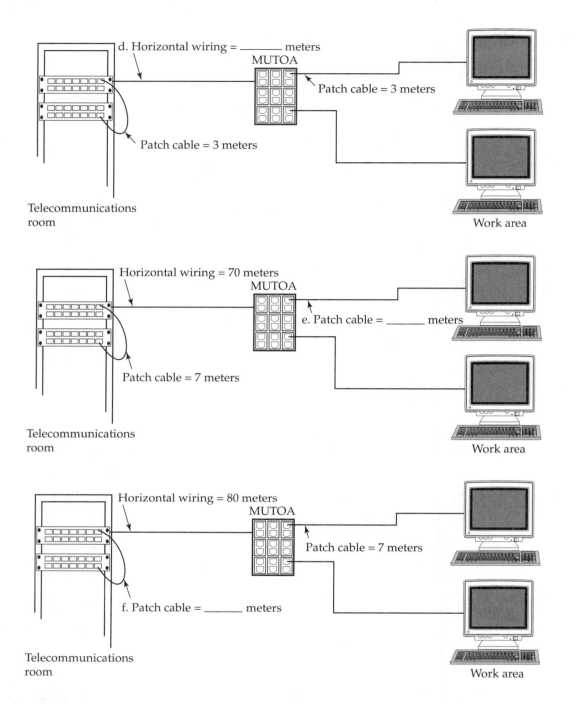

d. Horizontal wiring = _____ meters

MUTOA

Patch cable = 3 meters

Patch cable = 3 meters

Telecommunications room

Work area

Horizontal wiring = 70 meters

MUTOA

e. Patch cable = _____ meters

Patch cable = 7 meters

Telecommunications room

Work area

Horizontal wiring = 80 meters

MUTOA

Patch cable = 7 meters

f. Patch cable = _____ meters

Telecommunications room

Work area

Practice 19.5

Record the maximum backbone distance for each cable type.

90 meters	800 meters	2000 meters	3000 meters

1. multimode fiber-optic cable: _____

2. single-mode fiber-optic cable: _____

3. UTP or STP (data): _____

4. UTP or STP (voice): _____

Copyright by Goodheart-Willcox Co., Inc.

Instructions for Using the CompTIA Network+ Reference

The CompTIA Network+ Reference is designed to help you study for the CompTIA Network+ Certification exam. This material can also be used as a reference when completing the practice exercises in the Chapter Review section of this *Study Guide* or when studying for a classroom exam.

When using this section as a study guide, you may wish to approach your study by focusing on a topic or on a CompTIA Network+ objective. When focusing on a topic, be sure to review all related topics that are listed under Related Concepts. As you review the related topics, think about how they relate to the original topic.

When focusing on the CompTIA Network+ objectives, refer to the Network+ objective listed at the bottom of each reference page. Network+ objectives are presented in order throughout this section. However, because some objectives cover multiple concepts and only one concept is presented per reference page, the same Network+ objective may be repeated on consecutive pages. For example, the CompTIA Network+ objective 2-1 states the following:

2.1 Categorize standard cable types and their properties: Type (Cat 3, Cat 5, Cat 5e, Cat 6, STP, UTP; multimode fiber, single-mode fiber, coaxial, RG-59, RG-6, serial, plenum vs. non-plenum) and properties (transmission speeds, distance, duplex, noise immunity, frequency).

Since this objective contains multiple concepts, the *Study Guide* devotes seven reference pages to this objective and thus repeats the Network+ objective 2-1 on the bottom of each page. The following are the titles of the reference pages for this objective:

- Twisted Pair Cable
- STP vs. UTP
- Fiber-Optic Cable
- Single-Mode and Multimode
- Coaxial Cable
- Coaxial Cable Types
- Plenum-Rated Cables

Each reference page is identified with the CompTIA Network+ objective number and a letter from *A* to *Z*. This identification is located on the upper-right corner of each page. The letter *A* indicates the first topic related to the objective, the letter *B* indicates the second topic related to the objective, and so on. For example, the topics related to CompTIA Network+ objective 2-1 would be identified as follows:

2.1A   Twisted Pair Cable
2.1B   STP vs. UTP
2.1C   Fiber-Optic Cable
2.1D   Single-Mode and Multimode
2.1E   Coaxial Cable
2.1F   Coaxial Cable Types
2.1G   Plenum-Rated Cables

Therefore, be sure to check consecutive pages for coverage of the same objective you are studying. When using this section, in general, feel free to highlight text, record notes, and add to the illustrations. This will help you to better remember the material presented. If you decide to take the CompTIA Network+ Certification exam, carry this *Study Guide* with you for a last minute review.

These are just suggestions for using this section. This is *your Study Guide*. Use it in any way you feel it will be most effective. Be creative. For example, you may wish to choose a topic from the Table of Contents and then jot down everything you know about the topic. Then, you can compare your notes to the information presented in the reference section. You may even use the information presented to create your own study guide, arranging the information in a way that you can best remember it.

Copyright by Goodheart-Willcox Co., Inc.

Description

A networking protocol is a set of rules governing communication between devices on a network.

Examples

Networking Protocol	Function
ARP	Resolves IP addresses to MAC addresses.
DHCP	Assigns IP addresses automatically to hosts on a network.
DNS	Associates a host or domain name with an IP address, making it easy to identify and find hosts and networks.
FTP	Supports file transfers between a client and server.
HTTP(S)	Used for communications between a Web browser and a Web server. The *S* at the end of "https" means that the connection is secure and is using either SSL or TSL as the security mechanism.
ICMP	Part of the TCP/IP suite of protocols. It provides the ability to remotely troubleshoot and monitor devices on network systems.
IGMP	Supports multicasting by informing a multicast router of the names of the multicast group to which a host belongs.
IMAP4	E-mail access protocol that can manipulate e-mail while it is on the mail server. It also allows a user to access his or her e-mail and then leave the e-mail on the server.
NTP	Synchronizes time between network devices.
POP3	Simple e-mail access protocol designed to access a mail server and download e-mail to the e-mail client.
RTP (VoIP)	A standard and a protocol used to stream voice and video in real time.
SIP (VoIP)	A standard and a protocol for initiating, maintaining, and terminating the exchange of voice, multimedia, gaming, chat, and more.
SMTP	Transfers plain text e-mail from an e-mail client to a mail server and from a mail server to a mail server.
SNMP2/3	Allows an administrator to manage and monitor network devices and services from a single location.
SSH	Provides secure network services over an insecure network medium such as the Internet.
TCP	Connection-oriented protocol that ensures packets arrive intact and in correct order. Can break large amounts of data into smaller packets.
TCP/IP suite	Developed by the Defense Advanced Research Project Agency (DARPA) in the early 1970s and was designed to support communications over the Internet.
Telnet	Allows a user to manipulate files on a Telnet server.
TFTP	A lightweight version of FTP that does not require the use of a user name and password because it uses UDP packets for transferring data. It allows a client to transfer files, but not to view the directory listing at the FTP site.
TLS	Secures transactions between Web servers and individuals using the Internet for such purposes as credit card transactions.
UDP	Connectionless protocol that establishes a link but does not ensure data is delivered correctly. Sends a single packet to transmit control information and data.

Related Concepts

Port Numbers—1.2A	IPv4 Address—1.3B
IPv6 Address—1.3C	DHCP Server—3.1K
DNS Server—3.2E	ARP—5.1D
SSH—6.5A	HTTPS—6.5B
SNMP—6.5C	SFTP—6.5D
HTTP—6.5F	FTP—6.5G

Network+ Objective

1-1—Explain the function of common networking protocols: TCP, FTP, UDP, TCP/IP suite, DHCP, TFTP, DNS, HTTP(S), ARP, SIP (VoIP), RTP (VoIP), SSH, POP3, NTP, IMAP4, Telnet, SMTP, SNMP2/3, ICMP, IGMP, and TLS.

Copyright by Goodheart-Willcox Co., Inc.

Description

A port number is a number that is associated with the TCP/IP protocol and used to create a virtual connection between two computers running TCP/IP.

Examples

Port #	Service	Description
7	ECHO	Echo a reply
20	FTP	File Transfer Protocol data
21	FTP	File Transfer Protocol control commands
22	SSH	Secure Shell
23	TELNET	Terminal emulation connection
25	SMTP	Simple Mail Transfer Protoco
43	NICNAME	Who Is
49	LOGIN	Login Host Protocol
53	DNS	Domain Name Server
67	DHCP	Dynamic Host Configuration Protocol
69	TFTP	Trivia File Transfer Protocol
80	HTTP	Hypertext Transfer Protocol
110	POP	Post Office Protocol
119	NNTP	Network News Transfer Protocol
123	NTP	Network Time Protocol
137	NETBIOS	NetBIOS name service
143	IMAP4	Internet Message Access Protocol version 4
161	SNMP	Simple Network Management Protocol
389	LDAP	Lightweight Directory Access Protocol
443	HTTPS	HTTP Security
500	IPSEC	IP Security
1723	PPTP	Point-to-Point Tunneling Protocol
5631	pcAnywhere data	pcAnywhere data
5632	pcAnywhere status	pcAnywhere status
3389	Windows Remote Desktop	Remote access to desktops

Related Concepts

Networking Protocols—1.1A   DHCP Server—3.1K

DNS Server—3.2E   SSH—6.5A

HTTPS—6.5B   SNMP—6.5C

SFTP—6.5D   HTTP—6.5F

FTP—6.5G

Network+ Objective

1-2—Identify commonly used TCP and UDP default ports: TCP ports (FTP–20, 21; SSH–22; Telnet–23; SMTP–25; DNS–53; HTTP–80; POP3–110; NTP–123; IMAP4–143; HTTPS–443) and UDP ports (TFTP–69; DNS–53; BOOTPS/DHCP–67; SNMP–161).

Copyright by Goodheart-Willcox Co., Inc.

Description

A MAC address is a six-byte, hexadecimal number that uniquely identifies a network card. It is also called a physical ID or address. The first three bytes identify the network interface card's manufacturer, and the second three bytes uniquely identify the card.

Examples

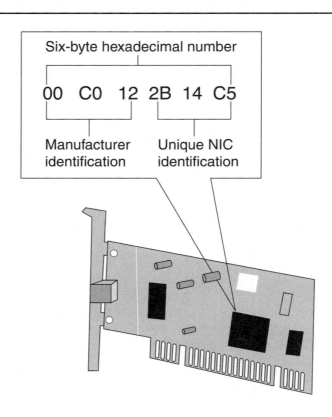

Related Concepts

Networking Protocols—1.1A	VLAN—2.7D
NIC—3.1D	Data Link Layer—4.1G
ARP—5.1D	Media Access Control Filter—6.3A

Network+ Objective

1.3—Identify the following address formats: IPv6, IPv4, and MAC addressing.

Description

An IPv4 address consists of four octets of binary numbers. These octets can be written in decimal form.

Examples

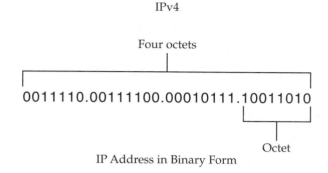

IPv4

Four octets

0011110.00111100.00010111.10011010

Octet

IP Address in Binary Form

30.60.23.154

IPv4 Decimal Form

Related Concepts

Subnetting—1.4A	Classful (IPv4) Addresses—1.4B
NAT—1.4D	Public and Private IP Addresses —1.4E
DHCP—1.4F	Network Layer—4.1F

Network+ Objective

1.3—Identify the following address formats: IPv6, IPv4, and MAC addressing.

1.3C   IPv6 Address

Description   An IPv6 address consists of 128 bits. The 128 bits are divided into 8 units of 16 bits. These units can be represented as a 4-digit hexadecimal number separated by colons.

Examples   The IPv6 addressing scheme.

The 128-bit IPv6 address is divided into eight 16-bit blocks each separated by a colon:

FE80:0000:0000:0000:4DE1:F01B:80FA:CCA3

A single 16-bit block containing all zeros can be expressed as a single zero:

FE80:0:0:0:4DE1:F01B:80FA:CCA3
         ↑

A series of 16-bit blocks containing only zeros can be expressed as a simple double colon:

FE80::4DE1:F01B:80FA:CCA3
     ↑

Only one double colon can be used in an IPv6 address:

FE80:0:0:0:A23D:0:0:CCA3
FE80::A23D:0:0:CCA3

Using a double colon more than once is illegal!!

Incorrect: FE80::A23D::CCA3
            ↑   ↑

**Related
Concepts**

Classless (IPv6) Addresses—1.4C

Unicast, Multicast, Anycast, and Broadcast—1.4G

Network Layer—4.1F

**Network+
Objective**

1.3—Identify the following address formats: IPv6, IPv4, and MAC addressing.

Description

Dividing a network into subnetworks, or subnets, is called *subnetting*. A subnet is a network created by borrowing bits from the host portion of an assigned network IP address. Subnetting allows multiple networks and host ranges to be created from a single, assigned IP address.

Examples

Assigned IP address: 130.200.86.64

Class B
subnet mask: **255.255.000.000**

Extended
Class B
subnet mask: **255.255.224.000**

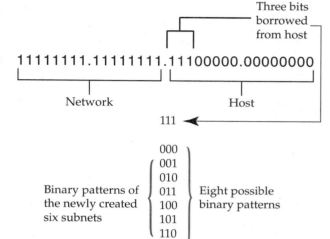

Three bits borrowed from host

11111111.11111111.11100000.00000000

Network   Host

111

Binary patterns of the newly created six subnets

000
001
010
011
100
101
110
111

Eight possible binary patterns

Subnet Network Address	Host Range	Broadcast Address
130.200.32.0	130.200.32.1 - 130.200.63.254	130.200.63.255
130.200.64.0	130.200.64.1 - 130.200.95.254	130.200.95.255
130.200.96.0	130.200.96.1 - 130.200.127.254	130.200.127.255
130.200.128.0	130.200.128.1 - 130.200.159.254	130.200.159.255
130.200.160.0	130.200.160.1 - 130.200.191.254	130.200.191.255
130.200.192.0	130.200.192.1 - 130.200.223.254	130.200.223.255

Related Concepts

IPv4 Address—1.3B

Classful (IPv4) Addresses—1.4B

Network+ Objective

1.4—Given a scenario, evaluate the proper use of the following addressing technologies and addressing schemes: Addressing technologies (subnetting, classful vs. classless, NAT, PAT, SNAT, public vs. private, DHCP) and addressing schemes (unicast, multicast, broadcast).

Copyright by Goodheart-Willcox Co., Inc.

1.4B　　　　Classful (IPv4) Addresses

Description

For the purpose of assigning IPv4 addresses, networks are divided into three major classifications: Class A, Class B, and Class C. Large networks are assigned a Class A classification. A Class A network can support up to 16 million hosts on each of 127 networks. Medium-sized networks are assigned a Class B classification. A Class B network supports up to 65,000 hosts on each of 16,000 networks. Small networks are assigned a Class C classification. A Class C network supports 254 hosts on each of 2 million networks.

Examples

Class	Range	Number of Networks	Number of Hosts
Class A	1–127	127	16,000,000
Class B	128–191	16,000	65,000
Class C	192–223	2,000,000	254

Related Concepts

IPv4 Address—1.3B　　　　Subnetting—1.4A

NAT—1.4D　　　　Public and Private IP Addresses—1.4E

DHCP—1.4F　　　　Network Layer—4.1F

Network+ Objective

1.4—Given a scenario, evaluate the proper use of the following addressing technologies and addressing schemes: Addressing technologies (subnetting, classful vs. classless, NAT, PAT, SNAT, public vs. private, DHCP) and addressing schemes (unicast, multicast, broadcast).

Description

IPv6 is referred to as a "classless IP addressing scheme" because there is no need for a subnet mask based on network class. IPv6 has been designed to not use a separate subnet mask, but it does use a prefix, which serves the same purpose as the IPv4 subnet mask. An IPv6 prefix is the portion of the address with a fixed value that informs network devices of what action to take. The IPv6 prefix is expressed as address/prefix. For example, FE80::/64 means that the first 64 bits represent the network address. You will see IPv6 addresses expressed in both forms: the entire IPv6 address or the Classless Inter-Domain Routing (CIDR).

Examples

Prefix	Address Type
2000::/3	Global unicast
FE80::/10	Link-local unicast
FC08::/10	Site-local unicast
FD08::/8	Unique-local unicast
FF00::/8	Multicast
FF01::1	Interface multicast local all nodes
FF02::1	Link-local multicast all nodes
FF01::2	Interface-local multicast all routers
FF02::2	Link-local multicast all routers
FF05::2	Site-local multicast all routers

Related Concepts

IPv6 Address—1.3C

Unicast, Multicast, Anycast, and Broadcast—1.4G

Network Layer—4.1F

Network+ Objective

1.4—Given a scenario, evaluate the proper use of the following addressing technologies and addressing schemes: Addressing technologies (subnetting, classful vs. classless, NAT, PAT, SNAT, public vs. private, DHCP) and addressing schemes (unicast, multicast, broadcast).

Description

Network Address Translation (NAT) is a protocol used to translate private network addresses into an assigned Internet address, and vice versa. NAT was especially designed for implementing private network configurations. It allows an unregistered private network address to communicate with a legally registered IP address. The three main advantages of using NAT are that NAT:

- Provides a firewall type of service by hiding internal IP addresses
- Allows computers on a network to share one common IP address to access the Internet without the need of multiple IP addresses to be assigned to the subnetwork
- Allows multiple ISDN connections to be combined into one Internet connection

Examples

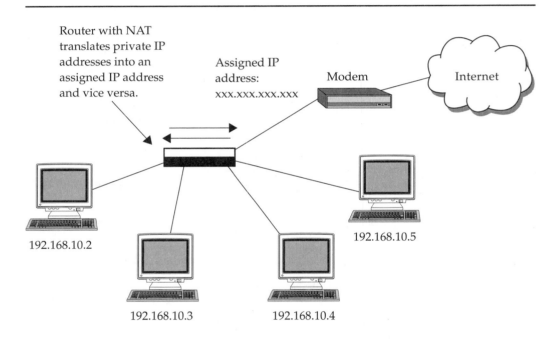

Related Concepts

IPv4 Address—1-3B	Subnetting—1.4A
Classful (IPv4) Addresses—1.4B	Public and Private IP Addresses—1.4E
DHCP—1.4F	Network Layer—4.1F

Network+ Objective

1.4—Given a scenario, evaluate the proper use of the following addressing technologies and addressing schemes: Addressing technologies (subnetting, classful vs. classless, NAT, PAT, SNAT, public vs. private, DHCP) and addressing schemes (unicast, multicast, broadcast).

Description

A number of IPv4 addresses are reserved for private networks. They are often used for offices sharing an Internet address or for experimentation. They are not valid for use as a direct connection to the Internet.

Examples

Class	Range	Number of Networks	Number of Hosts
Class A	1–127	127	16,000,000
Class B	128–191	16,000	65,000
Class C	192–223	2,000,000	254

Private IP Addresses

Class	Range	Subnet Mask
A	10.0.0.0–10.255.255.255	255.0.0.0
B	172.016.0.0–172.031.255.255	255.255.0.0
C	192.168.0.0–192.168.255.255	255.255.255.0

Related Concepts

IPv4 Address—1.3B

Router—3.1I

NAT—1.4D

Network+ Objective

1.4—Given a scenario, evaluate the proper use of the following addressing technologies and addressing schemes: Addressing technologies (subnetting, classful vs. classless, NAT, PAT, SNAT, public vs. private, DHCP) and addressing schemes (unicast, multicast, broadcast).

Description

Dynamic Host Configuration Protocol (DHCP) is a service that assigns IP addresses automatically to the hosts on a network. The IP address is randomly selected from a pool of addresses. The temporary IP address is returned to the pool when the lease expires.

Examples

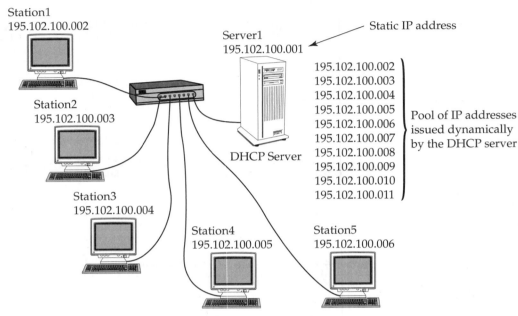

Each workstation receives a temporary IP address from the DHCP server

Related Concepts

IPv4 Address—1.3B	Classful (IPv4) Addresses—1.4B
DHCP Server—3.1K	

Network+ Objective

1.4—Given a scenario, evaluate the proper use of the following addressing technologies and addressing schemes: Addressing technologies (subnetting, classful vs. classless, NAT, PAT, SNAT, public vs. private, DHCP) and addressing schemes (unicast, multicast, broadcast).

Description

There are three broad classifications of IPv6 addresses: unicast, multicast, and anycast. A *unicast address* delivers packets to a single network address. A *multicast address* delivers packets to multiple addresses. An *anycast address* delivers packets to the nearest interface and is used mainly for supporting router functions. IPv4 uses broadcast and multicast addresses to distribute packets. A broadcast address sends packets to all network addresses. When messages are broadcast to all network nodes, a pattern of all ones is used in the destination address.

Examples

IPv6 Network Classifications

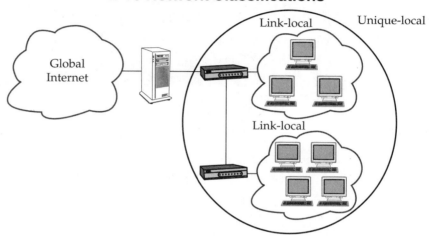

IPv6 Address Prefixes

Prefix	Address Type
2000::/3	Global unicast
FE80::/10	Link-local unicast
FC08::/10	Site-local unicast
FD08::/8	Unique-local unicast
FF00::/8	Multicast
FF01::1	Interface multicast local all nodes
FF02::1	Link-local multicast all nodes
FF01::2	Interface-local multicast all routers
FF02::2	Link-local multicast all routers
FF05::2	Site-local multicast all routers

Related Concepts

IPv6 Address—1.3C

Common IPv4 and IPv6 Routing Protocols—1.5A

Classless (IPv6) Addresses—1.4C

Network Layer—4.1F

Network+ Objective

1.4—Given a scenario, evaluate the proper use of the following addressing technologies and addressing schemes: Addressing technologies (subnetting, classful vs. classless, NAT, PAT, SNAT, public vs. private, DHCP) and addressing schemes (unicast, multicast, broadcast).

Copyright by Goodheart-Willcox Co., Inc.

Description

Two basic IPv4 and IPv6 routing protocol classifications are Interior Gateway Protocol (IGP) and Exterior Gateway Protocol (EGP). Two additional classifications are link state and distance vector.

Examples

Routing Protocol	Comment	IGP (Confined to an autonomous network)	EGP (Exchanges information between different autonomous networks)	Link State Protocol (Only transfers information about connections, and does not pass its routing table to other devices)	Distance Vector Protocol (Shares its routing table with other routers)
BGP	Exchanges routing information between different autonomous networks.		×		
EGP	Exchanges routing information between different autonomous networks.		×		
EIRGP	Guarantees loop-free operation. Cisco advertises EIGRP as a link state protocol and a distance vector protocol	×		×	×
IRGP	Allows a maximum hop count of 255 and uses a metric based on bandwidth, latency, route traffic, and reliability.	×			×
IS-IS	Detects router types as level 1 or level 2 when determining shortest route.	×		×	
OSPF	Can detect network link failures and then automatically determine next best path.	×		×	
RIP	Supports a maximum of 15 hops.	×			×
RIPng	IPv6 version of RIP.	×			×

Related Concepts

IGP vs. EGP—1.6A

Network+ Objective

1.5—Identify common IPv4 and IPv6 routing protocols: Link state (OSPF, IS-IS), distance vector (RIP, RIPv2, BGP), and hybrid (EIGRP).

Description

Two basic routing protocol classifications are Interior Gateway Protocol (IGP) and Exterior Gateway Protocol (EGP). IGP is confined to an autonomous network. EGP exchanges information between different autonomous networks.

Examples

Examples of IGP are RIP, IGRP, OSPF, and IS-IS. Examples of Exterior Gateway Protocol are BGP and EGP.

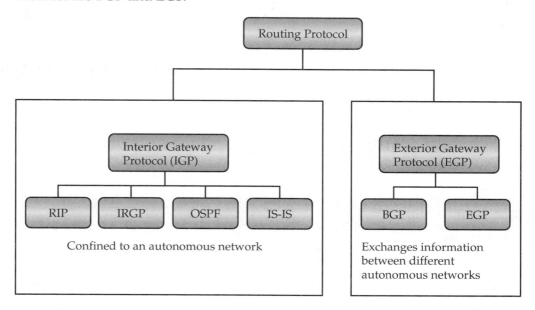

Related Concepts

Common IPv4 and IPv6 Routing Protocols—1.5A

Network+ Objective

1.6—Explain the purpose and properties of routing: IGP vs. EGP, static vs. dynamic, next hop, understanding routing tables and how they pertain to path selection, and explain convergence (steady state).

Description

Routers can be programmed to operate from static IP address tables or dynamic IP address tables. A static IP address table contains addresses that are entered manually. A dynamic IP address table contains addresses that are generated automatically by a software program that communicates with nearby routers.

Examples

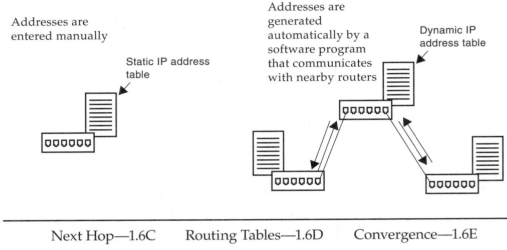

Related Concepts

Next Hop—1.6C   Routing Tables—1.6D   Convergence—1.6E

Router—3.1I   Route—5.1G

Network+ Objective

1.6—Explain the purpose and properties of routing: IGP vs. EGP, static vs. dynamic, next hop, understanding routing tables and how they pertain to path selection, and explain convergence (steady state).

Description

Hop is a measure of how many network devices, such as routers and gateways, a packet must pass through until it reaches its destination. The hop is the oldest and most basic metric used for determining the best route. When you issue a **tracert** command, you will see the number of hops that the **tracert** packet has passed through to reach its final destination.

Examples

Number of hops the **tracert** packet passed through to reach the final destination

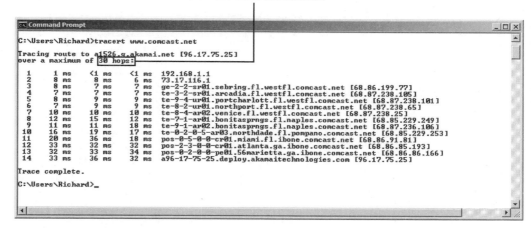

Related Concepts

Routing Tables—1.6D   Convergence—1.6E   Router—3.1I

Traceroute/Tracert—5.1A   Route—5.1G

Network+ Objective

1.6—Explain the purpose and properties of routing: IGP vs. EGP, static vs. dynamic, next hop, understanding routing tables and how they pertain to path selection, and explain convergence (steady state).

Description

The routing tables contain information about the other routers and networks. This information is processed by the router and then used to determine the best route to send the packet to its final destination.

Examples

The router metric is used to determine the best route

```
Command Prompt                                                          [─][□][✕]

C:\Users\Richard>route print
===========================================================================
Interface List
13...00 26 18 fd 4b b1 ......Realtek PCI GBE Family Controller
11...00 26 18 fd 50 da ......Realtek PCIe GBE Family Controller
 1...........................Software Loopback Interface 1
12...00 00 00 00 00 00 00 e0 Microsoft ISATAP Adapter
14...00 00 00 00 00 00 00 e0 Microsoft ISATAP Adapter #2
15...00 00 00 00 00 00 00 e0 Teredo Tunneling Pseudo-Interface
===========================================================================

IPv4 Route Table
===========================================================================
Active Routes:
Network Destination        Netmask          Gateway       Interface  Metric
          0.0.0.0          0.0.0.0      192.168.1.1   192.168.1.100      10
        127.0.0.0        255.0.0.0         On-link       127.0.0.1     306
        127.0.0.1  255.255.255.255         On-link       127.0.0.1     306
  127.255.255.255  255.255.255.255         On-link       127.0.0.1     306
      169.254.0.0      255.255.0.0         On-link   192.168.1.100     286
  169.254.255.255  255.255.255.255         On-link   192.168.1.100     266
      192.168.1.0    255.255.255.0         On-link   192.168.1.100     266
    192.168.1.100  255.255.255.255         On-link   192.168.1.100     266
    192.168.1.255  255.255.255.255         On-link   192.168.1.100     266
        224.0.0.0        240.0.0.0         On-link       127.0.0.1     306
        224.0.0.0        240.0.0.0         On-link   192.168.1.100     266
  255.255.255.255  255.255.255.255         On-link       127.0.0.1     306
  255.255.255.255  255.255.255.255         On-link   192.168.1.100     266
===========================================================================
Persistent Routes:
  None

IPv6 Route Table
===========================================================================
Active Routes:
 If Metric Network Destination      Gateway
 15     58 ::/0                     On-link
  1    306 ::1/128                  On-link
 15     58 2001::/32                On-link
 15    306 2001:0:4137:9e74:104b:b3d:51c5:bdcc/128
                                    On-link
 11    266 fe80::/64                On-link
 15    306 fe80::/64                On-link
 15    306 fe80::104b:b3d:51c5:bdcc/128
                                    On-link
 11    266 fe80::79f4:e012:74b4:5f1/128
                                    On-link
  1    306 ff00::/8                 On-link
 15    306 ff00::/8                 On-link
 11    266 ff00::/8                 On-link
===========================================================================
Persistent Routes:
  None

C:\Users\Richard>
```

Related Concepts

Static vs. Dynamic—1.6B	Next Hop—1.6C	Convergence—1.6E
Router—3.1I	Route—5.1G	

Network+ Objective

1.6—Explain the purpose and properties of routing: IGP vs. EGP, static vs. dynamic, next hop, understanding routing tables and how they pertain to path selection, and explain convergence (steady state).

Description

With dynamic routing, tables are constantly changing. When all dynamic routing tables contain the same information, a state of convergence is said to exist. Convergence is also referred to as *steady state*.

Examples

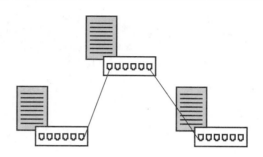

All dynamic routing tables contain the same information

Routers are in state of convergence

Related Concepts

Static vs. Dynamic—1.6B	Next Hop—1.6C	Routing Tables—1.6D
Router—3.1I	Route—5.1G	

Network+ Objective

1.6—Explain the purpose and properties of routing: IGP vs. EGP, static vs. dynamic, next hop, understanding routing tables and how they pertain to path selection, and explain convergence (steady state).

Description

Radio wave-based networks adhere to the 802.11 standard. The 802.11 standard consists of four classifications of wireless networks: 802.11a, 802.11b, 802.11g, and 802.11n.

Examples

802.11 Standard	Radio Frequency	Frequency Range	Data Rate	Range (approximate)	Transmission Method
802.11a	5 GHz	5.15 GHz–5.825 GHz	6 Mbps 9 Mbps 12 Mbps 18 Mbps 24 Mbps 36 Mbps 54 Mbps	50 m	OFDM
802.11b	2.4 GHz	2.4 GHz–2.4835 GHz	1 Mbps 2 Mbps 5.5 Mbps 11 Mbps	100 m	DSSS
802.11g	2.4 GHz	2.4 GHz–2.4835 GHz	1 Mbps 2 Mbps 5.5 Mbps 11 Mbps	100 m	DSSS
	5 GHz	5.15 GHz-5.825 GHz	54 Mbps	50 m	OFDM
802.11n	2.4 GHz	2.4 GHz–2.4835 GHz	All previous data rates up to 300 Mbps and possibly as high as 600 Mbps	300 m	OFDM
	5 GHz	5.15 GHz-5.825 GHz			

Related Concepts

Authentication—1.7B

Encryption—1.7D

Wireless Access Point—3.1H

Wireless Access Point Configuration—3.4B

RADIUS—6.4D

802.1x—6.4F

802.11x and RADIUS—1.7C

Wireless Channels—1.7E

Wireless Access Point Placement—3.4A

AAA—6.4C

TACACS+—6.4E

EAP—6.4H

Network+ Objective

1.7—Compare the characteristics of wireless communication standards: 802.11 a/b/g/n (speeds, distance, channels, frequency) and authentication and encryption (WPA, WEP, RADIUS, TKIP).

Description

Authentication is the process used to identify a user and ensure the user is who he or she claims to be. Wireless device authentication can be achieved in more than one way. The *IEEE 802.1x* draft standard provides a means for a client and server to authenticate with each other. *Wi-Fi Protected Access (WPA)* provides both authentication and encryption for wireless devices. *Wi-Fi Protected Access 2 (WPA2)* is an enhanced version of WPA. *TKIP* improves wireless security by constantly changing the security key rather than leaving it the same for all packets.

Examples

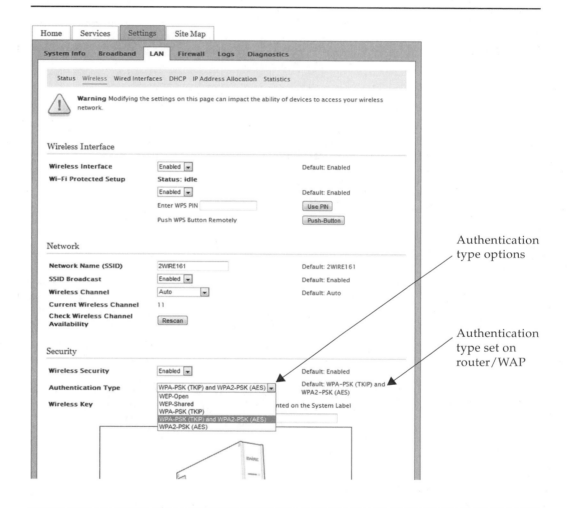

Related Concepts

802.11 a/b/g/n—1.7A	802.11x and RADIUS—1.7C
AAA—6.4C	RADIUS—6.4D
TACACS+—6.4E	802.1x—6.4F
EAP—6.4H	

Network+ Objective

1.7—Compare the characteristics of wireless communication standards: 802.11 a/b/g/n (speeds, distance, channels, frequency) and authentication and encryption (WPA, WEP, RADIUS, TKIP).

Description

802.1x is used for client/server-based networks. It allows the network server to authenticate a wireless network device when the wireless network device attempts to connect to the wired network through a WAP. 802.1x requires three components: supplicant, authenticator, and authentication server. The supplicant is the wireless network device that is requesting network access. The WAP functions as the authenticator and does not allow any type of access to the network without proper authentication. A server running Remote Authentication Dial-In User Service (RADIUS) acts as the authentication server.

Examples

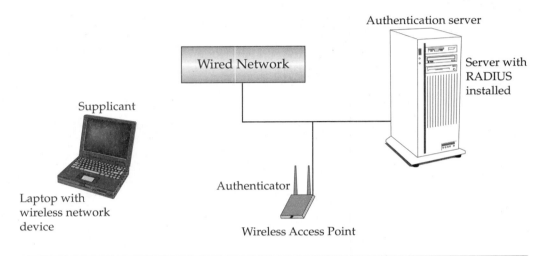

Related Concepts

802.11 a/b/g/n—1.7A	Authentication—1.7B
Client/Server—2.7B	AAA—6.4C
RADIUS—6.4D	802.1x—6.4F

Network+ Objective

1.7—Compare the characteristics of wireless communication standards: 802.11 a/b/g/n (speeds, distance, channels, frequency) and authentication and encryption (WPA, WEP, RADIUS, TKIP).

Description

Encryption is the method of using an algorithm to encode data. Wired Equivalent Privacy (WEP) was the first attempt to secure with encryption the data transferred across a wireless network. Wi-Fi Protected Access (WPA) uses a more complex encryption technique to protect data than WEP. It provides both authentication and encryption for wireless devices. Wi-Fi Protected Access 2 (WPA2) is an enhanced version of WPA.

Examples

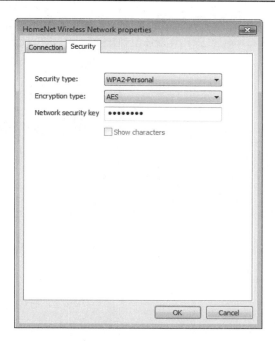

Related Concepts

802.11 a/b/g/n—1.7A

Network+ Objective

1.7—Compare the characteristics of wireless communication standards: 802.11 a/b/g/n (speeds, distance, channels, frequency) and authentication and encryption (WPA, WEP, RADIUS, TKIP).

Description

The bandwidth of a carrier wave is referred to as a *channel*. A channel is identified by the assigned frequency that represents the starting point of the band. The default wireless channel, or dedicated frequency, varies according to manufacturer. In the United States, the FCC has assigned 11 wireless channels for use with wireless devices. Each wireless device in the wireless network should be assigned the same channel. When wireless devices automatically configure themselves, they assign a specific channel to themselves. You can manually assign the wireless channel if necessary. For example, a specific channel may be experiencing radio interference, resulting in very low data speeds or not connecting at all. You can sometimes overcome the effects of the radio interference by changing the assigned channel.

Examples

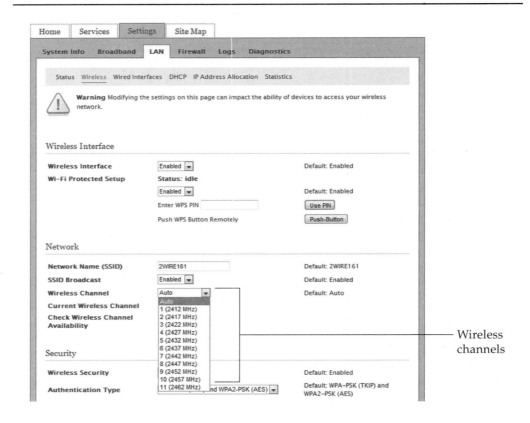

Wireless channels

Related Concepts

802.11 a/b/g/n—1.7A	Wireless Access Point—3.1H
Wireless Access Point Placement—3.4A	Wireless Access Point Configuration—3.4B

Network+ Objective

1.7—Compare the characteristics of wireless communication standards: 802.11 a/b/g/n (speeds, distance, channels, frequency) and authentication and encryption (WPA, WEP, RADIUS, TKIP).

Description

There are seven categories of twisted pair cable: Category 1 through Category 7. The categories are based on the physical design, such as the number of pairs or twists per foot, and the capabilities of the cable, such as the maximum frequency rating and the data rate. The maximum frequency rating and data rate are only two measurements of a cable's capabilities. Other measurements to consider are crosstalk, NEXT, and impedance.

Examples

Category	Type	Maximum Frequency Rating	Data Rate	Number of Pairs	Comments
Category 1	UTP	None	Less than 1 Mbps	2	Used for electrical signals representing voice transmission.
Category 2	UTP	1 MHz	4 Mbps	4	Used in earlier networks that were limited to 4 Mbps.
Category 3	UTP or STP	16 MHz	10 Mbps 16 Mbps	4	Can be found in existing networks rated at 10 Mbps and 16 Mbps and in some telephone installations.
Category 4	UTP or STP	20 MHz	16 Mbps	4	This cable type was only a slight improvement over Category 3.
Category 5	UTP or STP	100 MHz	100 Mbps 1000 Mbps (using 4 pairs)	4	Commonly used in 10BaseT and 100BaseTX network installations.
Category 5e	UTP or STP	100 MHz	100 Mbps 1000 Mbps (using 4 pairs)	4	This cable type is not a replacement for the Category 5 cable. It is an addendum to the cable classification.
Category 6	UTP or STP	250 MHz	1 Gbps	4	Has a plastic spine used to separate the conductors.
Category 6a	UTP or STP	500 MHz	10 Gbps	4	Introduced AXT.
Category 7	UTP or STP	600 MHz	10 Gbps	4	Each pair of twisted conductors is protected by foil shielding. Then, all four pairs are surrounded by foil or braided shielding.

Note: NS = No standard.

Copyright by Goodheart-Willcox Co., Inc.

Related Concepts

STP vs. UTP—2.1B	Network Connector Types—2.2A
568A and 568B—2.4A	Straight-Through, Crossover, and Rollover—2.4B
802.3 Copper Cable Classifications—2.6A	Backbone—2.8C
Patch Panel—2.8D	66 and 110 Block—2.8E
Wiring Termination—2.8K	Physical Layer—4.1H
Troubleshooting Connectivity Issues—4.7A	Network Hardware Tools—5.3A

Network+ Objective

2.1—Categorize standard cable types and their properties: Type (Cat 3, Cat 5, Cat 5e, Cat 6, STP, UTP, multimode fiber, single-mode fiber, coaxial, RG-59, RG-6, serial, plenum vs. non-plenum) and properties (transmission speeds, distance, duplex, noise immunity, frequency).

Copyright by Goodheart-Willcox Co., Inc.

Description

Twisted pair cable can be labeled as UTP (unshielded twisted pair) and STP (shielded twisted pair). Shielding can be applied over the entire cable assembly or over individual pairs of conductors. When shielding is applied to individual pairs of conductors, the shielding protects against crosstalk and outside sources of interference.

Examples

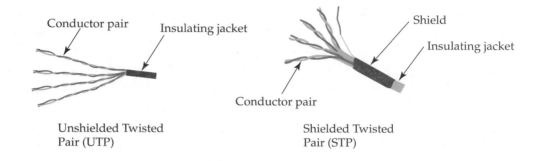

Conductor pair   Insulating jacket

Unshielded Twisted Pair (UTP)

Shield

Insulating jacket

Conductor pair

Shielded Twisted Pair (STP)

Related Concepts

Twisted Pair Cable—2.1A   Troubleshooting Connectivity Issues—4.7A

Network+ Objective

2.1—Categorize standard cable types and their properties: Type (Cat 3, Cat 5, Cat 5e, Cat 6, STP, UTP, multimode fiber, single-mode fiber, coaxial, RG-59, RG-6, serial, plenum vs. non-plenum) and properties (transmission speeds, distance, duplex, noise immunity, frequency).

Description

Fiber-optic cable consists of a glass or plastic core that carries pulses of light. It is primarily used for network backbones and long-distance runs.

Examples

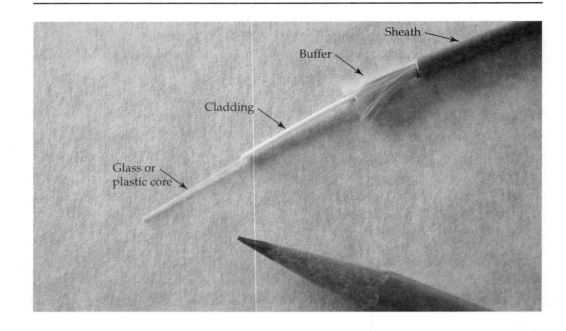

Related Concepts

Single-Mode and Multimode—2.1D	Network Connector Types—2.2A
802.3 Fiber-Optic Classifications—2.6B	Backbone—2.8C
Physical Layer—4.1H	Network Hardware Tools—5.3A

Network+ Objective

2.1—Categorize standard cable types and their properties: Type (Cat 3, Cat 5, Cat 5e, Cat 6, STP, UTP, multimode fiber, single-mode fiber, coaxial, RG-59, RG-6, serial, plenum vs. non-plenum) and properties (transmission speeds, distance, duplex, noise immunity, frequency).

Description

The two broad classifications of fiber-optic cable based on the diameter of the core are multimode and single-mode. Multimode fiber-optic cable has a larger core diameter than single-mode fiber-optic cable. A larger core diameter causes more light loss due to dispersion. Single-mode fiber-optic cable is much smaller in diameter than multimode cable. The diameter of single-mode fiber-optic cable is almost equal to the length of the light wave traveling through the cable. Because the core is designed to closely match the wavelength of the light wave, the light wave cannot readily disperse as it does in a large diameter core. The result is single-mode fiber-optic cable can carry light farther than multimode fiber-optic cable.

Examples

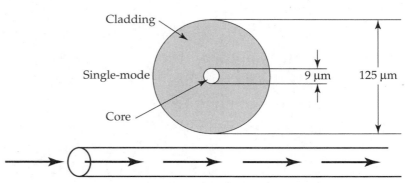

Single-mode fiber-optic cable has a small diameter and supports one light path.

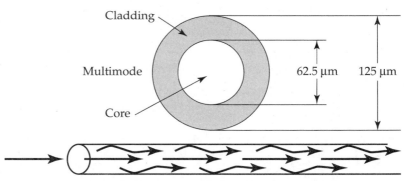

Multimode fiber-optic cable has a large diameter, causing multiple paths of light to be transmitted.

Related Concepts

Fiber-Optic Cable—2.1C

Network+ Objective

2.1—Categorize standard cable types and their properties: Type (Cat 3, Cat 5, Cat 5e, Cat 6, STP, UTP, multimode fiber, single-mode fiber, coaxial, RG-59, RG-6, serial, plenum vs. non-plenum) and properties (transmission speeds, distance, duplex, noise immunity, frequency).

Description

Coaxial cable, or coax, consists of a copper core conductor surrounded by an insulator referred to as a *dielectric*. The dielectric is covered with two shields: a foil shield and a braided copper shield. The shields protect the core from electromagnetic interference (EMI). The shields also prevent the cable from transmitting EMI to other cables. The entire cable assembly is covered by an insulating outer jacket, which protects the shielding.

Examples

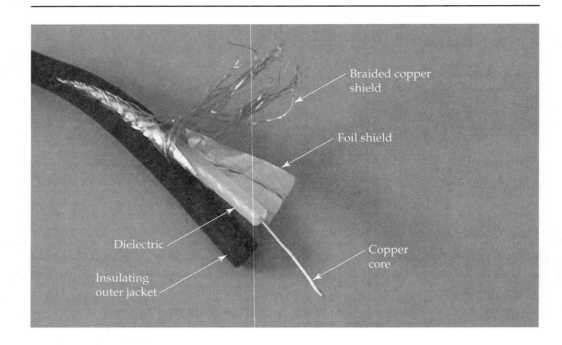

Related Concepts

Coaxial Cable Types—2.1F	Network Connector Types—2.2A
Physical Layer—4.1H	Network Hardware Tools—5.3A

Network+ Objective

2.1—Categorize standard cable types and their properties: Type (Cat 3, Cat 5, Cat 5e, Cat 6, STP, UTP, multimode fiber, single-mode fiber, coaxial, RG-59, RG-6, serial, plenum vs. non-plenum) and properties (transmission speeds, distance, duplex, noise immunity, frequency).

Description

There are several classifications of network coaxial cable. RG-6 has become the standard for Cable television (CATV) systems and satellite systems, replacing other types of cable such as RG-59 for new installations.

Examples

Cable	Common Name	Impedance	Actual Size in Diameter	Description
RG-6	Broadband	75 Ω	0.332	Used for Cable TV.
RG-8	Thicknet	50 Ω	0.405	Used for Ethernet networks.
RG-11	Thick coax	75 Ω	0.475	Used for Cable TV trunk lines.
RG-58	Thinnet	50 Ω	0.195	Used for Ethernet networks.
RG-59	CATV	75 Ω	0.242	Used for Cable TV and sometimes used for ARCnet.
RG-62	Baseband	93 Ω	0.249	Used for ARCnet.

Related Concepts

Coaxial Cable—2.1E   Network Connector Types—2.2A

Physical Layer—4.1H   Network Hardware Tools—5.3A

Network+ Objective

2.1—Categorize standard cable types and their properties: Type (Cat 3, Cat 5, Cat 5e, Cat 6, STP, UTP, multimode fiber, single-mode fiber, coaxial, RG-59, RG-6, serial, plenum vs. non-plenum) and properties (transmission speeds, distance, duplex, noise immunity, frequency).

Copyright by Goodheart-Willcox Co., Inc.

Description

Cables are often identified as plenum-rated. Plenum-rated means that the cable has a special type of insulation that will not give off toxic gases should the cable be consumed by fire. The term plenum-rated is derived from the plenum in a building. The plenum is the area above a drop ceiling and under a raised floor. Cables designed to pass through a building plenum must be plenum-rated.

Examples

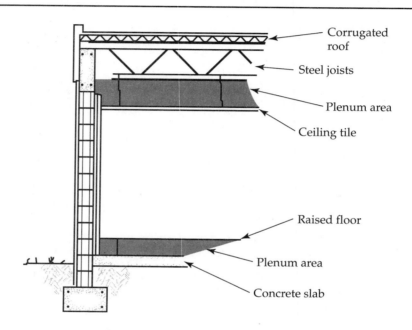

Related Concepts

Twisted Pair Cable—2.1A	Fiber-Optic Cable—2.1C
Coaxial Cable—2.1E	Coaxial Cable Types—2.1F

Network+ Objective

2.1—Categorize standard cable types and their properties: Type (Cat 3, Cat 5, Cat 5e, Cat 6, STP, UTP, multimode fiber, single-mode fiber, coaxial, RG-59, RG-6, serial, plenum vs. non-plenum) and properties (transmission speeds, distance, duplex, noise immunity, frequency).

Description

Network connectors attach to network media, such as coaxial cable, twisted pair cable, and fiber-optic cable, and are used to join the network media to a network device.

Examples

Twisted Pair

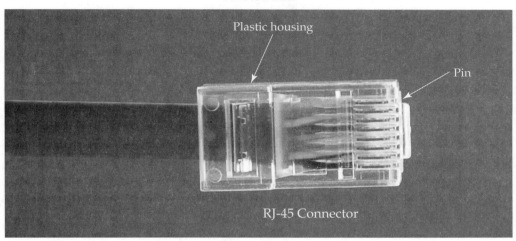

RJ-45 Connector

Coaxial Cable

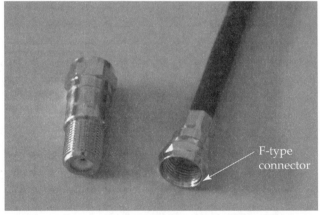

Fiber-Optic Cable Connectors

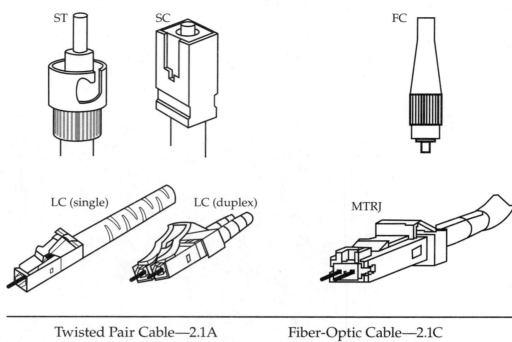

Networking Fundamentals Study Guide

Related Concepts	Twisted Pair Cable—2.1A	Fiber-Optic Cable—2.1C
	Coaxial Cable—2.1E	Coaxial Cable Types—2.1F

Network+ Objective

2.2—Identify common connector types: RJ-11, RJ-45, BNC, SC, ST, LC, and RS-232.

Copyright by Goodheart-Willcox Co., Inc.

Description

The physical arrangement of computers, computer-related devices, communication devices, and cabling in a network is referred to as *network topology*. The four major topologies are bus, ring, star, and mesh. Combining two or more of the four major topologies creates a hybrid topology. Point-to-point topology generally refers to two nodes connected directly to each other either by cable or by wireless means. A point-to-multipoint topology is when one node is connected directly to two or more nodes.

Examples

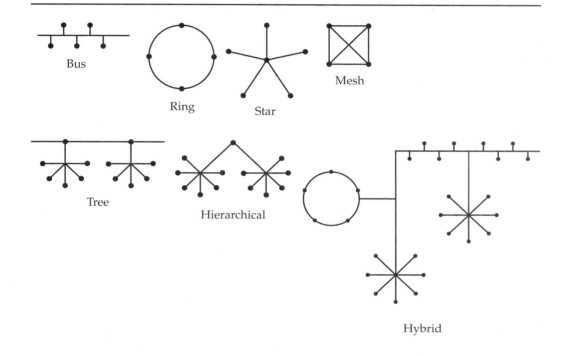

Related Concepts

Hub—3.1A	Switch—3.1F
Wireless Access Point—3.1H	

Network+ Objective

2.3—Identify common physical network topologies: Star, mesh, bus, ring, point-to-point, point-to-multipoint, and hybrid.

Description

The two main cable termination standards in use for twisted pair cable are 568A and 568B, as described by the TIA/EIA organization. Either standard can be used to make a straight-through cable, as long as the cable ends use the same standard. A crossover cable is created by using the 568A standard on one end and the 568B standard on the other.

Examples

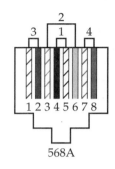

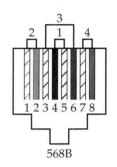

The difference between a 568A and 568B connection is the position of cable pairs 2 and 3.

Related Concepts

Straight-Through, Crossover, and Rollover—2.4B   Patch Panel—2.8D

66 and 110 Block—2.8E

Network+ Objective

2.4—Given a scenario, differentiate and implement appropriate wiring standards: 568A, 568B, straight vs. crossover, rollover, and loopback.

Description   UTP cables have two common classifications of assembly: straight-through and crossover. A rollover cable is a special cable in which the pin order is completely reversed on one end of the cable. Pin 1 connects to pin 8, pin 2 connects to pin 7, and so on. Like the straight-through and crossover cables, a rollover cable uses an RJ-45 connector on each end.

Examples

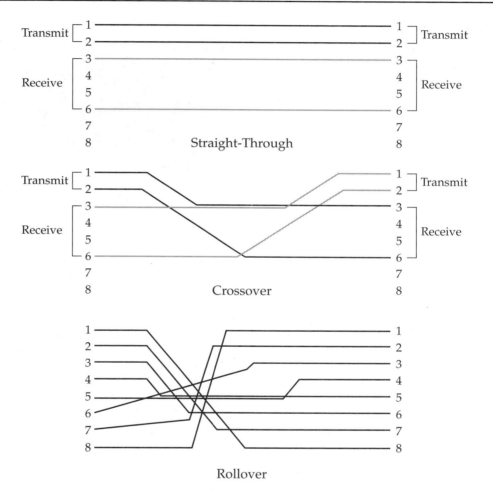

Related Concepts

568A and 568B—2.4A   Patch Panel—2.8D

66 and 110 Block—2.8E

Network+ Objective   2.4—Given a scenario, differentiate and implement appropriate wiring standards: 568A, 568B, straight vs. crossover, rollover, and loopback.

Copyright by Goodheart-Willcox Co., Inc.

Description

A loopback test checks a hardware device's ability to transmit and receive signals. It consists of diagnostic software and an adapter (connector) called a *loopback*. The loopback is plugged into the back of the network interface card. When the diagnostic software is run, the loopback completes the electrical circuit between the transmit and receive pins.

Examples

Related Concepts

NIC—3.1D

Network+ Objective

2.4—Given a scenario, differentiate and implement appropriate wiring standards: 568A, 568B, straight vs. crossover, rollover, and loopback.

Description

The worldwide communications system is quite complex, offering a variety of media to use and many different long-distance providers. While a LAN usually has a limited scope of communications media, a MAN and a WAN have a large variety of communications media and technologies from which to choose.

Examples

WAN Connection Technology	Access Method	Data Rate	Comments
ATM	Direct connection	25 Mbps–622 Mbps	Virtually private.
Cable Internet Service	Direct connection	Downstream: 27 Mbps–37 Mbps (theoretical). 300 kbps–500 kbps (actual) Upstream: 320 kbps–10 Mbps	TV Cable service. Requires a cable modem. Cable service uses MPEG-2 for data compression.
FDDI	Direct connection	100 Mbps	High reliability and bandwidth.
Fractional T1	Direct connection	64 kbps	T-carrier technology. Can use multiple channels to increase speed by increments of 64 kbps.
Frame Relay	Virtual connection	56 kbps–45 Mbps	Virtually private.
ISDN	Dial-up	64 kbps and 128 kbps	Requires a leased line and an ISDN modem. Can carry only one frequency.
PRI-ISDN	Direct connection	1.544 Mbps	Requires a leased line and an ISDN modem. Can carry only one frequency.
Public Switched Telephone Network (PSTN)	Dial-up	56 kbps	This is also known as Plain Old Telephone Service (POTS). Requires a telephone modem.
Satellite Internet Service	Direct connection	400 kbps–2 Mbps	May use a dial-up service to connect to the satellite Internet provider. Experiences propagation delay.
SONET	Direct connection	51 Mbps–9953 Mbps	Commonly used to span long distances such as across the nation and overseas.
T1	Direct connection	1.544 Mbps	T-carrier technology.
T3	Direct connection	44.736 Mbps	T-carrier technology.
X.25	Virtual connection	56 kbps	Packet switching, analog technology.
xDSL	Direct connection	1.544 Mbps–52 Mbps	Data rate depends on the version of DSL. Requires an xDSL modem. Limited distance from the DSL modem to the telephone company's Local Central Office is between 1,000 ft.–18,000 ft.

Related Concepts

Frame Relay—2.5B	T-Carrier—2.5C
xDSL—2.5D	Cable Modem—2.5E
Satellite—2.5F	OC-X—2.5G
ATM—2.5H	MPLS—2.5I
ISDN—2.5J	POTS/PSTN—2.5K
Packet and Circuit Switching—2.5L	

Network+ Objective

2.5—Categorize WAN technology types and properties: Type (Frame Relay, E1/T1, ADSL, SDSL, VDSL, Cable modem, satellite, E3/T3, OC-x, wireless, ATM, SONET, MPLS, BRI-ISDN, PRI-ISDN, POTS, PSTN), and properties (circuit switch, packet switch, speed, transmission media, distance).

Copyright by Goodheart-Willcox Co., Inc.

Description

Frame Relay is a packet switching protocol that typically uses leased lines such as T1 to carry data over long distances. Frame Relay allows for a data rate as high as 1.544 Mbps. Frame Relay data transfer speeds are limited to the media used. A T1 line has a bandwidth of 1.544 bps. T-3 is limited to 45 Mbps.

Examples

Frame Relay	X.25
Analog	Digital
56 kbps	56 kbps-1.544 kbps
Packet switching	Packet switching
Permanent virtual circuit	Permanent virtual circuit

Related Concepts

WAN Technology Types—2.5A   T-Carrier—2.5C

Network+ Objective

2.5—Categorize WAN technology types and properties: Type (Frame Relay, E1/T1, ADSL, SDSL, VDSL, Cable modem, satellite, E3/T3, OC-x, wireless, ATM, SONET, MPLS, BRI-ISDN, PRI-ISDN, POTS, PSTN), and properties (circuit switch, packet switch, speed, transmission media, distance).

Description

T-carrier is a leased line that follows one of the standards known as T1, fractional T1, T2, or T3. The T-carrier is a dedicated, permanent connection that is capable of providing a high bandwidth. The European counterpart to a T1 leased line is E1, which has a maximum rate of 2.048 Mbps. The Japanese counterpart is J1.

Examples

T-Carrier Standard	Number of T1 Lines	Number of Channels	Maximum Data Rate
T1	1	24	1.544 Mbps
T2	4	96	6.312 Mbps
T3	28	672	44.736 Mbps
T4	168	4032	274.176 Mbps

USA		Europe		Japan	
T1	1.544 Mbps	E1	2.048 Mbps	J1	1.544 Mbps
T2	6.312 Mbps	E2	8.448 Mbps	J2	6.312 Mbps
T3	44.736 Mbps	E3	34.368 Mbps	J3	32.064 Mbps
T4	274.176 Mbps	E4	139.264 Mbps	J4	97.728 Mbps
NA	NA	E5	564.992 Mbps	J5	397.200 Mbps

Related Concepts

WAN Technology Types—2.5A   Frame Relay—2.5B

Network+ Objective

2.5—Categorize WAN technology types and properties: Type (Frame Relay, E1/T1, ADSL, SDSL, VDSL, Cable modem, satellite, E3/T3, OC-x, wireless, ATM, SONET, MPLS, BRI-ISDN, PRI-ISDN, POTS, PSTN), and properties (circuit switch, packet switch, speed, transmission media, distance).

Description

Digital Subscriber Line (DSL) is a leased line dedicated to networking that uses multiple frequencies as separate channels on the existing telephone local loop. The multiple channels combine to carry more data than the original telephone modem design.

Examples

DSL Type	Description	Upstream Data Rate	Downstream Data Rate	Maximum Distance between DSL Modem and Central Office
ADSL	Asymmetrical DSL	1.544 Mbps	1.5 Mbps–8 Mbps	12,000 ft.–18,000 ft.
SDSL	Symmetric DSL	1.544 Mbps	1.544 Mbps	10,000 ft.
HDSL	High bit-rate DSL	1.544 Mbps	1.544 Mbps	14,000 ft.
VDSL	Very high bit-rate DSL	1.5 Mbps–2.3 Mbps	13 Mbps–52 Mbps	1000 ft.–4500 ft.

Related Concepts

WAN Technology Types—2.5A   POTS/PSTN—2.5K

Modem—3.1C

Network+ Objective

2.5—Categorize WAN technology types and properties: Type (Frame Relay, E1/T1, ADSL, SDSL, VDSL, Cable modem, satellite, E3/T3, OC-x, wireless, ATM, SONET, MPLS, BRI-ISDN, PRI-ISDN, POTS, PSTN), and properties (circuit switch, packet switch, speed, transmission media, distance).

Copyright by Goodheart-Willcox Co., Inc.

Description

A Cable modem uses the Cable television distribution system to provide Internet access. Cable Internet service is an asymmetrical form of communication. The term *asymmetrical* is used to describe Cable Internet service communication because the uplink and downlink have two different transfer speeds. Upstream connections vary between 320 kbps and 10 Mbps, while downstream data rates vary between 27 Mbps and 36 Mbps.

Examples

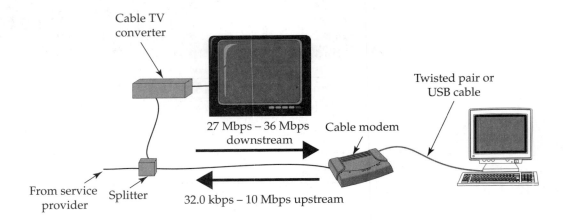

Related Concepts

WAN Technology Types—2.5A	Modem—3.1C

Network+ Objective

2.5—Categorize WAN technology types and properties: Type (Frame Relay, E1/T1, ADSL, SDSL, VDSL, Cable modem, satellite, E3/T3, OC-x, wireless, ATM, SONET, MPLS, BRI-ISDN, PRI-ISDN, POTS, PSTN), and properties (circuit switch, packet switch, speed, transmission media, distance).

Description

A satellite system can be used for Internet access and for data communication. A typical satellite system consists of a satellite dish at the satellite service provider location, a satellite, and a satellite dish at the consumer location. Typical download speeds for consumer satellite communications are 400 kbps to 500 kbps. Upload speeds are limited to the particular land-based technology used for upload.

Examples

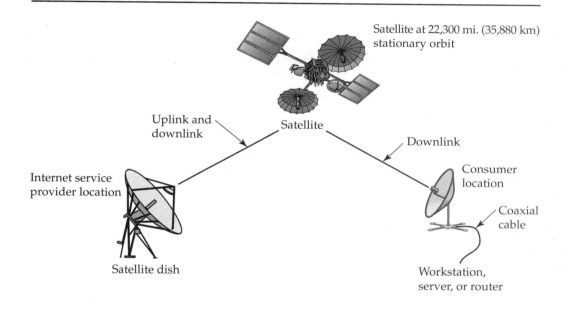

Related Concepts

WAN Technology Types—2.5A

Network+ Objective

2.5—Categorize WAN technology types and properties: Type (Frame Relay, E1/T1, ADSL, SDSL, VDSL, Cable modem, satellite, E3/T3, OC-x, wireless, ATM, SONET, MPLS, BRI-ISDN, PRI-ISDN, POTS, PSTN), and properties (circuit switch, packet switch, speed, transmission media, distance).

Description

Synchronous Optical Network (SONET) is similar to T-carrier in that special termination equipment, such as a multiplexer, is needed at the customer location; however, SONET bases its technology on fiber-optic cable. SONET often uses multiplexer technology to carry a mix of data, voice, and video on the same channel and is designed as a ring topology similar to the dual-ring structure of FDDI. SONET levels are identified by OC and the number of the level, such as OC-1 for SONET level 1. SONET is the standard choice for connecting global-sized networks spanning across the nation and oceans.

Examples

SONET Level	Maximum Data Rate
OC-1	51.84 Mbps
OC-3	145.52 Mbps
OC-12	622 Mbps
OC-24	1244 Mbps
OC-48	2488 Mbps
OC-192	9953 Mbps

Related Concepts

Fiber-Optic Cable—2.1C   Single-Mode and Multimode—2.1D

WAN Technology Types—2.5A

Network+ Objective

2.5—Categorize WAN technology types and properties: Type (Frame Relay, E1/T1, ADSL, SDSL, VDSL, Cable modem, satellite, E3/T3, OC-x, wireless, ATM, SONET, MPLS, BRI-ISDN, PRI-ISDN, POTS, PSTN), and properties (circuit switch, packet switch, speed, transmission media, distance).

Description

Asynchronous Transfer Mode (ATM) is a widely used protocol that is especially designed for carrying audio, video, and multimedia. It can support a bandwidth of 622 Mbps. ATM is designed to divide text and audio/video into cells of 53 bytes each. Cells are placed in sequence giving higher priority to the audio/video cells.

Examples

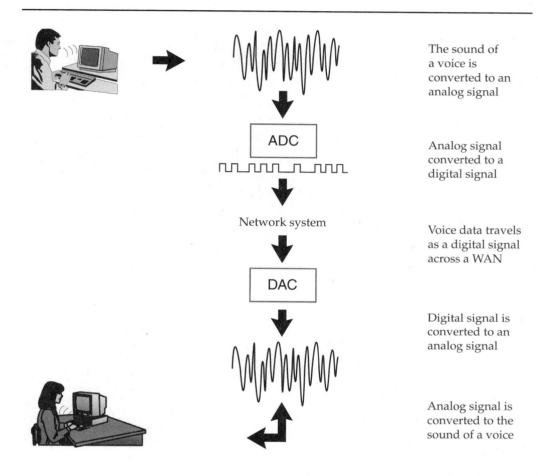

The sound of a voice is converted to an analog signal

ADC

Analog signal converted to a digital signal

Network system

Voice data travels as a digital signal across a WAN

DAC

Digital signal is converted to an analog signal

Analog signal is converted to the sound of a voice

Related Concepts

WAN Technology Types—2.5A

Network+ Objective

2.5—Categorize WAN technology types and properties: Type (Frame Relay, E1/T1, ADSL, SDSL, VDSL, Cable modem, satellite, E3/T3, OC-x, wireless, ATM, SONET, MPLS, BRI-ISDN, PRI-ISDN, POTS, PSTN), and properties (circuit switch, packet switch, speed, transmission media, distance).

Description

Multi-Protocol Label Switching (MPLS) is a routing protocol that allows a label to be attached to an IP packet in order to route the packet to a specific destination. MPLS is not intended by design for routing on a local area network but rather for moving packets from point to point across large network systems controlled by a single authority.

Examples

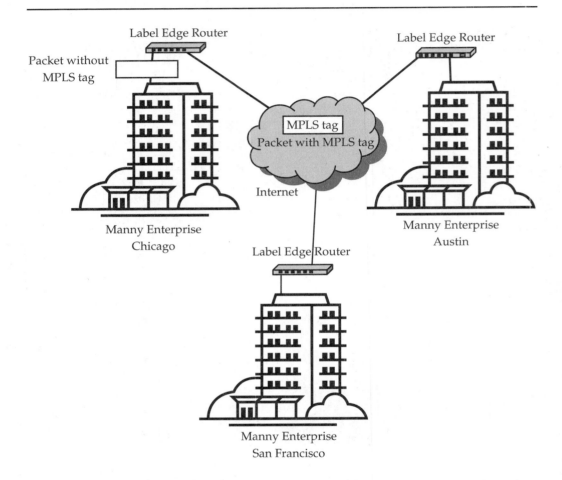

Related Concepts

WAN Technology Types—2.5A

Network+ Objective

2.5—Categorize WAN technology types and properties: Type (Frame Relay, E1/T1, ADSL, SDSL, VDSL, Cable modem, satellite, E3/T3, OC-x, wireless, ATM, SONET, MPLS, BRI-ISDN, PRI-ISDN, POTS, PSTN), and properties (circuit switch, packet switch, speed, transmission media, distance).

Description

Integrated Services Digital Network (ISDN) is a long-distance technology that provides a means for a fully digital transmission over channels that are capable of speeds of up to 64 kbps.

Examples

Two B channels at 64 kbps each

64 kbps
+64 kbps
128 kbps   Maximum data rate

One D channel at 16 kbps

Basic Rate ISDN (BRI-ISDN) Cable

ISDN Type	Maximum Speed	Comment
BRI-ISDN	128 kbps	Contains two B (bearer) channels and one D (delta) channel
PRI-ISDN	1.544 Mbps	Contains twenty-three B (bearer) channels and one D (delta) channel
B-ISDN	>1.5 Mbps	Can carry multiple frequencies, such as voice, data, and video

Related Concepts

WAN Technology Types—2.5A   Modem—3.1C

Network+ Objective

2.5—Categorize WAN technology types and properties: Type (Frame Relay, E1/T1, ADSL, SDSL, VDSL, Cable modem, satellite, E3/T3, OC-x, wireless, ATM, SONET, MPLS, BRI-ISDN, PRI-ISDN, POTS, PSTN), and properties (circuit switch, packet switch, speed, transmission media, distance).

Description

Public Switched Telephone Network (PSTN), or Plain Old Telephone Service (POTS), is the older telephone system that uses twisted pair cabling and analog signals rather than digital. Typically, the PSTN is used when making a dial-up connection. A dial-up connection is a type of connection made using a traditional telephone line to reach a distant computer or network system.

Examples

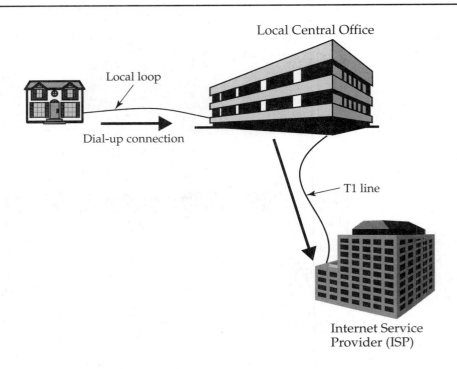

Local Central Office

Local loop

Dial-up connection

T1 line

Internet Service Provider (ISP)

Related Concepts

Twisted Pair Cable—2.1A	STP vs. UTP—2.1B
WAN Technology Types—2.5A	Modem—3.1C

Network+ Objective

2.5—Categorize WAN technology types and properties: Type (Frame Relay, E1/T1, ADSL, SDSL, VDSL, Cable modem, satellite, E3/T3, OC-x, wireless, ATM, SONET, MPLS, BRI-ISDN, PRI-ISDN, POTS, PSTN), and properties (circuit switch, packet switch, speed, transmission media, distance).

Description

Two main categories describing the way data are routed between two points are packet switching and circuit switching. *Circuit switching* establishes a permanent connection between two points for the duration of the data transfer period. *Packet switching* breaks the data transmission into smaller parts called *packets*. Each packet has a source and destination address and a sequence number attached to it. The packets are sent out onto the Internet and may each take a different route to their destination.

Examples

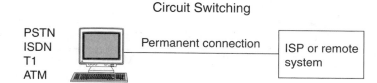

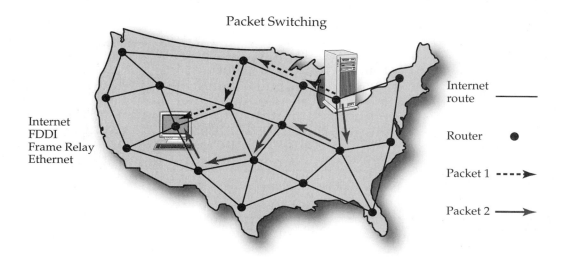

Related Concepts

WAN Technology Types—2.5A	T-Carrier—2.5C
ATM—2.5H	ISDN—2.5J
POTS/PSTN—2.5K	

Network+ Objective

2.5—Categorize WAN technology types and properties: Type (Frame Relay, E1/T1, ADSL, SDSL, VDSL, Cable modem, satellite, E3/T3, OC-x, wireless, ATM, SONET, MPLS, BRI-ISDN, PRI-ISDN, POTS, PSTN), and properties (circuit switch, packet switch, speed, transmission media, distance).

Copyright by Goodheart-Willcox Co., Inc.

Description

The IEEE 802.3 standard comprises various Ethernet classifications. These classifications differ by data rate, topology, and media type and are named with short descriptions, such as 1000BaseT and 10GBaseT.

Examples

Category	Classification	Data Rate	Maximum Segment Length	Minimum Segment Length	Cable Type	Topology
10 Mbps	10Base2	10 Mbps	185 m	0.5 m	RG-58 (thinnet)	Bus
	10Base5	10 Mbps	500 m	2.5 m	RG-8 (thicknet)	Bus
	10BaseT	10 Mbps	100 m	0.6 m	Category 3, 4, and 5	Star
Fast Ethernet	100BaseT4	100 Mbps	100 m	0.6 m	Category 3, 4, and 5	Star
	100BaseTX	100 Mbps	100 m	0.6 m	Category 5	Star
Gigabit Ethernet	1000BaseCX	1000 Mbps	25 m	0.6 m	Category 5	Star
	1000BaseT	1000 Mbps	100 m	0.6 m	Category 5e	Star
10 Gigabit Ethernet	10GBaseT	10 Gbps	55 m	0.6 m	Category 6	Star
	10GBaseT	10 Gbps	100 m	0.6 m	Category 6a	Star

Note: 1000BaseCX is obsolete and is no longer recognized.

Related Concepts

Twisted Pair Cable—2.1A   STP vs. UTP—2.1B

Coaxial Cable—2.1E   Coaxial Cable Types—2.1F

Network Connector Types—2.2A   Network Topologies—2.3A

CSMA/CD—2.6C   Collision Domain—2.6D

Bonding—2.6E   Hub—3.1A

Switch—3.1F   Data Link Layer—4.1G

Physical Layer—4.1H

Network+ Objective

2.6—Categorize LAN technology types and properties: Types (Ethernet, 10BaseT, 100BaseTX, 100BaseFX, 1000BaseT, 1000BaseX, 10GBaseSR, 10GBaseLR, 10GBaseER, 10GBaseSW, 10GBaseLW, 10GBaseEW, 10GBaseT) and properties (CSMA/CD, broadcast, collision, bonding, speed, distance).

Description

In 2002, the IEEE amended the 802.3 Ethernet standard to include 10 Gigabit Ethernet. The amended standard is known as IEEE 802.3ae. The IEEE 802.3ae standard only recognizes fiber-optic cables. It does not recognize copper core cables.

Examples

Standard	Single-mode (S) or Multimode (M)	Core Diameter in Microns	Wavelength in Nanometers (nm)	Cable Distance	Remarks
10BaseFL	M	62.5 50	850	2000 m	Early generic fiber-optic standard.
100BaseFX	M	62.5 50	1300	2000 m	Known as Fast Ethernet.
1000BaseSX	M	62.5 50	850	300 m	Known as Gigabit Ethernet.
1000BaseLX	M	62.5 50	1300	550 m	Known as Gigabit Ethernet.
1000BaseLX	S	9	1300	5 km	Known as Gigabit Ethernet.
10GBaseSR	M	62.5 50	850	66–300	Known as 10 Gigabit Ethernet. Distance dependent on bandwidth.
10GBaseLR	S	9	1310	10 km	Known as 10 Gigabit Ethernet.
10GBaseER	S	9	1310	40 km	Known as 10 Gigabit Ethernet.
10GBaseSW	M	50 62.5	850	300 m 33 m	Commonly used inside commercial buildings.
10GBaseLW	S	9	1310	10 km	Has a long wave-length and is used relatively long distances.
10GBaseW	S	9	1550	40 km	Used for "long-haul" connections.

Note: Companies may calculate greater distances based on manufacturer cable specifications and equipment requirements. Such engineering is common in long-haul communication systems such as long-distance telecommunications industries.

Related Concepts

Fiber-Optic Cable—2.1C   Single-Mode and Multimode—2.1D

Network Connector Types—2.2A   Network Topologies—2.3A

CSMA/CD—2.6C   Data Link Layer—4.1G

Physical Layer—4.1H

Network+ Objective

2.6—Categorize LAN technology types and properties: Types (Ethernet, 10BaseT, 100BaseTX, 100BaseFX, 1000BaseT, 1000BaseX, 10GBaseSR, 10GBaseLR, 10GBaseER, 10GBaseSW, 10GBaseLW, 10GBaseEW, 10GBaseT) and properties (CSMA/CD, broadcast, collision, bonding, speed, distance).

Description

Ethernet networks use the CSMA/CD access method to control and ensure the delivery of data. CSMA/CD is a broadcast method of communication. When a computer sends data to another computer, it does so by broadcasting the information to all the computers on the network. This is similar to one person yelling in a room full of people "Bob, do you hear me?" Everyone in the room hears Bob's name being called, but only Bob will reply if he is in the room.

Examples

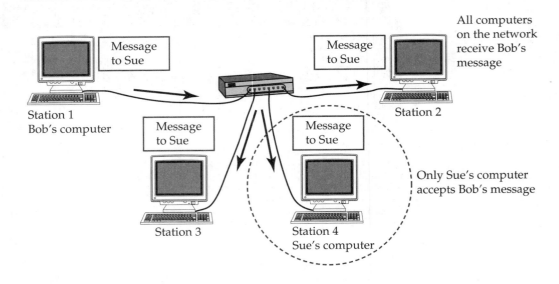

Related Concepts

MAC Address—1.3A

Data Link Layer—4.1G

Collision Domain—2.6D

Network+ Objective

2.6—Categorize LAN technology types and properties: Types (Ethernet, 10BaseT, 100BaseTX, 100BaseFX, 1000BaseT, 1000BaseX, 10GBaseSR, 10GBaseLR, 10GBaseER, 10GBaseSW, 10GBaseLW, 10GBaseEW, 10GBaseT) and properties (CSMA/CD, broadcast, collision, bonding, speed, distance).

Description

The section of a network where collisions occur is referred to as a *collision domain*. A collision domain consists of computers that can directly communicate with each other using broadcasts. The collision domain can be isolated by equipment that controls or limits the broadcasts. Equipment such as switches and routers controls broadcasts by limiting the extent or physical boundary of a collision domain.

Examples

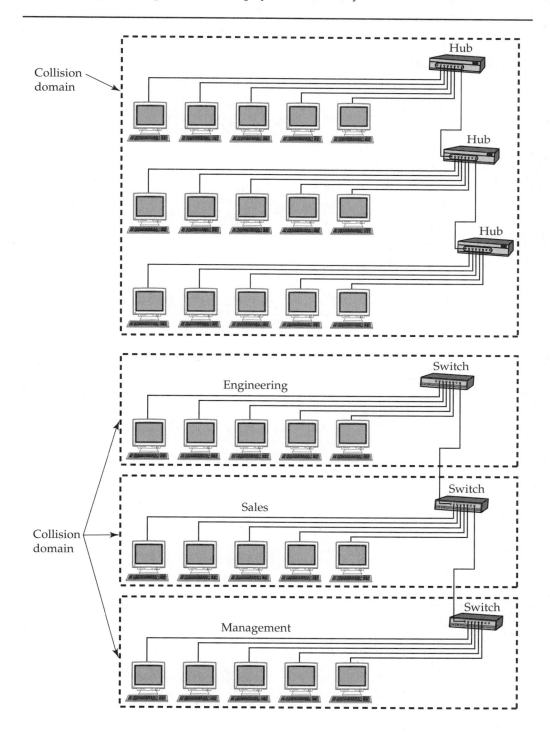

Related Concepts

CSMA/CD—2.6C	Switch—3.1F
Router—3.1I	

Network+ Objective

2.6—Categorize LAN technology types and properties: Types (Ethernet, 10BaseT, 100BaseTX, 100BaseFX, 1000BaseT, 1000BaseX, 10GBaseSR, 10GBaseLR, 10GBaseER, 10GBaseSW, 10GBaseLW, 10GBaseEW, 10GBaseT) and properties (CSMA/CD, broadcast, collision, bonding, speed, distance).

Copyright by Goodheart-Willcox Co., Inc.

Description

STP and coaxial cable requires equipment to be bonded and grounded before the shielding can be effective. The ground path must be continuous from the equipment to which the cable is attached to the central ground in the electrical system. If the ground path is not continuous, the shielding will not effectively protect the network cables from electrical and radio interference.

Examples

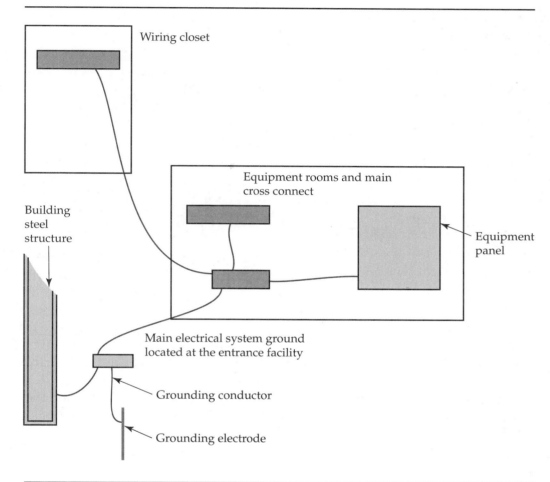

Wiring closet

Building steel structure

Equipment rooms and main cross connect

Equipment panel

Main electrical system ground located at the entrance facility

Grounding conductor

Grounding electrode

Related Concepts

Twisted Pair Cable—2.1A	STP vs. UTP—2.1B
Coaxial Cable—2.1E	Coaxial Cable Types—2.1F

Network+ Objective

2.6—Categorize LAN technology types and properties: Types (Ethernet, 10BaseT, 100BaseTX, 100BaseFX, 1000BaseT, 1000BaseX, 10GBaseSR, 10GBaseLR, 10GBaseER, 10GBaseSW, 10GBaseLW, 10GBaseEW, 10GBaseT) and properties (CSMA/CD, broadcast, collision, bonding, speed, distance).

Description

All computers are considered peers or equals in a peer-to-peer network. A computer in a peer-to-peer network can serve as both a client and a server. Each computer is considered equal because each computer's user has equal authority to share his or her computer's resources with other users on the network. Peer-to-peer networks are often referred to as workgroups.

Examples

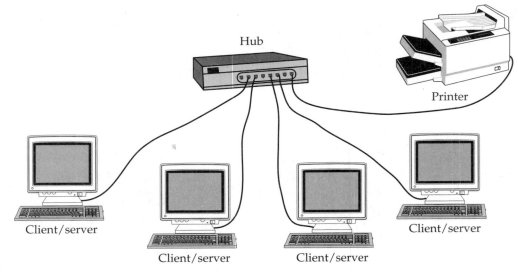

Peer-to-Peer Network

Related Concepts

Client/Server—2.7B

Network+ Objective

2.7—Explain common logical network topologies and their characteristics: Peer-to-peer, client/server, VPN, and VLAN.

Description

The client/server network consists of computers connected via a network to one or more servers. As its name implies, the server provides services to networked computers, or clients. Typical services are security, database applications, data storage, Internet access, Web page hosting, and e-mail.

Examples

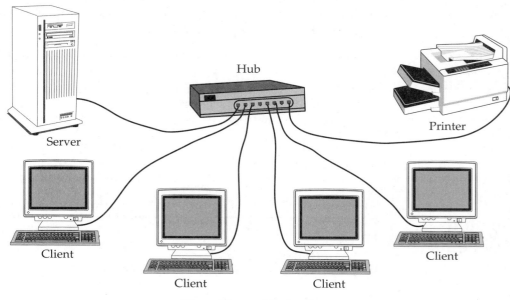

Client/Server Network

Related Concepts

Peer-to-Peer—2.7A

Network+ Objective

2.7—Explain common logical network topologies and their characteristics: Peer-to-peer, client/server, VPN, and VLAN.

Description

A Virtual Private Network (VPN) is a simulated, independent network created by software over a public network. A VPN is created through a software package that provides security. Adding special equipment, such as a firewall, can further increase the security of the VPN. All operating systems support a form of VPN. Four of the most common protocols used in a VPN are PPTP, L2F, L2TP, and IPSec. These protocols allow a VPN to provide four basic features common to all VPN connections: authentication, access control, confidentiality, and data integrity.

Examples

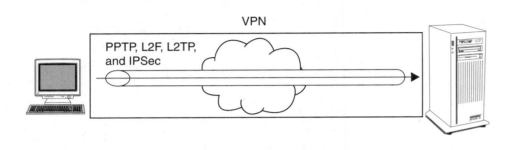

Related Concepts

Firewall—3.1J	L2TP—6.3C
PPTP—6.3D	IPSec—6.3E

Network+ Objective

2.7—Explain common logical network topologies and their characteristics: Peer-to-peer, client/server, VPN, and VLAN.

Description

A Virtual Local Area Network (VLAN) is a broadcast domain created by one or more switches based on logical (MAC) addresses. VLANs are typically used to improve network performance by reducing the size of collision domains. VLANs can also be used to create secure subnets on shared network media.

Examples

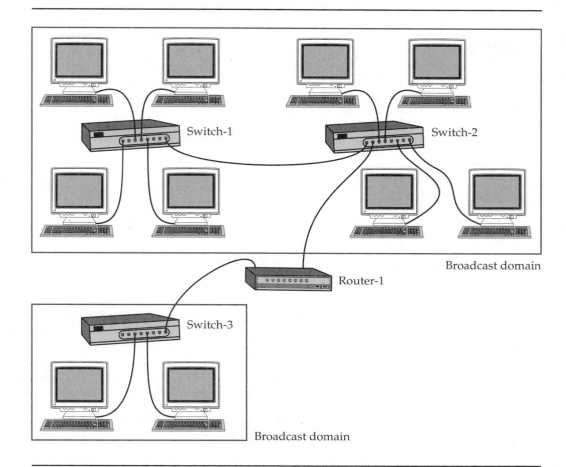

Broadcast domain

Broadcast domain

Related Concepts

MAC Address—1.3A	Subnetting—1.4A
Collision Domain—2.6D	Switch—3.1F
Trunking—3.3C	

Network+ Objective

2.7—Explain common logical network topologies and their characteristics: Peer-to-peer, client/server, VPN, and VLAN.

Description

A horizontal cross connect provides a mechanical means of connecting horizontal cabling systems to other cables or equipment. All work areas connect to the telecommunications closet horizontal cross connects. A horizontal cross connect is used to connect horizontal cabling to a backbone or to system equipment such as a router, switch, bridge, or server.

Examples

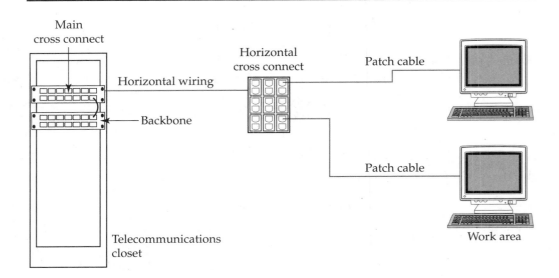

Related Concepts

Horizontal Wiring—2.8B	Backbone—2.8C
Wiring Termination—2.8K	Switch—3.1F
Bridge—3.1G	Router—3.1I

Network+ Objective

2.8—Install components of wiring distribution: Vertical and horizontal cross connects, patch panels, 66 block, MDFs, IDFs, 25 pair, 100 pair, 110 block, demarc, demarc extension, smart jack, verify wiring installation, and verify wiring termination.

Description

Horizontal wiring refers to the section of cable that runs from individual work areas to the telecommunications closet. Horizontal cable distance is limited to 90 meters for the horizontal run from the telecommunications outlet to the telecommunications closet. The maximum total distance is 100 meters.

Examples

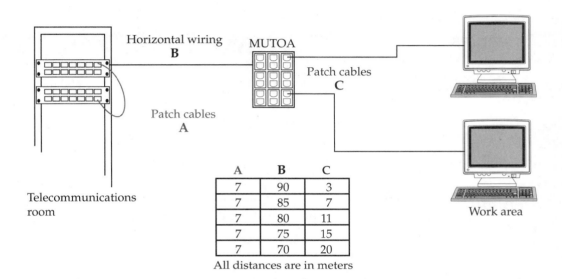

A	B	C
7	90	3
7	85	7
7	80	11
7	75	15
7	70	20

All distances are in meters

Related Concepts

Horizontal Cross Connect—2.8A   Patch Panel—2.8D

66 and 110 Block—2.8E

Network+ Objective

2.8—Install components of wiring distribution: Vertical and horizontal cross connects, patch panels, 66 block, MDFs, IDFs, 25 pair, 100 pair, 110 block, demarc, demarc extension, smart jack, verify wiring installation, and verify wiring termination.

Copyright by Goodheart-Willcox Co., Inc.

Description

A network backbone is located between the telecommunications closets, equipment rooms, and main entrance facility. The backbone connects these areas and does not serve individual workstations. A backbone can run horizontally and vertically through a building. The most widely accepted material used for network backbones is fiber-optic cable.

Examples

Cable Type	Distance
UTP Category 3 or higher (Category 5, 5e, 6, or 6e recommended)	800 meters (voice)
	90 meters (data)
STP Category 3 or higher (Category 5, 5e, 6, or 6e recommended)	800 meters (voice)
	90 meters (data)
Multimode or 62.5/125 fiber-optic cable	2000 meters
Single-mode fiber-optic cable	3000 meters

Related Concepts

Fiber-Optic Cable—2.1C   Single-Mode and Multimode—2.1D

Horizontal Cross Connect—2.8A   Horizontal Wiring—2.8B

Network+ Objective

2.8—Install components of wiring distribution: Vertical and horizontal cross connects, patch panels, 66 block, MDFs, IDFs, 25 pair, 100 pair, 110 block, demarc, demarc extension, smart jack, verify wiring installation, and verify wiring termination.

Description

A typical patch panel is a rack-mounted wiring device for network systems. The device has RJ-45 jacks on the front and a matching series of connections on the back. Patch panel cables are used for making connections between the front of the patch panel and equipment. The back of the panel is where the horizontal run cable is terminated.

Examples

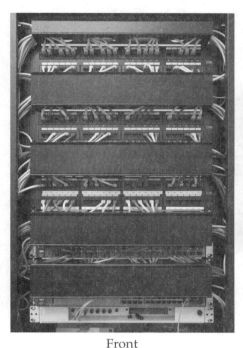

Front

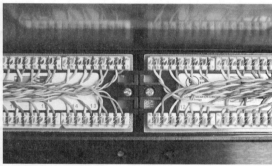

Back

Related Concepts

Twisted Pair Cable—2.1A   Network Connector Types—2.2A

66 and 110 Block—2.8E   MDF—2.8F

Wiring Termination—2.8K

Network+ Objective

2.8—Install components of wiring distribution: Vertical and horizontal cross connects, patch panels, 66 block, MDFs, IDFs, 25 pair, 100 pair, 110 block, demarc, demarc extension, smart jack, verify wiring installation, and verify wiring termination.

Description

There are two main types of punch down blocks: 66 and 110. The 66 block is older than the 110 block. The 110 block was designed to support higher cable frequencies and is less prone to crosstalk. It is the preferred style for network cable such as Cat 5, Cat 5e, and Cat 6. The 66 block was originally designed for telephone communications and is limited to Cat 3 or earlier types of twisted pair cable. It does not support high frequencies.

Examples

Punch down tool

66 Block

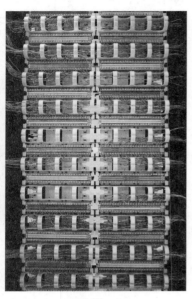

110 Block

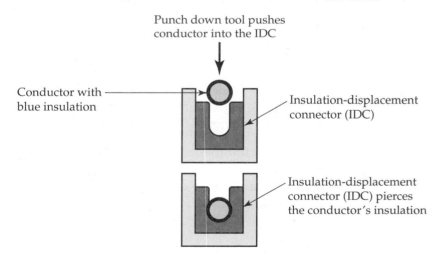

Punch down tool pushes conductor into the IDC

Conductor with blue insulation

Insulation-displacement connector (IDC)

Insulation-displacement connector (IDC) pierces the conductor's insulation

Related Concepts

Twisted Pair Cable—2.1A   Patch Panel—2.8D

Wiring Termination—2.8K

Network+ Objective

2.8—Install components of wiring distribution: Vertical and horizontal cross connects, patch panels, 66 block, MDFs, IDFs, 25 pair, 100 pair, 110 block, demarc, demarc extension, smart jack, verify wiring installation, and verify wiring termination.

Description

The Main Distribution Frame (MDF) is the cable connection point where the private telecommunications cables come into a building and then connect or distribute to other areas in the building. The MDF typically consists of a cable rack and physical cable connections for the individual cable conductors. The MDF is usually located in the main entrance room.

Examples

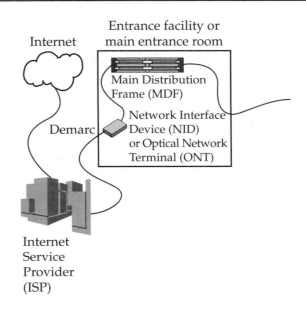

Internet

Entrance facility or main entrance room

Main Distribution Frame (MDF)

Demarc

Network Interface Device (NID) or Optical Network Terminal (ONT)

Internet Service Provider (ISP)

Related Concepts

IDF—2.8G

Network+ Objective

2.8—Install components of wiring distribution: Vertical and horizontal cross connects, patch panels, 66 block, MDFs, IDFs, 25 pair, 100 pair, 110 block, demarc, demarc extension, smart jack, verify wiring installation, and verify wiring termination.

Description

An Intermediate Distribution Frame (IDF) acts as the connection point from the Main Distribution Frame (MDF) and distributes cable runs to all areas on a specific floor. For example, when a multistory building requires telecommunications, each floor would have an IDF that connects to the MDF in the main entrance facility or main entrance room.

Examples

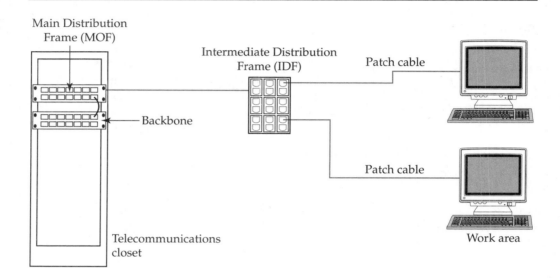

Related Concepts

MDF—2.8F

Network+ Objective

2.8—Install components of wiring distribution: Vertical and horizontal cross connects, patch panels, 66 block, MDFs, IDFs, 25 pair, 100 pair, 110 block, demarc, demarc extension, smart jack, verify wiring installation, and verify wiring termination.

Description

Demarcation point, or demarc, is the spot where the customer equipment or cable meets the telecommunications provider cable or equipment. Both the smart jack and the Optical Network Terminal (ONT) can be identified as the demarcation point.

Examples

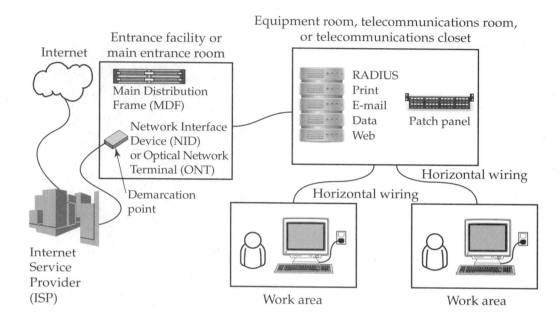

Related Concepts

Smart Jack—2.8I

Network+ Objective

2.8—Install components of wiring distribution: Vertical and horizontal cross connects, patch panels, 66 block, MDFs, IDFs, 25 pair, 100 pair, 110 block, demarc, demarc extension, smart jack, verify wiring installation, and verify wiring termination.

Copyright by Goodheart-Willcox Co., Inc.

Description

A smart jack is considered an intelligent connection point because it incorporates additional electronics that allow it to perform specific functions. For example, a smart jack can perform a loopback test remotely from the service provider without the need to send a technician to the smart jack location. Smart jacks are commonly used for T1 and DSL terminations.

Examples

Related Concepts

Demarcation Point—2.8H

Network+ Objective

2.8—Install components of wiring distribution: Vertical and horizontal cross connects, patch panels, 66 block, MDFs, IDFs, 25 pair, 100 pair, 110 block, demarc, demarc extension, smart jack, verify wiring installation, and verify wiring termination.

Description

There are many organizations that write standards for communications and network systems. The standards of these organizations are often incorporated into the contract specifications for network installation.

Examples

Standard	Description
TIA/EIA 569-A	Commercial Building Standard for Telecommunications Pathways and Spaces
TIA/EIA 568-B.1-2000	Commercial Building Telecommunications Cabling Standard
TIA/EIA 606-A	Administration Standard for Commercial Telecommunications Infrastructure
TIA/EIA 607-A	Commercial Building Grounding and Bonding Requirements for Telecommunications
TSB-75	Additional Horizontal Cabling Practices for Open Offices

Related Concepts

Twisted Pair Cable—2.1A   STP vs. UTP—2.1B

Plenum-Rated Cables—2.1G   568A and 568B—2.4A

Bonding—2.6E   Horizontal Cross Connect—2.8A

Horizontal Wiring—2.8B   Backbone—2.8C

Patch Panel—2.8D   66 and 110 Block—2.8E

MDF—2.8F   IDF—2.8G

Demarcation Point—2.8H   Smart Jack—2.8I

Network+ Objective

2.8—Install components of wiring distribution: Vertical and horizontal cross connects, patch panels, 66 block, MDFs, IDFs, 25 pair, 100 pair, 110 block, demarc, demarc extension, smart jack, verify wiring installation, and verify wiring termination.

Description

The back of the patch panel is where the horizontal run cable is terminated. The individual wires of twisted pair cable are pushed into the connections on the back of the patch panel using a punch down tool. The connections found on the back of patch panels are also found in RJ-45 outlets and punch down blocks.

Examples

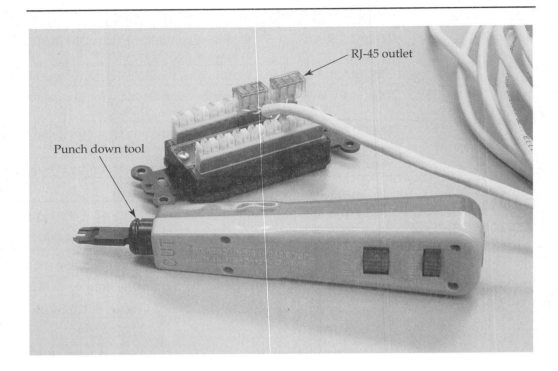

RJ-45 outlet

Punch down tool

Related Concepts

Twisted Pair Cable—2.1A	568A and 568B—2.4A
Patch Panel—2.8D	66 and 110 Block—2.8E

Network+ Objective

2.8—Install components of wiring distribution: Vertical and horizontal cross connects, patch panels, 66 block, MDFs, IDFs, 25 pair, 100 pair, 110 block, demarc, demarc extension, smart jack, verify wiring installation, and verify wiring termination.

Description

A hub is a central connection point where all network cables are concentrated. It is classified as either active or passive. A passive hub simply acts as a central connection point for network cables. Packets transmitted from one node are passed to all nodes connected to the passive hub and through the hub to other sections of the network. An active hub, sometimes called an *intelligent hub* or *switch*, is designed with a power supply. The active hub not only acts as a central connection point for the network cabling, it also regenerates digital signals like a repeater. The active hub can also determine whether a packet should remain in the isolated section of the network or pass the packet through the hub to another section of the network.

Examples

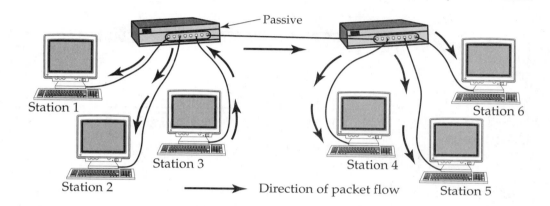

Passive

Station 1
Station 2
Station 3
Station 4
Station 5
Station 6

Direction of packet flow

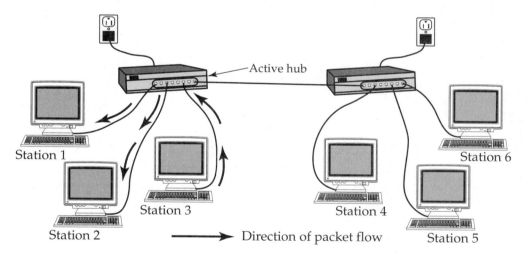

Active hub

Station 1
Station 2
Station 3
Station 4
Station 5
Station 6

Direction of packet flow

Related Concepts

Twisted Pair Cable—2.1A	Network Connector Types—2.2A
Network Topologies—2.3A	Straight-Through, Crossover, and Rollover—2.4B
Repeater—3.1B	Switch—3.1F
OSI Model—4.1A	Physical Layer—4.1H

Network+ Objective

3.1—Install, configure, and differentiate between common network devices: Hub, repeater, modem, NIC, media converters, basic switch, bridge, wireless access point, basic router, basic firewall, and basic DHCP server.

Copyright by Goodheart-Willcox Co., Inc.

Description   The repeater amplifies or reshapes the weak signal into its original strength and form. A repeater allows the network media to exceed its recommended maximum length.

Examples

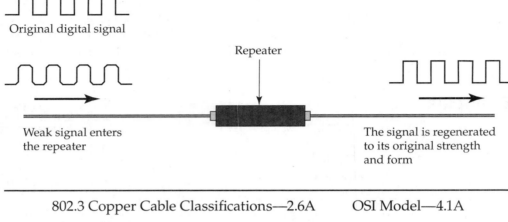

Original digital signal

Repeater

Weak signal enters the repeater

The signal is regenerated to its original strength and form

Related Concepts

802.3 Copper Cable Classifications—2.6A   OSI Model—4.1A

Physical Layer—4.1H

Network+ Objective   3.1—Install, configure, and differentiate between common network devices: Hub, repeater, modem, NIC, media converters, basic switch, bridge, wireless access point, basic router, basic firewall, and basic DHCP server.

Description

A modem is a device that allows a computer to connect to the Internet by converting digital signals from the computer to signals compatible with the infrastructure used to reach an Internet Service Provider. Examples of modems are dial-up, Cable, DSL, and ISDN.

Examples

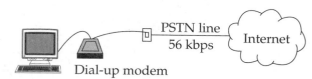

Dial-up

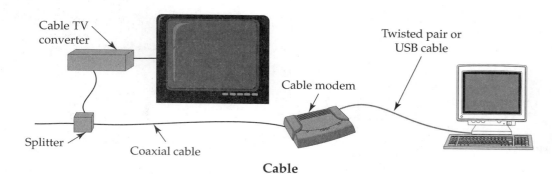

Cable

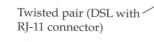

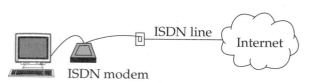

ISDN

Related Concepts

WAN Technology Types—2.5A	xDSL—2.5D
Cable Modem—2.5E	ISDN—2.5J
POTS/PSTN—2.5K	

Network+ Objective

3.1—Install, configure, and differentiate between common network devices: Hub, repeater, modem, NIC, media converters, basic switch, bridge, wireless access point, basic router, basic firewall, and basic DHCP server.

Copyright by Goodheart-Willcox Co., Inc.

Description

A network interface card (NIC) contains the electronic components needed to send and receive a digital signal. A network card is known by many other names such as a *network host adapter*, *network expansion card*, and *network adapter card*.

Examples

(Courtesy of Cisco System, Inc.)

Related Concepts

MAC Address—1.3A	Network Connector Types—2.2A
OSI Model—4.1A	Data Link Layer—4.1G

Network+ Objective

3.1—Install, configure, and differentiate between common network devices: Hub, repeater, modem, NIC, media converters, basic switch, bridge, wireless access point, basic router, basic firewall, and basic DHCP server.

Description   A media converter changes one type of electrical signal into another or interfaces one cable type to another.

Examples

(Courtesy of TRENDnet)

Related Concepts

Twisted Pair Cable—2.1A	Fiber-Optic Cable—2.1C
Coaxial Cable—2.1E	

Network+ Objective   3.1—Install, configure, and differentiate between common network devices: Hub, repeater, modem, NIC, media converters, basic switch, bridge, wireless access point, basic router, basic firewall, and basic DHCP server.

Copyright by Goodheart-Willcox Co., Inc.

Description

A switch filters network traffic or creates subnetworks from a larger network. Some LANs can easily have hundreds or even thousands of nodes. A switch can be used to divide the transmission paths to improve data delivery. When switches form logical networks from a large network, they are called *virtual networks* or *virtual LANs*.

Examples

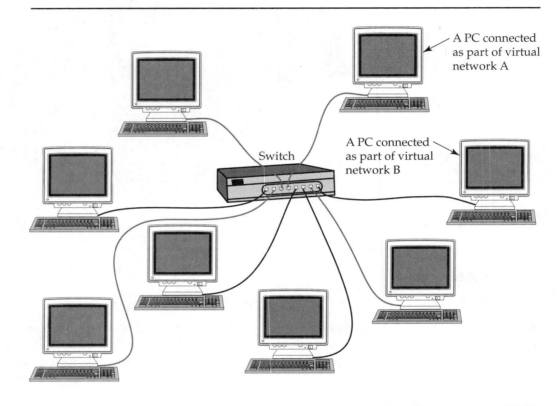

Switch

A PC connected as part of virtual network A

A PC connected as part of virtual network B

Related Concepts

VLAN—2.7D	Hub—3.1A
OSI Model—4.1A	Data Link Layer—4.1G

Network+ Objective

3.1—Install, configure, and differentiate between common network devices: Hub, repeater, modem, NIC, media converters, basic switch, bridge, wireless access point, basic router, basic firewall, and basic DHCP server.

Description

A bridge can be used to divide the network into smaller segments, reducing the chance of collisions. A bridge controls the flow of network traffic between two segments by reading the destination of a network packet. The bridge either allows a packet to pass through to the other segment or restricts the packet to the originating segment.

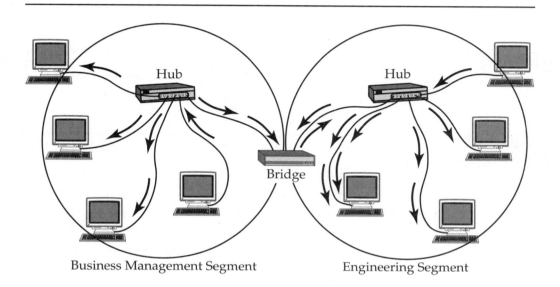

Business Management Segment   Engineering Segment

Related Concepts

OSI Model—4.1A	Data Link Layer—4.1G

Network+ Objective

3.1—Install, configure, and differentiate between common network devices: Hub, repeater, modem, NIC, media converters, basic switch, bridge, wireless access point, basic router, basic firewall, and basic DHCP server.

3.1H   Wireless Access Point

Description   A Wireless Access Point (WAP) is a device that provides a connection between a wireless network and a cable-based network and controls the flow of all packets on the wireless network.

Examples

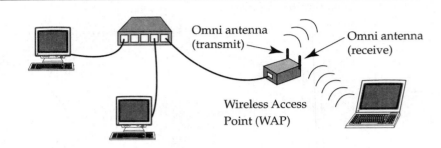

Related Concepts

802.11 a/b/g/n—1.7A	802.11x and RADIUS—1.7C
Wireless Channels—1.7E	Wireless Access Point Placement—3.4A
Wireless Access Point Configuration—3.4B	OSI Model—4.1A
Data Link Layer—4.1G	

Network+ Objective   3.1—Install, configure, and differentiate between common network devices: Hub, repeater, modem, NIC, media converters, basic switch, bridge, wireless access point, basic router, basic firewall, and basic DHCP server.

Description

A router navigates packets across large networks, such as the Internet, using the most efficient route. It maintains a table of information containing the location of other routers and their identification. Routers are typically installed between LANs, but may be installed inside a LAN if traffic conditions warrant their installation. Routers "route" data packets across WANs using the TCP/IP protocol addressing scheme.

Examples

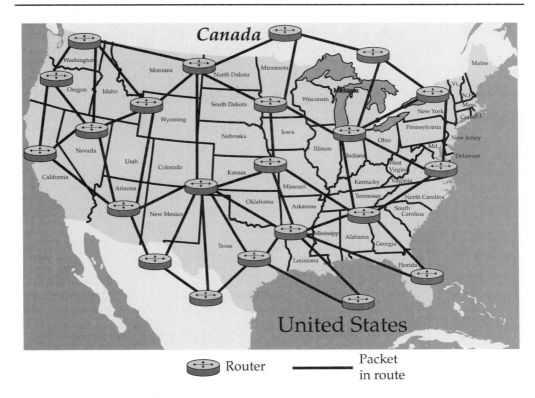

Router — Packet in route

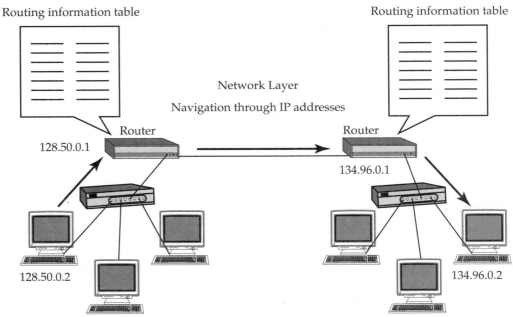

Related Concepts

IPv4 Address—1.3B	IPv6 Address—1.3C
Common IPv4 and IPv6 Routing Protocols—1.5A	IGP vs. EGP—1.6A
Static vs. Dynamic—1.6B	Next Hop—1.6C
Routing Tables—1.6D	Convergence—1.6E
OSI Model—4.1A	Network Layer—4.1F

Network+ Objective

3.1—Install, configure, and differentiate between common network devices: Hub, repeater, modem, NIC, media converters, basic switch, bridge, wireless access point, basic router, basic firewall, and basic DHCP server.

Copyright by Goodheart-Willcox Co., Inc.

Description

A firewall is designed to monitor and pass or block packets as they enter or leave a network system. A firewall may consist of either hardware or software or a combination of both. Servers, routers, and individual computers may be used as firewalls.

Examples

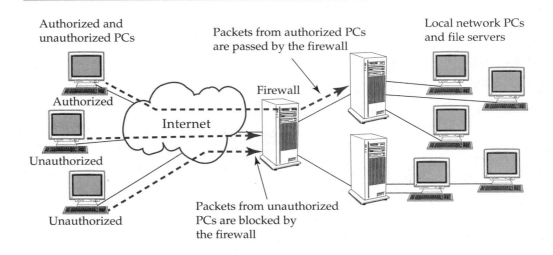

Related Concepts

Intrusion Detection and Intrusion Prevention Systems—6.1A

Common Firewall Features—6.2A

Network+ Objective

3.1—Install, configure, and differentiate between common network devices: Hub, repeater, modem, NIC, media converters, basic switch, bridge, wireless access point, basic router, basic firewall, and basic DHCP server.

Copyright by Goodheart-Willcox Co., Inc.

Description

A DHCP server automatically assigns IP addresses to computers on the network. The act of automatically assigning IP addresses is known as *dynamic addressing*. The DHCP server has a pool, or list, of IP addresses to draw from. Each computer that logs on to the network is assigned an address from the pool. The IP address assignment is temporary. The address is released after a period of time and may be reissued to another computer.

Examples

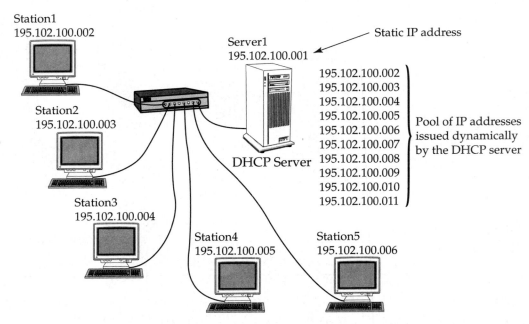

Each workstation receives a temporary IP address from the DHCP server

Related Concepts

IPv4 Address—1.3B	DHCP—1.4F

Network+ Objective

3.1—Install, configure, and differentiate between common network devices: Hub, repeater, modem, NIC, media converters, basic switch, bridge, wireless access point, basic router, basic firewall, and basic DHCP server.

Description

A multilayer switch has an additional electronic chip known as an *Application Specific Integrated Circuit (ASIC)*. The addition of the ASIC gives the layer 2 switch additional capabilities typically found at upper levels of the OSI model. Multilayer switches are generally limited to a specific task and have limited programmable functions. They are referred to by many different names such as *layer 3 switch*, *4-7 switch*, *layer 7 switch*, *URL switch*, *Web content switch*, and *content switch*.

Examples

OSI Model Layer	Switch Type
Application	Layer 4-7 switch (content switch)
Presentation	Layer 4-7 switch (content switch)
Session	Layer 4-7 switch (content switch)
Transport	Layer 4-7 switch (content switch)
Network	Layer 3 switch
Data Link	Layer 2 switch
Physical	NA

Related Concepts

Switch—3.1F   Multifunction Network Devices—3.2D

OSI Model—4.1A   Application Layer—4.1B

Presentation Layer—4.1C   Session Layer—4.1D

Transport Layer—4.1E   Network Layer—4.1F

Data Link Layer—4.1G

Network+ Objective

3.2—Identify the functions of specialized network devices: Multilayer switch, content switch, IDS/IPS, load balancer, multifunction network devices, DNS server, bandwidth shaper, proxy server, and CSU/DSU.

Description

An Intrusion Detection System (IDS) is a passive system; it only detects unauthorized activity. An Intrusion Prevention System (IPS) is a reactive system; it not only detects unauthorized activity, but also performs some function to stop the activity.

Examples

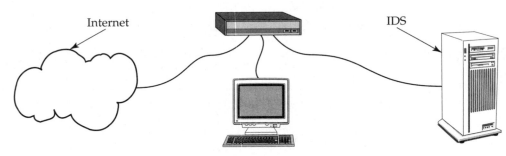

Intrusion Detection System

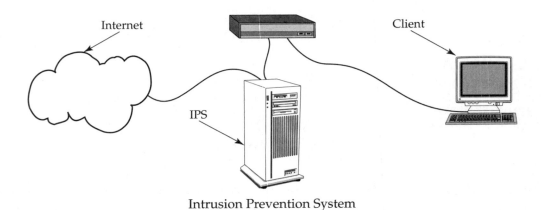

Intrusion Prevention System

Related Concepts

Intrusion Detection and Intrusion Prevention Systems—6.1A

Common Firewall Features—6.2A   Antivirus Software—6.6H

Network+ Objective

3.2—Identify the functions of specialized network devices: Multilayer switch, content switch, IDS/IPS, load balancer, multifunction network devices, DNS server, bandwidth shaper, proxy server, and CSU/DSU.

Description

Load balancing is balancing the demand of network clients to utilize system resources, such as files or CPU processing. For example, additional servers can be installed to share the processing load. When additional servers are configured for load balancing, they are often referred to as *server clusters* or *server farms*.

Examples

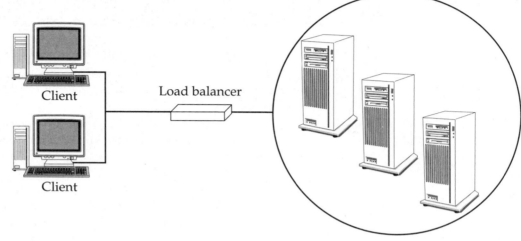

Server farm or server cluster

Related Concepts

Network Performance Optimization—4.5A

Network+ Objective

3.2—Identify the functions of specialized network devices: Multilayer switch, content switch, IDS/IPS, load balancer, multifunction network devices, DNS server, bandwidth shaper, proxy server, and CSU/DSU.

Description

Often, network devices are identified as performing other functions in addition to their intended purpose. For example, a network gateway can also perform functions associated with a firewall by filtering packets based on IP address, port number, or MAC address.

Examples

Multifunction Device	Description
Media converter	Changes one type of electrical signal into another or interfaces one cable type to another. Some media converters may even act as a repeater.
Multilayer switch	An enhanced switch designed to perform more than basic switch functions, such as making decisions about routing a packet based on packet content.
Brouter	Combines router and bridge functions. It functions as a bridge by restricting or passing packets to other sections of a LAN based on the MAC address. It functions as a router by forwarding packets based on the IP address.
Hub	Normally a layer 1 device, it may be reclassified as a layer 2 device when it acts as an intelligent hub. Intelligent hubs make decisions based on MAC addresses and behave more like a switch.
Router	Can be programmed to perform a much wider amount of functions than a switch. For example, routers can be programmed to filter network traffic and can be used to create more networks. Routers can be used to create logical networks and subnets, limit broadcast domains, and create new broadcast domains.

Related Concepts

Port Numbers—1.2A   MAC Address—1.3A

IPv4 Address—1.3B   IPv6 Address—1.3C

Multilayer Switch—3.2A   Common Firewall Features—6.2A

Media Access Control Filter—6.3A

Network+ Objective

3.2—Identify the functions of specialized network devices: Multilayer switch, content switch, IDS/IPS, load balancer, multifunction network devices, DNS server, bandwidth shaper, proxy server, and CSU/DSU.

Description

A DNS server resolves host names to IP addresses, making it easy to identify and find hosts and networks. DNS root servers are located at the top of the domain name hierarchy structure. The root domain server stores the ultimate database for resolving an Internet domain name to a specific IP address. A top-level domain server stores DNS information of all top-level domains. A second-level domain server stores DNS information of all second-level domains.

Examples

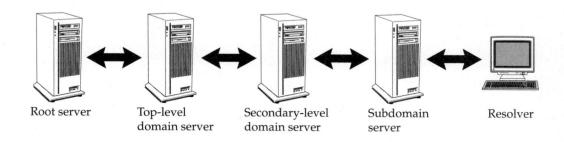

Root server   Top-level domain server   Secondary-level domain server   Subdomain server   Resolver

Related Concepts

Networking Protocols—1.1A   Port Numbers—1.2A

IPv4 Address—1.3B

Network+ Objective

3.2—Identify the functions of specialized network devices: Multilayer switch, content switch, IDS/IPS, load balancer, multifunction network devices, DNS server, bandwidth shaper, proxy server, and CSU/DSU.

Description

A bandwidth shaper, or traffic shaper, is used to prioritize network packets to ensure quality of service for time-sensitive applications such as VoIP. A bandwidth shaper prioritizes network traffic by protocol or assigned switch port or port number. Bandwidth shaping can be accomplished with hardware or software and is used to control the bandwidth through a particular device such as a gateway, shared Internet connection, network switch, or router.

Examples

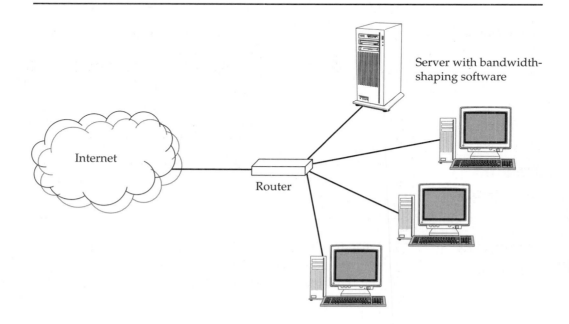

Server with bandwidth-shaping software

Internet

Router

Related Concepts

Port Numbers—1.2A	Switch—3.1F
Router—3.1I	Network Performance Optimization—4.5A

Network+ Objective

3.2—Identify the functions of specialized network devices: Multilayer switch, content switch, IDS/IPS, load balancer, multifunction network devices, DNS server, bandwidth shaper, proxy server, and CSU/DSU.

Description

A proxy server is a firewall component that is typically installed on a server and resides between the Internet server and the LAN hosts. It appears as a destination host while hiding the address of the true host inside the LAN. The proxy server can be configured to allow packets to flow into and out of the network if they meet certain conditions. The conditions configured can be items such as specific IP addresses, certain protocols, and server names or URLs. Proxy servers may also cache information, like frequently visited Web sites.

Examples

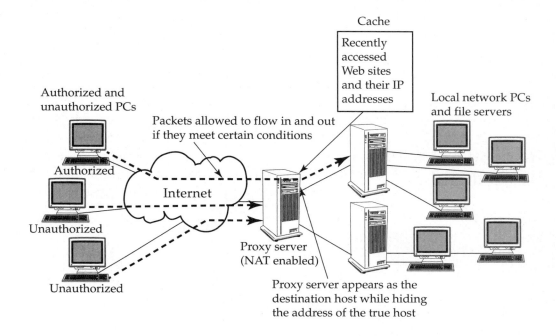

Related Concepts

NAT—1.4D	Firewall—3.1J
Network Performance Optimization—4.5A	Common Firewall Features—6.2A

Network+ Objective

3.2—Identify the functions of specialized network devices: Multilayer switch, content switch, IDS/IPS, load balancer, multifunction network devices, DNS server, bandwidth shaper, proxy server, and CSU/DSU.

Description

A Channel Service Unit/Data Service Unit (CSU/DSU) converts signals from a LAN to signals that can be carried by a T1 line, and vice versa.

Examples

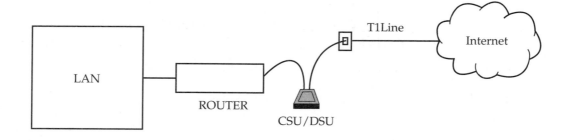

Related Concepts

T-Carrier—2.5C

Network+ Objective

3.2—Identify the functions of specialized network devices: Multilayer switch, content switch, IDS/IPS, load balancer, multifunction network devices, DNS server, bandwidth shaper, proxy server, and CSU/DSU.

Description

Power over Ethernet (PoE) is an IEEE standard that specifies the supply of small amounts of electrical power to network devices such as cameras, IP phones, Wireless Access Points, speakers, and phone chargers.

Examples

Related Concepts

Switch—3.1F	Wireless Access Point—3.1H

Network+ Objective

3.3—Explain the advanced features of a switch: PoE, spanning tree, VLAN, trunking, port mirroring, and port authentication.

3.3B Spanning Tree Protocol

Description   Spanning Tree Protocol (STP) is a layer 2 protocol designed to manage networks based on MAC addresses and to prevent bridge loops.

Examples

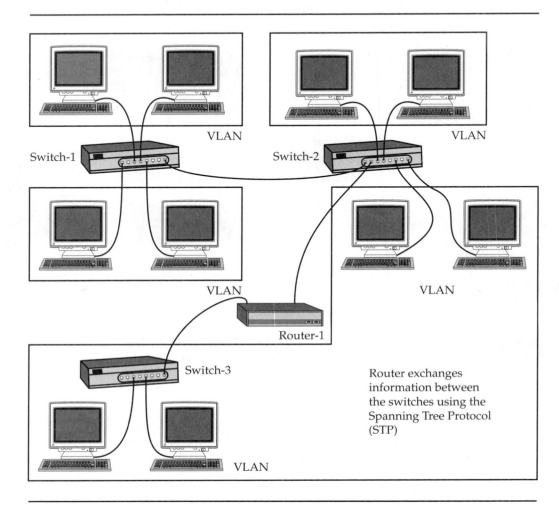

Related Concepts

MAC Address—1.3A	Switch—3.1F
OSI Model—4.1A	Data Link Layer—4.1G

Network+ Objective   3.3—Explain the advanced features of a switch: PoE, spanning tree, VLAN trunking, port mirroring, and port authentication.

Description

Trunking is the technique of connecting different VLANs together using a single network link. Switches are connected to each other through a router or routers. The router then can be used to exchange information between switches using the Spanning Tree Protocol (STP). The cable that is used for trunking is referred to as the *trunk*. The ports used for trunking are referred to as the *trunk ports*.

Examples

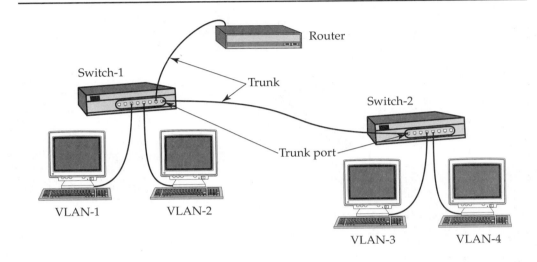

Related Concepts

VLAN—2.7D	Switch—3.1F
Router—3.1I	Spanning Tree Protocol—3.3B

Network+ Objective

3.3—Explain the advanced features of a switch: PoE, spanning tree, VLAN, trunking, port mirroring, and port authentication.

Copyright by Goodheart-Willcox Co., Inc.

Description

RADIUS is referred to as a "port authentication" standard. Some switches have an advanced feature referred to as "port authentication." Port authentication is a method in which a switch restricts access through a specific switch port until access is authenticated by a RADIUS or TACACS+ server.

Examples

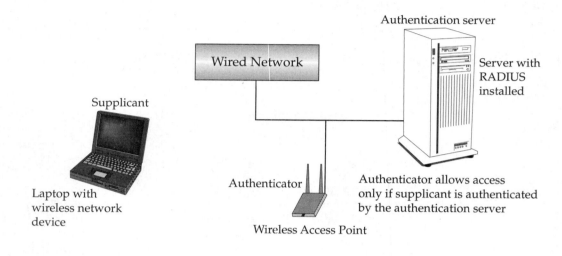

Authentication server

Wired Network

Server with RADIUS installed

Supplicant

Authenticator

Authenticator allows access only if supplicant is authenticated by the authentication server

Laptop with wireless network device

Wireless Access Point

Related Concepts

Switch—3.1F

TACACS+—6.4E

RADIUS—6.4D

Network+ Objective

3.3—Explain the advanced features of a switch: PoE, spanning tree, VLAN, trunking, port mirroring, and port authentication.

Description

In an infrastructure wireless network, the Wireless Access Point (WAP) must be in the common overlap area of the wireless network computers. The WAP controls all communication. The range of a wireless network can be extended by adding additional WAPs.

Examples

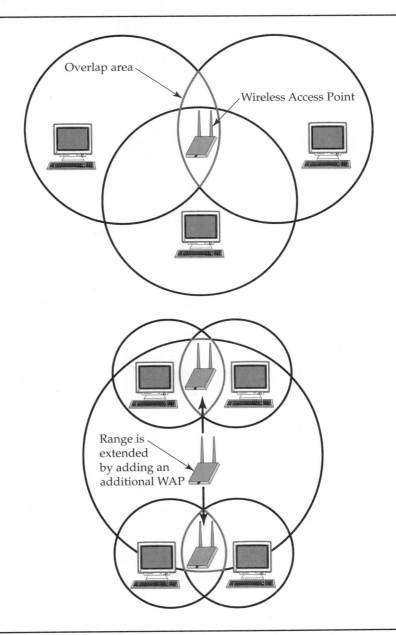

Related Concepts

802.11 a/b/g/n—1.7A	Wireless Access Point—3.1H

Network+ Objective

3.4—Implement a basic wireless network: Install client, access point placement, install access point (configure appropriate encryption, configure channels and frequencies, set ESSID and beacon), and verify installation.

Description

When configuring a Wireless Access Point, the configuration software for the device will prompt for an SSID, security type, and a security key.

Examples

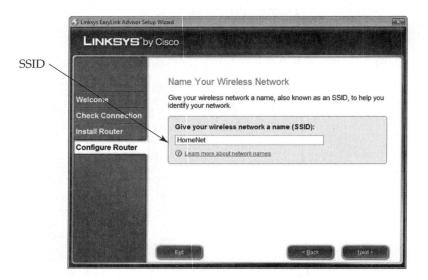

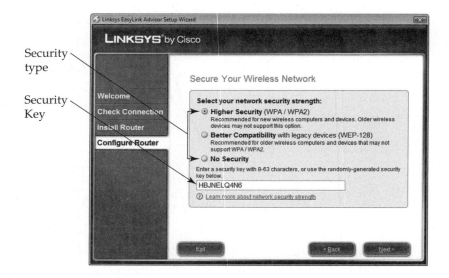

Related Concepts

802.11 a/b/g/n—1.7A	Authentication—1.7B
802.11x and RADIUS—1.7C	Encryption—1.7D
Wireless Channels—1.7E	Wireless Access Point—3.1H
802.1x—6.4F	EAP—6.4H

Network+ Objective

3.4—Implement a basic wireless network: Install client, access point placement, install access point (configure appropriate encryption, configure channels and frequencies, set ESSID and beacon), and verify installation.

Description

The OSI model describes how hardware and software should work together to form a network communications system. It serves as a guide for troubleshooting and designing networks. The OSI model consists of seven layers. Each layer in the OSI model is assigned a specific function.

Examples

OSI Layer	Function	Hardware	Protocols	Keywords
Application	User interface	Gateways	HTTP, FTP, WWW, SNAP, SMB, SMTP, Telnet, POP, IMAP	Browser, e-mail, network applications
Presentation	Convert to common format such as ASCII, data encryption, and compression	Gateways	MPEG, WAV, MIDI, QuickTime	ASCII, Unicode, EBCDIC, CODEC, and bit order
Session	Establish and close communication between two nodes Coordinates communication	Gateways	NFS, DNS, SQL, RPC, NetBIOS, X.25, SMB	Establish and terminate a communication session, log on, user name, password, authentication, assign services through port numbers
Transport	Sequence packets Ensure error free delivery Takes over after the session has been established	Gateways (layer 4 switches)	TCP, UDP, SPX	Segments, windowing, flow control, transport packets, error checking (if required), port numbers
Network	Navigates outside of the LAN	Routers (layer 3 switches)	IP, IPX, AppleTalk, ICMP, RIP, RIPv2, ARP, OSPF, IGRP, RARP, BGP, NLSP, IS-IS, EIRGP	IP address, routing, packets, datagrams, network address, packet switching, logical address, best and shortest route
Data Link	Prepares data for media access Defines frame format	Bridges, switches, Wireless Access Points, network interface cards	CSMA/CD, CSMA/CA, LLDP	MAC address, hardware address, LLC, CRC, frame types, frames, topologies, contention
Physical	The physical aspect of the network	Copper core cable, fiber-optic cable, wireless, hubs, repeaters, transceivers, amplifiers, transducers	NA	Bit, byte, cable, media, topology, transmission, voltage, digital signals

Copyright by Goodheart-Willcox Co., Inc.

Related Concepts

Application Layer—4.1B	Presentation Layer—4.1C
Session Layer—4.1D	Transport Layer—4.1E
Network Layer—4.1F	Data Link Layer—4.1G
Physical Layer—4.1H	

Network+ Objective

4.1—Explain the function of each layer of the OSI model: Layer 1—physical, Layer 2—data link, Layer 3—network, Layer 4—transport, Layer 5—session, Layer 6—presentation, and Layer 7—application.

Copyright by Goodheart-Willcox Co., Inc.

Description

The application layer is the layer of the OSI model that works with specific networking applications such as Web browser programs, file transfer programs, and e-mail.

Examples

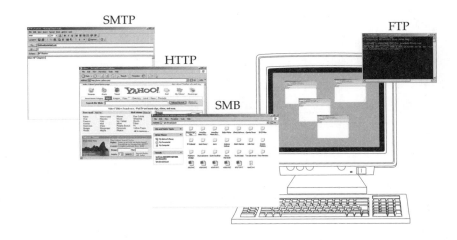

Related Concepts

OSI Model—4.1A

Network+ Objective

4.1—Explain the function of each layer of the OSI model: Layer 1—physical, Layer 2—data link, Layer 3—network, Layer 4—transport, Layer 5—session, Layer 6—presentation, and Layer 7—application.

Description

The presentation layer is the layer of the OSI model that ensures character-code recognition. It is responsible for converting character codes into a code that is recognizable by a computer that uses a different character code.

Examples

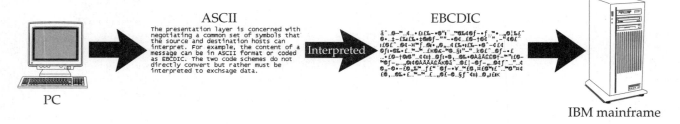

PC

IBM mainframe

Related Concepts

OSI Model—4.1A

Network+ Objective

4.1—Explain the function of each layer of the OSI model: Layer 1—physical, Layer 2—data link, Layer 3—network, Layer 4—transport, Layer 5—session, Layer 6—presentation, and Layer 7—application.

Description

The session layer is the layer of the OSI model layer that establishes, maintains, and terminates the connection with the destination.

Examples

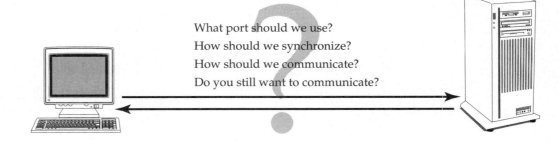

What port should we use?
How should we synchronize?
How should we communicate?
Do you still want to communicate?

Related Concepts

OSI Model—4.1A

Network+ Objective

4.1—Explain the function of each layer of the OSI model: Layer 1—physical, Layer 2—data link, Layer 3—network, Layer 4—transport, Layer 5—session, Layer 6—presentation, and Layer 7—application.

Description

The transport layer is a layer of the OSI model layer that ensures reliable data by sequencing packets and reassembling them into their correct order.

Examples

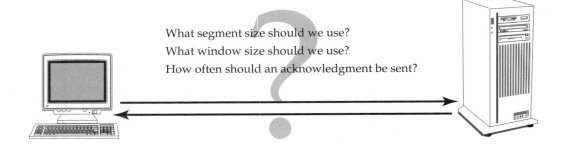

What segment size should we use?
What window size should we use?
How often should an acknowledgment be sent?

Related Concepts

OSI Model—4.1A

Network+ Objective

4.1—Explain the function of each layer of the OSI model: Layer 1—physical, Layer 2—data link, Layer 3—network, Layer 4—transport, Layer 5—session, Layer 6—presentation, and Layer 7—application.

Description

The network layer is a layer of the OSI model layer that is responsible for routing packets from one network to another using the IP addressing format.

Examples

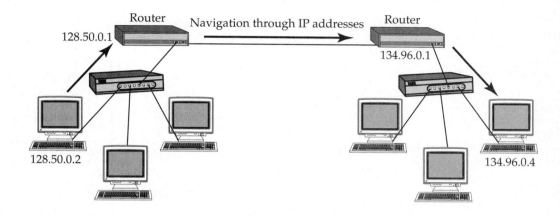

Related Concepts

OSI Model—4.1A

Network+ Objective

4.1—Explain the function of each layer of the OSI model: Layer 1—physical, Layer 2—data link, Layer 3—network, Layer 4—transport, Layer 5—session, Layer 6—presentation, and Layer 7—application.

Copyright by Goodheart-Willcox Co., Inc.

Description

The data link layer is a layer of the OSI model layer that describes how the raw data is packaged for transfer from one network interface card to another. The data link layer contains information such as the addresses of the source and destination and the size of the packet. The data link layer provides for error checking.

Examples

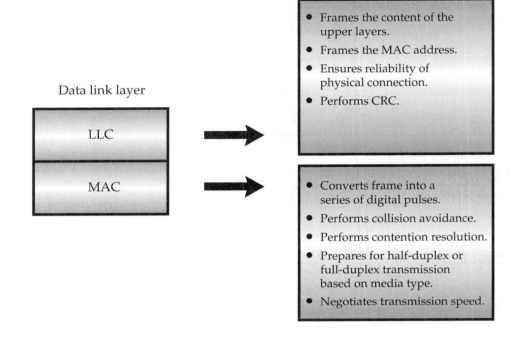

Data link layer

LLC

MAC

- Frames the content of the upper layers.
- Frames the MAC address.
- Ensures reliability of physical connection.
- Performs CRC.

- Converts frame into a series of digital pulses.
- Performs collision avoidance.
- Performs contention resolution.
- Prepares for half-duplex or full-duplex transmission based on media type.
- Negotiates transmission speed.

Related Concepts

MAC Address—1.3A   OSI Model—4.1A

Network+ Objective

4.1—Explain the function of each layer of the OSI model: Layer 1—physical, Layer 2—data link, Layer 3—network, Layer 4—transport, Layer 5—session, Layer 6—presentation, and Layer 7—application.

Description

The physical layer is a layer of the OSI model that provides the path for the raw digital pulses that are moved along cables and connectors. The various network topologies and IEEE standards for equipment are also identified at this layer. Exact dimensions of connectors, materials, voltage level, frequency, data rates, Baseband and Broadband signaling techniques, and any other concerns about the physical communications circuit between the destination and source is described at this layer.

Examples

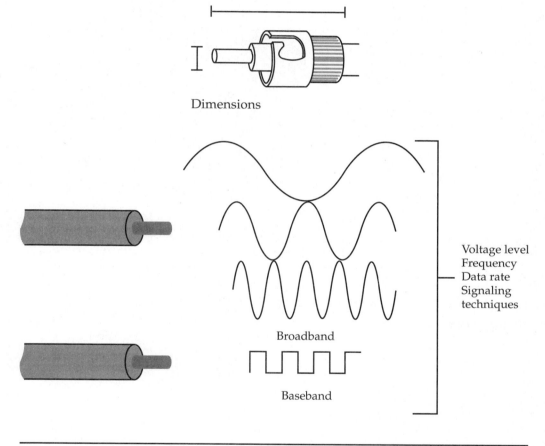

Dimensions

Broadband

Baseband

Voltage level
Frequency
Data rate
Signaling
techniques

Related Concepts

Twisted Pair Cable—2.1A	Fiber-Optic Cable—2.1C
Coaxial Cable—2.1E	Network Connector Types—2.2A
Network Topologies—2.3A	OSI Model—4.1A

Network+ Objective

4.1—Explain the function of each layer of the OSI model: Layer 1—physical, Layer 2—data link, Layer 3—network, Layer 4—transport, Layer 5—session, Layer 6—presentation, and Layer 7—application.

4.2A   Physical and Logical Network Diagrams

Description

There are many utilities and case studies available to help with network design. A network designer can use the Microsoft Visio program to design the physical structure and directory structure of a network.

Examples

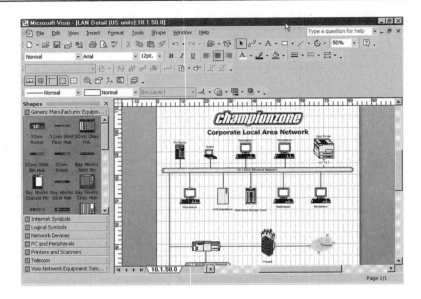

Related Concepts

Configuration Management Documentation—4.3A

Network+ Objective

4.2—Identify types of configuration management documentation: Wiring schematics; physical and logical network diagrams; baselines; policies, procedures, and configurations; and regulations.

Description

A baseline is a measurement of performance characteristics that can be used at a later date to objectively determine if the network or server is performing satisfactorily. Baseline of the system should be established as soon as a new network or server is installed and is operational. After that, the baseline information should be routinely collected and reviewed to predict events that could affect network or server performance.

Examples

Network Segment ID _____

Date and Time Period _____

Segment	Value	Comments
Peak Utilization		
Average Utilization		
Frame Size Peak		
Frame Size Average		
Number of Protocols		
Number of Nodes		
Most Active 10 Nodes		
Collisions		
Packets Dropped		

Related Concepts

Network Monitoring Utilities—4.4A

Network+ Objective

4.2—Identify types of configuration management documentation: Wiring schematics; physical and logical network diagrams; baselines; policies, procedures, and configurations; and regulations.

Copyright by Goodheart-Willcox Co., Inc.

Description

A network administrator's best protection for the network is a combination of user policies and antivirus software. Policies outline how users are to use and not use their workstation and the network. Basically, policies and procedures are a list of dos and don'ts for the user. Typically, these are called an *Acceptable Use Policy*. An Acceptable Use Policy helps protect a system against malware.

Examples

Acceptable Use Policy

- Do *not* open any e-mail file attachments from unknown sources.

- Do *not* download any files from unknown sources.

- Update antivirus software on a regular basis.

- Never open e-mail advertisements, chain letters, or junk mail.

- Do *not* click icons embedded in files or e-mails.

- Do *not* open any e-mail attachments with an exe, com, bat, vbs, shs, pif, ovl extension or double extensions such as in GreatPicture.jpg.exe. If you doubt the authenticity of an e-mail, check with the indicated source before opening the e-mail, especially an attachment.

Related Concepts

Configuration Management Documentation—4.3A

Network+ Objective

4.2—Identify types of configuration management documentation: Wiring schematics; physical and logical network diagrams; baselines; policies, procedures, and configurations; and regulations.

Description

There are several security standards and laws aimed at securing user personal data such as medical records, banking records, health records, and credit card information. Many states have their own laws related to personal data security.

Examples

Regulation	Descriptions
Health Insurance Portability and Accountability Act (HIPAA)	A set of standards designed to protect health records.
Payment Card Industry Data Security Standard (PCI DSS)	A set of credit card security standards designed to protect credit card information.
California SB 1386 Act	A legislative act that requires all organizations that own or have access to personal information of California residents to notify the person of any breach of security of his or her personal data.
Sarbanes-Oxley (SOX)	A legislative act that imposes standards on financial institutions to secure personal financial records. As part of the legislative act, the IT portion of the organization is required to perform routine security checks of the network system and data storage.

Related Concepts

Intrusion Detection and Intrusion Prevention Systems—6.1A

Common Firewall Features—6.2A

Network+ Objective

4.2—Identify types of configuration management documentation: Wiring schematics; physical and logical network diagrams; baselines; policies, procedures, and configurations; and regulations.

Description

Always keep an up-to-date and complete set of documentation for the existing network and associated equipment. One of the most important items to assist you when troubleshooting a large network system is a detailed site plan that has all of the major networking devices identified. Documentation also acts as a history of the system. For example, if a network interface card is replaced by another brand or version, you have a record available. The record can be used to update equipment inventories and equipment descriptions. Software programs, such as HelpSTAR, are available to help an administrator keep track of service requests, computer inventory, and history.

Examples

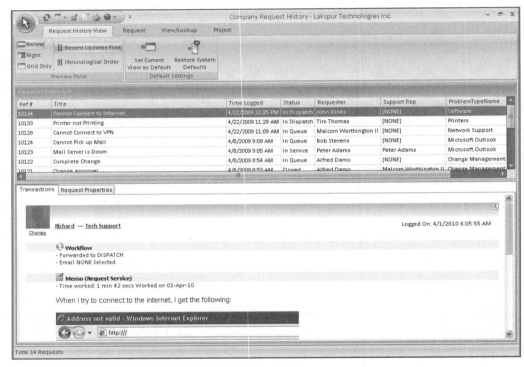

HelpSTAR

Related Concepts

Physical and Logical Network Diagrams—4.2A   Baselines—4.2B

Network+ Objective

4.3—Given a scenario, evaluate the network based on configuration management documentation: Compare wiring schematics, physical and logical network diagrams, baselines, policies and procedures, and configurations to network devices and infrastructure. Update wiring schematics, physical and logical network diagrams, configurations, and job logs as needed.

Description

Network events need to be monitored to detect and predict problems. The exact problems can vary a great deal, from simple user problems to detecting an intruder's attempts to break into the system. All major operating systems have monitoring utilities. There are also many good third-party tools available. Monitoring tools not only monitor events but also record the events into a log, which is then saved as a file. Event logs can be used to assist in analyzing system problems involving hardware, software, and security issues.

Examples

Monitoring Utility	Windows OS	Description
Performance Monitor or Reliability and Performance Monitor	Windows Vista Windows 7 Windows Server 2008 R2	Can be used to predict system failure or to isolate the cause of poor performance. When used properly, the administrator can schedule routine hardware replacements, additions, and upgrades that will minimally affect user access. Can also be configured to send alerts to the system administrator when resources are critical.
Windows Task Manager	Windows XP Windows Vista Windows 7 Windows Server 2003 Windows Server 2008	Provides a quick view of system performance and can also show what software applications, processes, and services are running.
Microsoft Network Monitor	Windows XP SP3 Windows XP 64-bit Windows Vista SP1 Windows Vista 64-bit editions SP1 Windows 7 Windows Server 2003 SP2 Windows Server 2003 SP2 64-bit edition Windows Server 2008 Windows Server 2008 R2 Windows Server 2008 R2 (Itanium-based systems)	A full protocol analyzer with many features found only in very expensive third-party protocol analyzers. It can be used to establish a baseline of information about network performance. Microsoft Network Monitor is not installed by default but can be downloaded from the Microsoft Web site for free.
Event Viewer	Windows XP Windows Vista Windows 7 Windows Server 2003 Windows Server 2008	Records events that occur during the operation of the server or desktop system. Some typical events are the starting or stopping of a service, user logon activities, share access, file access, and hardware and software information. Event Viewer is an excellent utility for troubleshooting system failures.

Copyright by Goodheart-Willcox Co., Inc.

Related Concepts

Network+ Objective

Baselines—4.2B   Configuration Management Documentation—4.3A

4.4—Conduct network monitoring to identify performance and connectivity issues using the following: Network monitoring utilities (packet sniffers, connectivity software, load testing, throughput testers) and system logs, history logs, and event logs.

Copyright by Goodheart-Willcox Co., Inc.

Description

Methods such as traffic shaping; incorporating the QoS protocol, caching engines, fault tolerant devices; load balancing; and increasing the amount of server resources can be used to overcome network performance problems.

Examples

Performance Optimization Method	Reason or Need	Description
Traffic Shaping	VoIP and video applications and latency sensitivity	Prioritizes network packets to ensure quality of service for time-sensitive applications such as VoIP.
Quality of Service (QoS) Protocol	VoIP and video applications and latency sensitivity	Developed to minimize latency, the QoS protocol gives time-sensitive packets, such as those carrying telephone conversations, a higher priority than data packets.
Load Balancing	High-bandwidth applications	Balances the demand of network clients to utilize system resources such as files or CPU processing by adding more servers to share the processing load.
High Availability	High-bandwidth applications	Increasing the amount of server resources available to users by adding more memory or configuring more hard disk drives and mapping users to the additional drives.
Caching Engines	High-bandwidth applications	Network proxy servers can be used to store IP and URL addresses in their cache to expedite the connection process.
Fault Tolerance	Uptime	A system's ability to continue operation during a system hardware or software error can be achieved with some RAID systems, server clustering, and UPS units.

Related Concepts

Load Balancer—3.2C

Network+ Objective

4.5—Explain different methods and rationales for network performance optimization: Methods (QoS, traffic shaping, load balancing, high availability, caching engines, fault tolerance), reasons (latency sensitivity, high-bandwidth applications, VoIP, video applications), and uptime.

4.6A   Network Troubleshooting Methodology

Description

A troubleshooting strategy is a general list of steps to follow when presented with a problem scenario. CompTIA suggests nine steps for troubleshooting a network problem.

Examples

> **Given a scenario, implement the following network troubleshooting methodology:**
> 1. Information gathering—identify symptoms and problems.
> 2. Identify the affected areas of the network.
> 3. Determine if anything has changed.
> 4. Establish the most probable cause.
> 5. Determine if escalation is necessary.
> 6. Create an action plan and solution identifying potential effects.
> 7. Implement and test the solution.
> 8. Identify the results and effects of the solution.
> 9. Document the solution and the entire process.

Related Concepts

Troubleshooting Connectivity Issues—4.7A	Traceroute/Tracert—5.1A
Ipconfig/Ifconfig—5.1B	Ping—5.1C
ARP—5.1D	Nslookup—5.1E
Pathping—5.1F	Route—5.1G
Nbtstat—5.1H	Netstat—5.1I
Network Hardware Tools—5.3A	

Network+ Objective

4.6—Given a scenario, implement the following network troubleshooting methodology: Information gathering—identify symptoms and problems, identify the affected areas of the network, determine if anything has changed, establish the most probable cause, determine if escalation is necessary, create an action plan and solution identifying potential effects, implement and test the solution, identify the results and effects of the solution, and document the solution and the entire process.

Description

Connectivity problems include physical issues, logical issues, and wireless issues. If an issue is beyond the technician's expertise, the issue should be escalated to someone with the appropriate expertise.

Examples

Connectivity Issue	Description
Physical Issues	
Crosstalk	Interference that comes from neighboring conductors inside a wire's insulating jacket.
Near-End Crosstalk	A measurement of the reflected loss at the near end, or input end, of a cable.
Attenuation	The loss of signal strength.
Collision	A condition that occurs when two computers transmit data at the same time.
Short	A wiring fault that occurs in cabling when two conductors are improperly connected, resulting in a shorter circuit path.
Open	A wiring fault that occurs when the length of a conductor has an open spot.
Impedance mismatch (echo)	The effect of connecting two different electronic audio systems that have different electronic characteristics.
Interference	An undesired electromagnetic signal imposed on a desired signal that distorts or corrupts the desired signal.
Logical Issues	
Port duplex mismatch	When one device is configured to communicate in full-duplex mode and the other device in half-duplex mode.
Incorrect VLAN	An incorrectly-configured VLAN assignment, commonly due to technician error when configuring the switch.
Incorrect IP address	A host with an incorrect IP address may not be able to access other hosts on the network or may not be recognized by the security system.
Wrong gateway	A host configured with the wrong gateway address will not be able to access the Internet.
Wrong DNS	Configuring a host for the wrong DNS server can cause Internet access problems.
Wrong subnet mask	Configuring a host for the wrong subnet mask can prevent the host from accessing hosts on the local network.

(Continued.)

Copyright by Goodheart-Willcox Co., Inc.

Connectivity Issue	Description
Wireless Issues	
Interference	Packet loss is generally caused by radio interference or excessive distance between two devices.
Incorrect encryption	When encryption is enabled on a wireless device such as a WAP, all devices expected to communicate with the WAP must have a matching encryption passphrase or security key.
Incorrect channel	For wireless devices to be able to communicate with one another, all devices must use the same channel.
ESSID mismatch	When two or more Wireless Access Points (WAPs) are used to support roaming and are connected to a common wired network, they must have matching SSIDs.
Distance	Packet loss is generally caused by radio interference or excessive distance between two devices.
Bounce	A condition where a wireless signal reflects off metal objects, some types of glass, and certain building materials, thus corrupting the wireless signal.
Incorrect antenna placement	For nodes to communicate with each other on a wireless network, all nodes must be inside the same broadcast area.

Related Concepts

Network Troubleshooting Methodology—4.6A   Traceroute/Tracert—5.1A

Ipconfig/Ifconfig—5.1B   Ping—5.1C

Pathping—5.1F   Route—5.1G

Network Hardware Tools—5.3A

Network+ Objective

4.7—Given a scenario, troubleshoot common connectivity issues and select an appropriate solution: Physical issues (crosstalk, near-end crosstalk, attenuation, collisions, shorts, open, impedance mismatch, interference), logical issues (port speed, port duplex mismatch, incorrect VLAN, incorrect IP address, wrong gateway, wrong DNS, wrong subnet mask), issues that should be identified but escalated (switching loop, routing loop, route problems, proxy ARP, broadcast storms), and wireless issues (interference, incorrect encryption, incorrect channel, incorrect frequency, ESSID mismatch, standard mismatch, distance, bounce, incorrect antenna placement).

Copyright by Goodheart-Willcox Co., Inc.

5.1A   Traceroute/Tracert

Description

The traceroute/tracert utility is good for troubleshooting a path to a distant destination. The trace route utility also displays the approximate hop lapse times between points along the route. The amount of time delay can help analyze network failure or problems caused by excessive time delays. The **traceroute** command is used on UNIX/Linux systems, and the **tracert** command is used on Microsoft systems.

Examples

Analyze network failure or problems caused by excessive time delays.

Related Concepts

Next Hop—1.6C

Router—3.1I

Troubleshooting Connectivity Issues—4.7A

Route—5.1G

Routing Tables—1.6D

Network Troubleshooting Methodology—4.6A

Pathping—5.1F

Network+ Objective

5.1—Given a scenario, select the appropriate command line interface tool and interpret the output to verify functionality: **traceroute, ipconfig, ifconfig, ping, arp, nslookup, hostname, dig, mtr, route, nbtstat,** and **netstat.**

Description

Windows operating systems use the **ipconfig** command issued from the command prompt to run the IP Configuration utility. The assigned IPv4 address, the subnet mask, and the default gateway address are displayed. To reveal more information about the connection, use the **ipconfig/all** command. UNIX/Linux operating systems use the **ifconfig** command.

Examples

Verify assigned IP address subnet mask and default gateway.

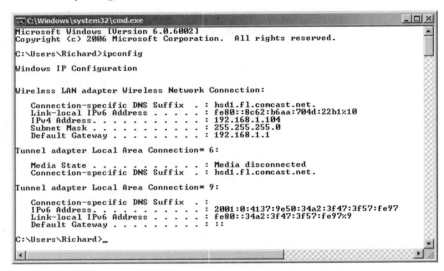

Related Concepts

MAC Address—1.3A

IPv6 Address—1.3C

IPv4 Address—1.3B

Network Troubleshooting Methodology—4.6A

Troubleshooting Connectivity Issues—4.7A

Network+ Objective

5.1—Given a scenario, select the appropriate command line interface tool and interpret the output to verify functionality: **traceroute**, **ipconfig**, **ifconfig**, **ping**, **arp**, **nslookup**, **hostname**, **dig**, **mtr**, **route**, **nbtstat**, and **netstat**.

Description

The **ping** command is used to verify that a connection exists between the destination and the source. It is also used to verify that the TCP/IP protocol is configured for the network interface card at the host and to check the proper operation of the network interface card.

Examples

Check proper operation of the network interface card.

```
C:\WINDOWS\system32\command.com                                    _ □ ×
Microsoft(R) Windows DOS
(C)Copyright Microsoft Corp 1990-2001.

C:\DOCUME~1>ping localhost

Pinging EDIT84.gwp.com [127.0.0.1] with 32 bytes of data:

Reply from 127.0.0.1: bytes=32 time<1ms TTL=64
Reply from 127.0.0.1: bytes=32 time<1ms TTL=64
Reply from 127.0.0.1: bytes=32 time<1ms TTL=64
Reply from 127.0.0.1: bytes=32 time<1ms TTL=64

Ping statistics for 127.0.0.1:
    Packets: Sent = 4, Received = 4, Lost = 0 (0% loss),
Approximate round trip times in milli-seconds:
    Minimum = 0ms, Maximum = 0ms, Average = 0ms

C:\DOCUME~1>
```

Check connection state of network.

```
C:\>ping 192.168.1.1

Pinging 192.168.1.1 with 32 bytes of data:

Reply from 192.168.1.1: bytes=32 time<1ms TTL=150
Reply from 192.168.1.1: bytes=32 time<1ms TTL=150
Reply from 192.168.1.1: bytes=32 time<1ms TTL=150
Reply from 192.168.1.1: bytes=32 time<1ms TTL=150

Ping statistics for 192.168.1.1:
    Packets: Sent = 4, Received = 4, Lost = 0 (0% loss),
Approximate round trip times in milli-seconds:
    Minimum = 0ms, Maximum = 0ms, Average = 0ms
```

Related Concepts

IPv4 Address—1.3B	IPv6 Address—1.3C
NIC—3.1D	Network Troubleshooting Methodology—4.6A
Troubleshooting Connectivity Issues—4.7A	Pathping—5.1F

Network+ Objective

5.1—Given a scenario, select the appropriate command line interface tool and interpret the output to verify functionality: **traceroute**, **ipconfig**, **ifconfig**, **ping**, **arp**, **nslookup**, **hostname**, **dig**, **mtr**, **route**, **nbtstat**, and **netstat**.

Description

The **arp** command lists entries in the ARP cache. It can be used to troubleshoot problems with multiple IP assignments and to solve host communications problems.

Examples

Solve host communication problems.
Identify stations with multiple IP addresses.

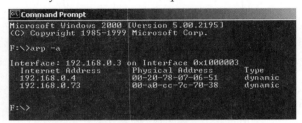

Related Concepts

Networking Protocols—1.1A

IPv6 Address—1.3C

Troubleshooting Connectivity Issues—4.7A

IPv4 Address—1.3B

Network Troubleshooting Methodology—4.6A

Network+ Objective

5.1—Given a scenario, select the appropriate command line interface tool and interpret the output to verify functionality: **traceroute, ipconfig, ifconfig, ping, arp, nslookup, hostname, dig, mtr, route, nbtstat,** and **netstat.**

Description

The **nslookup** command is a UNIX/Linux utility used to query domain servers when seeking information about domain names and IP addresses. The **nslookup** command maps, or resolves, domain names to IP addresses. This is a convenient tool when looking for information about a particular domain or IP addresses. Two UNIX/Linux tools that perform a similar function as **nslookup** are **dig** (Domain Information Digger) and **host**.

Examples

Query a domain server about a domain name.

Display the network's default DNS server.

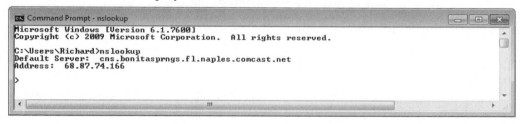

Related Concepts

IPv4 Address—1.3B   DNS Server—3.2E

Network+ Objective

5.1—Given a scenario, select the appropriate command line interface tool and interpret the output to verify functionality: **traceroute**, **ipconfig**, **ifconfig**, **ping**, **arp**, **nslookup**, **hostname**, **dig**, **mtr**, **route**, **nbtstat**, and **netstat**.

Description

The **pathping** command is a combination of the **ping** and **tracert** commands. It sends an ICMP echo request message to all routers and gateways along the path to the destination address. The results are quite detailed when compared with **ping** or **tracert** and help to identify the exact device causing the bottleneck. UNIX/Linux systems use a similar command as **pathping** called **mtr**.

Examples

Identify the source of network latency.

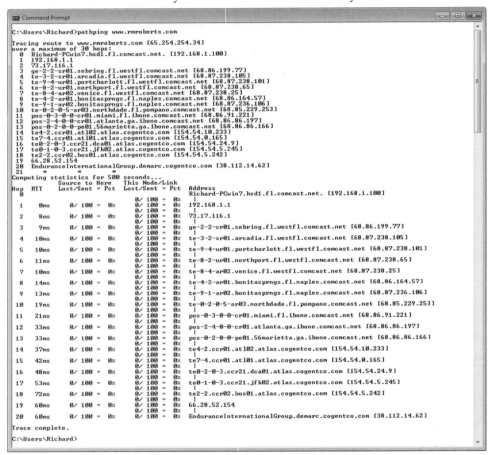

Related Concepts

IPv4 Address—1.3B

Routing Tables—1.6D

Router—3.1I

Troubleshooting Connectivity Issues—4.7A

Ping—5.1C

Next Hop—1.6C

NIC—3.1D

Network Troubleshooting Methodology—4.6A

Traceroute/Tracert—5.1A

Network+ Objective

5.1—Given a scenario, select the appropriate command line interface tool and interpret the output to verify functionality: **traceroute, ipconfig, ifconfig, ping, arp, nslookup, hostname, dig, mtr, route, nbtstat,** and **netstat**.

Description

The **route** command is used to view information contained in the local routing table. The **route print** command displays both IPv4 and IPv6 addresses, subnet masks, the default gateway, and the assigned IP address of the default gateway.

Examples

View information contained in the local routing table.

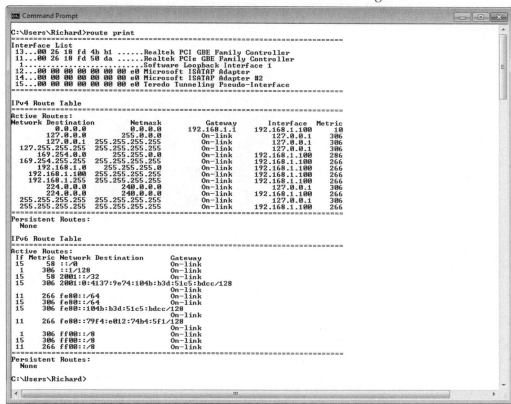

Related Concepts

IPv4 Address—1.3B

Next Hop—1.6C

Router—3.1I

Troubleshooting Connectivity Issues—4.7A

IPv6 Address—1.3C

Routing Tables—1.6D

Network Troubleshooting Methodology—4.6A

Pathping—5.1F

Network+ Objective

5.1—Given a scenario, select the appropriate command line interface tool and interpret the output to verify functionality: **traceroute**, **ipconfig**, **ifconfig**, **ping**, **arp**, **nslookup**, **hostname**, **dig**, **mtr**, **route**, **nbtstat**, and **netstat**.

Description

The **nbtstat** command displays NetBIOS over TCP/IP statistics and information gathered from broadcasts, NetBIOS cache, and WINS services. It can be a very handy tool for verifying that the WINS server is functioning properly or that NetBIOS over TCP has been configured correctly for the network interface card.

Examples

Verify WINS server is functioning.
Verify NetBIOS over TCP has been configured correctly.

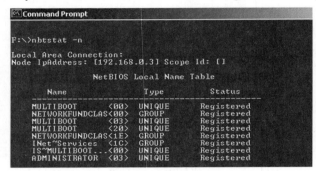

Related Concepts

IPv4 Address—1.3B	NIC—3.1D
Network Troubleshooting Methodology—4.6A	Troubleshooting Connectivity Issues—4.7A

Network+ Objective

5.1—Given a scenario, select the appropriate command line interface tool and interpret the output to verify functionality: **traceroute**, **ipconfig**, **ifconfig**, **ping**, **arp**, **nslookup**, **hostname**, **dig**, **mtr**, **route**, **nbtstat**, and **netstat**.

Description

The **netstat** command displays information about active TCP/IP connections. The **netstat** command displays Ethernet statistics for IP, TCP, ICMP, and UDP for IPv4 and IPv6. It can be used to determine network problems such as excessive broadcasts on the network. It also allows the user to monitor network connections.

Examples

Identify excessive broadcasts. Monitor network connections. Check the status of a service.

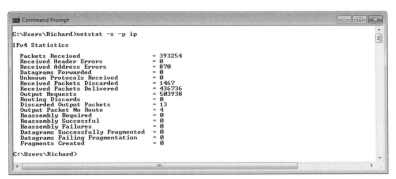

netstat switch	Description
-a	Displays all active TCP and UDP connections.
-e	Displays Ethernet statistics.
-f	Displays the Fully Qualified Domain Name (FQDN).
-n	Displays active TCP connections expressed numerically.
-p	Displays active connections for a specific protocol.
-s	Displays statistics by protocol.
-r	Displays contents of routing table.
/?	Displays help.

Related Concepts

Networking Protocols—1.1A

IPv4 Address—1.3B

Troubleshooting Connectivity Issues—4.7A

Port Numbers—1.2A

Network Troubleshooting Methodology—4.6A

Port Scanner—5.2D

Network+ Objective

5.1—Given a scenario, select the appropriate command line interface tool and interpret the output to verify functionality: **traceroute**, **ipconfig**, **ifconfig**, **ping**, **arp**, **nslookup**, **hostname**, **dig**, **mtr**, **route**, **nbtstat**, and **netstat**.

5.2A   Packet Sniffers

Description

A packet sniffer is a network monitoring utility that captures data packets as they travel across a network. A packet sniffer provides a vast amount of information such as packet size, protocol, and the source and destination address expressed as an IP address and a MAC address.

Examples

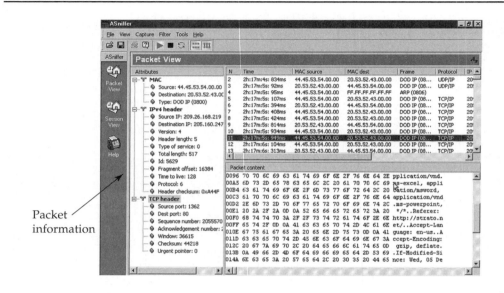

Packet information

Related Concepts

Networking Protocols—1.1A	Port Numbers—1.2A
MAC Address—1.3A	IPv4 Address—1.3B
IPv6 Address—1.3C	Network Monitoring Utilities—4.4A

Network+ Objective

5.2—Explain the purpose of network scanners: Packet sniffers, intrusion detection software, intrusion prevention software, and port scanners.

Description

An Intrusion Detection System (IDS) is a passive system, which only detects unauthorized activity. Microsoft Event Viewer is a type of IDS system. It monitors activities on a host computer but does not prevent unauthorized activity.

Examples

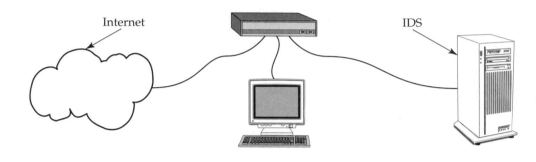

Related Concepts

Network Monitoring Utilities—4.4A   Intrusion Prevention System—5.2C

Port Scanner—5.2D

Network+ Objective

5.2—Explain the purpose of network scanners: Packet sniffers, intrusion detection software, intrusion prevention software, and port scanners.

Copyright by Goodheart-Willcox Co., Inc.

Description

An Intrusion Prevention System (IPS) is a reactive system, which means it not only detects unauthorized activity, it also performs some function to stop the activity. For example, most antivirus software programs not only detect unauthorized activity such as an attempt to download and install malware, they can also remove malware.

Examples

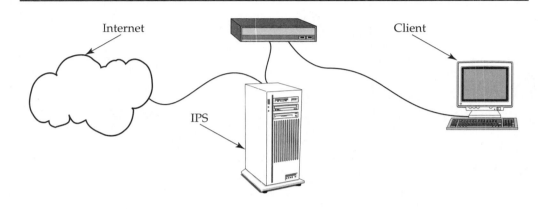

Related Concepts

Network Monitoring Utilities—4.4A	Intrusion Detection System—5.2B
Intrusion Detection and Intrusion Prevention Systems—6.1A	Common Firewall Features—6.2A
Antivirus Software—6.6H	

Network+ Objective

5.2—Explain the purpose of network scanners: Packet sniffers, intrusion detection software, intrusion prevention software, and port scanners.

Description

A port scanner is a software program that scans a network's TCP/IP ports to uncover open unused ports. Open ports can be a way for intruders to gain access to the network system. Open ports are one of the most common security problems for any site. All unused ports should be closed, and all ports should be monitored for activity. A third-party utility or the **netstat** utility can be used to check for open ports.

Examples

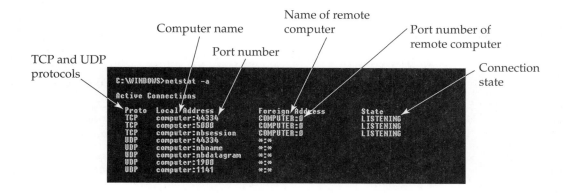

Related Concepts

Port Numbers—1.2A

Netstat—5.1I

Intrusion Detection and Intrusion Prevention Systems—6.1A

Network Monitoring Utilities—4.4A

Intrusion Detection System—5.2B

Network+ Objective

5.2—Explain the purpose of network scanners: Packet sniffers, intrusion detection software, intrusion prevention software, and port scanners.

Copyright by Goodheart-Willcox Co., Inc.

Description

Troubleshooting requires not only knowledge about the various utilities and tools available, but also their application.

Examples

Tool	Application
Cable tester	A network cable tester performs a series of checks of cable integrity. Cable faults such as opens, shorts, and grounds can be quickly determined and located. Many cable testers can also check for crosstalk, radio interference, EMI, and excessive cable lengths and can determine the exact location of a cable fault.
Protocol analyzer	Used to capture and monitor data frames traveling across the network media. While most protocol analyzers monitor only TCP/IP, more sophisticated protocol analyzers can monitor hundreds of different protocols.
TDR	Used to test copper core network cable by sending an electronic pulse down the copper core cable and then reads signal bounce to locate cable faults.
OTDR	Used to locate faults in the fiber-optic cable core.
Toner probe	Used to trace the exact location of cable runs inside walls, ceilings, or under the floor or to identify unmarked cables.
Punch down tool	Used for pushing individual twisted pair wires into an insulation-displacement connector (IDC) and automatically trimming conductor excess.
Cable stripper	Used to strip the insulation from a cable.
Snips	Used to cut cable.

Related Concepts

Network Troubleshooting Methodology—4.6A

Troubleshooting Connectivity Issues—4.7A

Network+ Objective

5.3—Given a scenario, utilize the appropriate hardware tools: Cable testers, protocol analyzer, certifiers, TDR, OTDR, multimeter, toner probe, butt set, punch down tool, cable stripper, snips, voltage event recorder, and temperature monitor.

Description

All security protection systems, both software and hardware, can be classified as either Intrusion Detection System (IDS) or Intrusion Prevention System (IPS). The detection system can be either host-based or network-based. A host-based system is installed on the individual computer and monitors and prevents unauthorized activity. Network-based systems monitor and protect the entire network.

Examples

Security System	IDS/IPS Classification	Function
Network-based firewall	IPS	Passes or blocks packets as they enter or leave a network system.
Host-based firewall	IPS	Passes or blocks packets as they enter or leave the host device.
VPN concentrator	IPS	Creates a private connection over a public network. PPTP, L2F, L2TP, and IPSec protocols allow a VPN to provide four basic features common to all VPN connections: authentication, access control, confidentiality, and data integrity.

Related Concepts

Network Monitoring Utilities—4.4A   Netstat—5.1I

Intrusion Detection System—5.2B   Intrusion Prevention System—5.2C

Port Scanner—5.2D   Common Firewall Features—6.2A

Antivirus Software—6.6H

Network+ Objective

6.1—Explain the function of hardware and software security devices: Network-based firewall, host-based firewall, IDS, IPS, and VPN concentrator.

Common Firewall Features

Description

There are several classifications of firewalls, such as packet filter, application gateway, content filter, and circuit level gateway. A typical firewall consists of two or more filtering techniques. Often, network devices are identified as performing firewall functions in addition to their intended purpose. For example, a network gateway can also perform functions associated with a firewall by filtering packets based on IP address, port number, or MAC address.

Examples

Firewall Feature	Function
Application gateway	Provides security for specific applications such as FTP and Telnet.
Circuit-level gateway	Monitors a connection until the connection is successfully established between the destination and source host. After the connection is established, packets can flow freely between the two hosts.
Content filter	Provides security based on the packet contents.
DMZ	The area of a network that permits access from a host located outside the local area network. It is not protected by the firewall.
Firewall signature identification	Works in similar fashion as antivirus protection by intercepting a packet and comparing it to specific malware attributes. When the attributes match, it removes the packet.
Packet filter	Inspects each packet as it passes through the firewall and then accepts or rejects the packet based on a set of rules.
Stateful packet inspection	Inspects the sequence of packets in order to detect missing packets or an altered sequence of packets.
Stateless packet inspection	Inspects and filters attributes such as IP address, port number, and protocols.

Related Concepts

Port Numbers—1.2A   MAC Address—1.3A

IPv4 Address—1.3B   IPv6 Address—1.3C

Firewall—3.1J   Multifunction Network Devices—3.2D

Network+ Objective

6.2—Explain common features of a firewall: Application layer vs. network layer, stateful vs. stateless, scanning services, content filtering, signature identification, and zones.

Description

A Media Access Control (MAC) filter is a feature that allows or restricts WAP access based on the MAC address of a wireless network card. To set up a MAC filter, an administrator creates an Access Control List (ACL). The ACL contains a list of MAC addresses belonging to authorized wireless network devices. The ACL is stored in the Wireless Access Point (WAP). When a wireless network device attempts to access the network through the WAP, the WAP checks the ACL to see if the wireless network device is authorized to access the network.

Examples

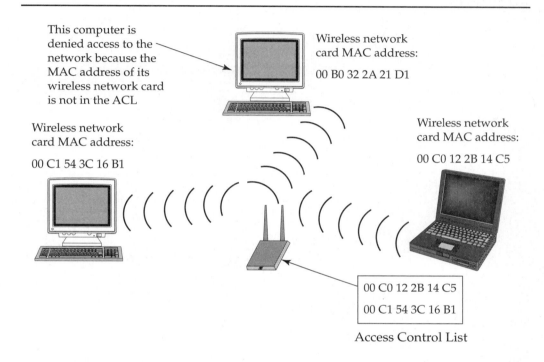

This computer is denied access to the network because the MAC address of its wireless network card is not in the ACL

Wireless network card MAC address:

00 C1 54 3C 16 B1

Wireless network card MAC address:

00 B0 32 2A 21 D1

Wireless network card MAC address:

00 C0 12 2B 14 C5

00 C0 12 2B 14 C5
00 C1 54 3C 16 B1

Access Control List

Related Concepts

MAC Address—1.3A	802.11 a/b/g/n—1.7A
Authentication—1.7B	NIC—3.1D
Wireless Access Point—3.1H	

Network+ Objective

6.3—Explain the methods of network access security: Filtering (ACL, MAC filtering, IP filtering), tunneling and encryption (SSL VPN, L2TP, PPTP, IPSec), and remote access (RAS, RDP, PPPoE, PPP, VNC, ICA).

Description

Security Sockets Layer (SSL) is a security protocol used to authenticate clients and servers and to encrypt data. SSL was first introduced and developed by Netscape Communications Corporation. It was designed to secure transactions between Web servers and individuals using the Internet for such purposes as credit card transactions.

Examples

Indicates
Web Server is
using SSL

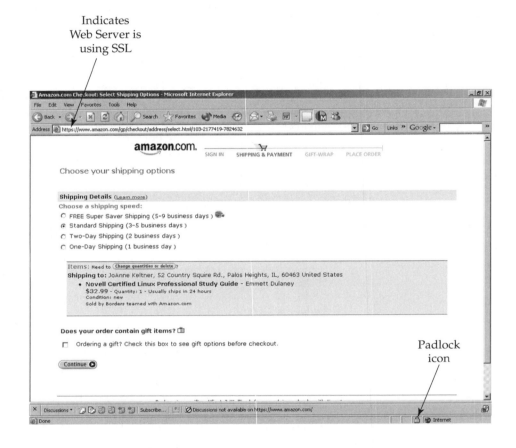

Padlock
icon

Related Concepts

Port Numbers—1.2A	HTTPS—6.5B

Network+ Objective

6.3—Explain the methods of network access security: Filtering (ACL, MAC filtering, IP filtering), tunneling and encryption (SSL VPN, L2TP, PPTP, IPSec), and remote access (RAS, RDP, PPPoE, PPP, VNC, ICA).

Description   Layer 2 Tunneling Protocol (L2TP) is a tunneling protocol that uses IPSec to encrypt the contents of the encapsulated PPP protocol.

Examples

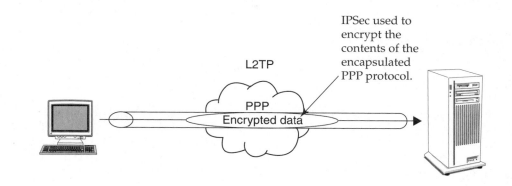

IPSec used to encrypt the contents of the encapsulated PPP protocol.

L2TP

PPP
Encrypted data

Related Concepts

IPSec—6.3E   PPP—6.3I

Network+ Objective

6.3—Explain the methods of network access security: Filtering (ACL, MAC filtering, IP filtering), tunneling and encryption (SSL VPN, L2TP, PPTP, IPSec), and remote access (RAS, RDP, PPPoE, PPP, VNC, ICA).

Description

Point-to-Point Tunneling Protocol (PPTP) is a remote access protocol that is an enhanced version of PPP. It is designed to enhance security and to make use of a virtually private network using the public Internet.

Examples

Related Concepts

VPN—2.7C   PPP—6.3I

Network+ Objective

6.3—Explain the methods of network access security: Filtering (ACL, MAC filtering, IP filtering), tunneling and encryption (SSL VPN, L2TP, PPTP, IPSec), and remote access (RAS, RDP, PPPoE, PPP, VNC, ICA).

Description

Security (IPSec) is an IETF standard for securing point-to-point connections in an IP-based network using encryption techniques. There are two standard modes of IPSec implementation: transport mode and tunnel mode. In tunnel mode, the payload and the header, which contains routing information, is encrypted. In transport mode, only the payload is encrypted. Some of the more common security technologies that can be implemented with IPSec are ESP, IKE, AH, MDS, SHA-1, 3DES, AES, and more. The two common protocols associated with IPSec are Encapsulated Security Payload (ESP) and Authentication Header (AH). Authentication can also be verified using Kerberos, a preshared key, or digital certificate.

Examples

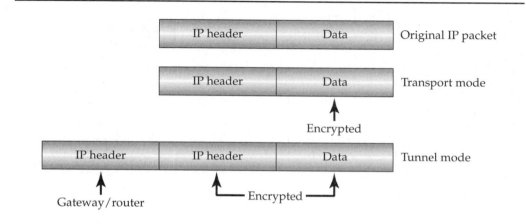

Related Concepts

VPN—2.7C

Network+ Objective

6.3—Explain the methods of network access security: Filtering (ACL, MAC filtering, IP filtering), tunneling and encryption (SSL VPN, L2TP, PPTP, IPSec), and remote access (RAS, RDP, PPPoE, PPP, VNC, ICA).

Description

The Remote Access Service (RAS) allows users to dial into a remote access server and use the network as if their computers were on the remote access user's LAN.

Examples

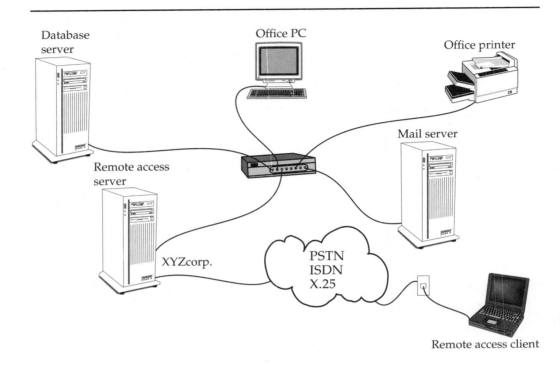

Related Concepts

T-Carrier—2.5C   POTS/PSTN—2.5K

Network+ Objective

6.3—Explain the methods of network access security: Filtering (ACL, MAC filtering, IP filtering), tunneling and encryption (SSL VPN, L2TP, PPTP, IPSec), and remote access (RAS, RDP, PPPoE, PPP, VNC, ICA).

Description

The Remote Desktop Protocol (RDP) is a presentation protocol that allows Windows computers to communicate directly with Windows-based clients. The Remote Desktop Protocol is transmitted across any TCP/IP connection. RDP provides security by encrypting the contents of packets sent across the TCP/IP network. Port 3389 is the default port used for RDP and must be opened when a firewall is used.

Examples

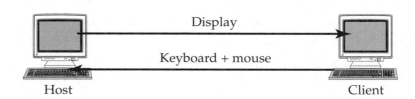

Host   Client

Related Concepts

Port Numbers—1.2A   Firewall—3.1J

PPP—6.3I

Network+ Objective

6.3—Explain the methods of network access security: Filtering (ACL, MAC filtering, IP filtering), tunneling and encryption (SSL VPN, L2TP, PPTP, IPSec), and remote access (RAS, RDP, PPPoE, PPP, VNC, ICA).

Description

Point-to-Point Protocol over Ethernet (PPPoE) provides one or more hosts on an Ethernet network the ability to establish an individual PPP connection with an ISP. PPPoE frames the PPP protocol so that the PPP frame can travel over an Ethernet network.

Examples

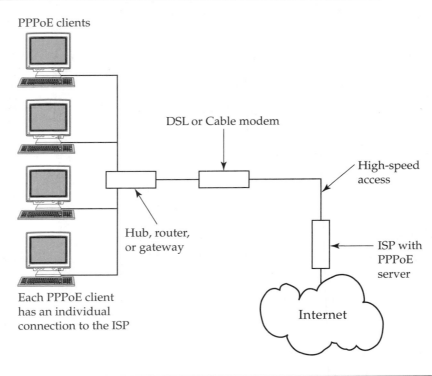

PPPoE clients

DSL or Cable modem

High-speed access

Hub, router, or gateway

ISP with PPPoE server

Each PPPoE client has an individual connection to the ISP

Internet

Related Concepts

NAT—1.4D	xDSL—2.5D
Cable Modem—2.5E	PPP—6.3I

Network+ Objective

6.3—Explain the methods of network access security: Filtering (ACL, MAC filtering, IP filtering), tunneling and encryption (SSL VPN, L2TP, PPTP, IPSec), and remote access (RAS, RDP, PPPoE, PPP, VNC, ICA).

Description

Point-to-Point Protocol (PPP) enables a PC to connect to a remote network using a serial line connection, typically through a telephone line. It can support multiple protocols such as IPX, AppleTalk, and TCP/IP.

Examples

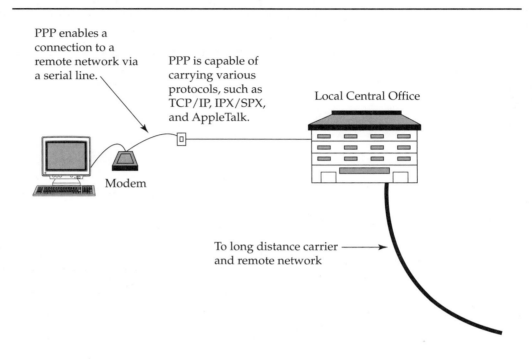

PPP enables a connection to a remote network via a serial line.

PPP is capable of carrying various protocols, such as TCP/IP, IPX/SPX, and AppleTalk.

Local Central Office

Modem

To long distance carrier and remote network

Related Concepts

Networking Protocols—1.1A   POTS/PSTN—2.5K

Network+ Objective

6.3—Explain the methods of network access security: Filtering (ACL, MAC filtering, IP filtering), tunneling and encryption (SSL VPN, L2TP, PPTP, IPSec), and remote access (RAS, RDP, PPPoE, PPP, VNC, ICA).

Description

A virtual network connection (VNC) is a term used to describe the broad category of remote connection systems that allow a user to connect to a network device, such as a server or a desktop computer from a remote device such as a laptop, palmtop, or cell phone. Typically, the user attaches to the remote network either wirelessly or through an Internet connection. Because the remote user is not actually a physical part of the network the user is accessing, the connection is considered "virtual."

Examples

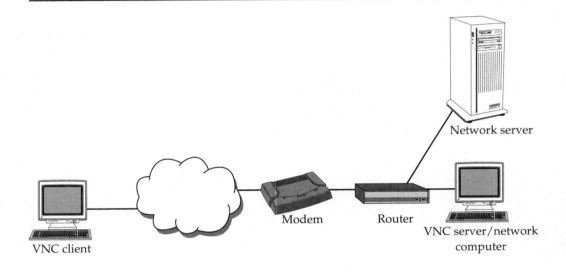

Network server

Modem   Router

VNC client   VNC server/network computer

Related Concepts

RDP—6.3G	ICA—6.3K

Network+ Objective

6.3—Explain the methods of network access security: Filtering (ACL, MAC filtering, IP filtering), tunneling and encryption (SSL VPN, L2TP, PPTP, IPSec), and remote access (RAS, RDP, PPPoE, PPP, VNC, ICA).

Description

Independent Computer Architecture (ICA) is a proprietary protocol designed by Citrix Systems to support the exchange of software applications between a server and client. Citrix ICA and Microsoft Remote Desktop Protocol (RDP) are the two main choices for this application.

Examples

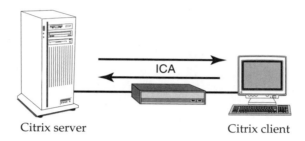

Citrix server   Citrix client

Related Concepts

RDP—6.3G

Network+ Objective

6.3—Explain the methods of network access security: Filtering (ACL, MAC filtering, IP filtering), tunneling and encryption (SSL VPN, L2TP, PPTP, IPSec), and remote access (RAS, RDP, PPPoE, PPP, VNC, ICA).

Description

Public Key Infrastructure (PKI) is the use of public keys (encryption keys) to create a secure environment for the exchange of data between network devices. PKI is a form of encryption and authentication. There are two main types of key encryption methods: symmetric-key encryption and asymmetric-key encryption.

Examples

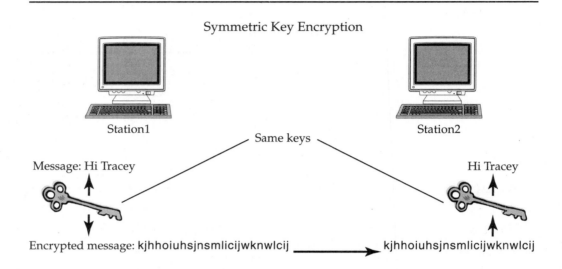

Symmetric Key Encryption

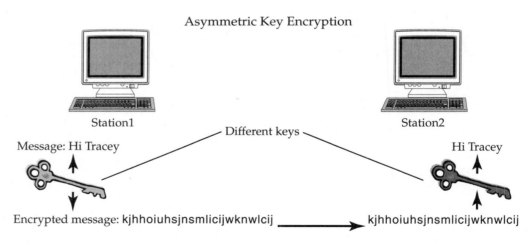

Asymmetric Key Encryption

Related Concepts

Kerberos—6.4B	AAA—6.4C
RADIUS—6.4D	TACACS+—6.4E
802.1x—6.4F	CHAP and MS-CHAP—6.4G
EAP—6.4H	

Network+ Objective

6.4—Explain methods of user authentication: PKI, Kerberos, AAA (RADIUS, TACACS+), network access control (802.1x), CHAP, MS-CHAP, and EAP.

Description

Kerberos is a security authentication system that provides both authentication and encryption services. It uses a two-way method of authentication.

Examples

Kerberos

Credit card number:
123-4567-7890

Data before the encryption key is applied

Encryption key

Tofh&l(l)pWSth47%m%fk&
gd!~sjiFkbL80DgBW$fJ^g
KLA#&GH48Ui(m0E3gHB

Data after the encryption key is applied

Tofh&l(l)pWSth47%m%fk&
gd!~sjiFkbL80DgBW$fJ^g
KLA#&GH48Ui(m0E3gHB

Data transmitted in encrypted form

Decryption key

Credit card number:
123-4567-7890

Data after decryption key is applied

Related Concepts

PKI—6.4A	AAA—6.4C
RADIUS—6.4D	TACACS+—6.4E
802.1x—6.4F	CHAP and MS-CHAP—6.4G
EAP—6.4H	

Network+ Objective

6.4—Explain methods of user authentication: PKI, Kerberos, AAA (RADIUS, TACACS+), network access control (802.1x), CHAP, MS-CHAP, and EAP.

Description

Authentication, Authorization, and Accounting (AAA), also known as *triple A*, is a security standard that consists of three parts: authentication, authorization, and accounting. *Authentication* is the process of verifying the identity of the user. It incorporates various authentication models typically designed around a user name and user password. *Authorization* is the process of identifying which system resources a user may use. User share permissions are an example of authorization. *Accounting* is a system that tracks what resources a user accesses and keeps a record of user activity.

Examples

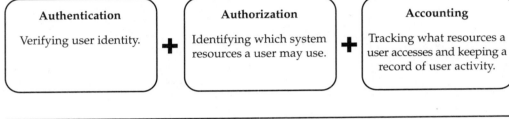

Authentication		Authorization		Accounting
Verifying user identity.	**+**	Identifying which system resources a user may use.	**+**	Tracking what resources a user accesses and keeping a record of user activity.

Related Concepts

PKI—6.4A   Kerberos—6.4B

RADIUS—6.4D   TACACS+—6.4E

802.1x—6.4F   CHAP and MS-CHAP—6.4G

EAP—6.4H

Network+ Objective

6.4—Explain methods of user authentication: PKI, Kerberos, AAA (RADIUS, TACACS+), network access control (802.1x), CHAP, MS-CHAP, and EAP.

Description

Remote Authentication Dial-In User Service (RADIUS) is a service that allows remote access servers to authenticate to a central server. RADIUS is referred to as a "port authentication" standard. Microsoft refers to it as an "802.1x security standard." 802.1x requires three components: supplicant, authenticator, and authentication server. The *supplicant* is the wireless network device that is requesting network access. The WAP functions as the *authenticator* and does not allow any type of access to the network without proper authentication. A server running Remote Authentication Dial-In User Service (RADIUS) acts as the *authentication server*.

Examples

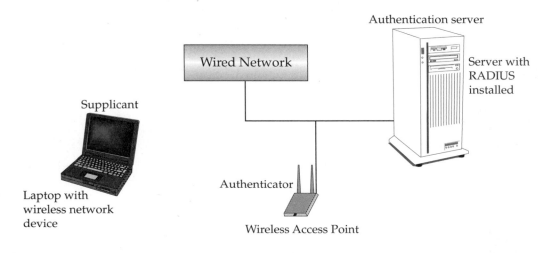

Related Concepts

PKI—6.4A	Kerberos—6.4B
AAA—6.4C	TACACS+—6.4E
802.1x—6.4F	CHAP and MS-CHAP—6.4G
EAP—6.4H	

Network+ Objective

6.4—Explain methods of user authentication: PKI, Kerberos, AAA (RADIUS, TACACS+), network access control (802.1x), CHAP, MS-CHAP, and EAP.

Copyright by Goodheart-Willcox Co., Inc.

Description

TACACS+ is a Cisco proprietary client/server security method that directs client requests to the authentication server in similar fashion as Microsoft RADIUS. It is an alternative to RADIUS for security.

Examples

RADIUS	TACACS+
Uses connectionless UDP.	Uses connection-oriented TCP.
Uses one database for authentication, authorization, and accounting.	Uses separate databases for authentication, authorization, and accounting.
Encrypts only the password.	Encrypts the entire exchange of logon packets.
Uses a token-based authentication method.	Uses a token-based authentication method.

Related Concepts

PKI—6.4A	Kerberos—6.4B
AAA—6.4C	RADIUS—6.4D
802.1x—6.4F	CHAP and MS-CHAP—6.4G
EAP—6.4H	

Network+ Objective

6.4—Explain methods of user authentication: PKI, Kerberos, AAA (RADIUS, TACACS+), network access control (802.1x), CHAP, MS-CHAP, and EAP.

Description

802.1x provides port-based, network access control, which supports authentication for Ethernet network access. 802.1x is primarily used for client/server-based networks. It allows the network server to authenticate a wireless network device when the wireless network device attempts to connect to the wired network through a WAP. 802.1x requires three components: supplicant, authenticator, and authentication server.

Examples

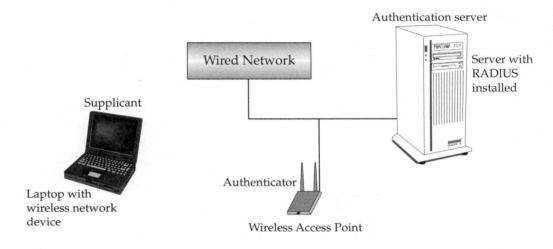

Related Concepts

PKI—6.4A	Kerberos—6.4B
AAA—6.4C	RADIUS—6.4D
TACACS+—6.4E	CHAP and MS-CHAP—6.4G
EAP—6.4H	

Network+ Objective

6.4—Explain methods of user authentication: PKI, Kerberos, AAA (RADIUS, TACACS+), network access control (802.1x), CHAP, MS-CHAP, and EAP.

Copyright by Goodheart-Willcox Co., Inc.

Description

Challenge Handshake Authentication Protocol (CHAP) is an authentication protocol that sends an encrypted string of characters representing the user name and password. It does not send the actual user name and password. Microsoft Challenge Handshake Authentication Protocol (MS-CHAP) is an enhanced version of CHAP that encrypts not only the user name and password but also the data package. MS-CHAP must be used with Microsoft operating systems.

Examples

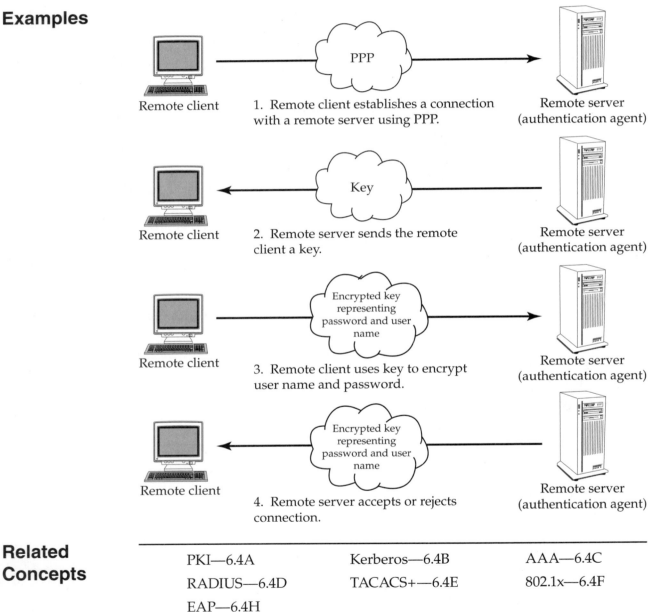

Remote client   1. Remote client establishes a connection with a remote server using PPP.   Remote server (authentication agent)

Remote client   2. Remote server sends the remote client a key.   Remote server (authentication agent)

Remote client   3. Remote client uses key to encrypt user name and password.   Remote server (authentication agent)

Remote client   4. Remote server accepts or rejects connection.   Remote server (authentication agent)

Related Concepts

PKI—6.4A	Kerberos—6.4B	AAA—6.4C
RADIUS—6.4D	TACACS+—6.4E	802.1x—6.4F
EAP—6.4H		

Network+ Objective

6.4—Explain methods of user authentication: PKI, Kerberos, AAA (RADIUS, TACACS+), network access control (802.1x), CHAP, MS-CHAP, and EAP.

Description

Extensible Authentication Protocol (EAP) ensures authorized access to the network system and network resources. It is used on both wired and wireless network systems. There are numerous variations of the original EAP standard such as EAP-MD5, EAP-TLS, EAP-IKEv2, EAP-AKA, EAP-FAST, and EAP-SIM. The most commonly encountered variations are PEAP and LEAP.

Examples

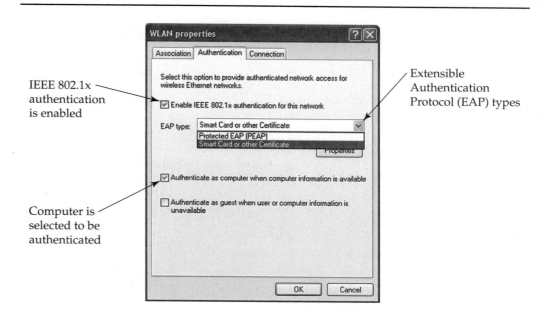

IEEE 802.1x authentication is enabled

Extensible Authentication Protocol (EAP) types

Computer is selected to be authenticated

Related Concepts

PKI—6.4A	Kerberos—6.4B	AAA—6.4C
RADIUS—6.4D	TACACS+—6.4E	802.1x—6.4F
CHAP and MS-CHAP—6.4G		

Network+ Objective

6.4—Explain methods of user authentication: PKI, Kerberos, AAA (RADIUS, TACACS+), network access control (802.1x), CHAP, MS-CHAP, and EAP.

Description

Secure Shell (SSH) provides secure network services over an insecure network medium, such as the Internet. SSH was originally designed for UNIX systems to replace Remote Login (**rlogin**), Remote Shell (**rsh**), and Remote Copy (**rcp**). SSH is associated with TCP/IP port 22. It requires the use of a private and a public key and a password.

Examples

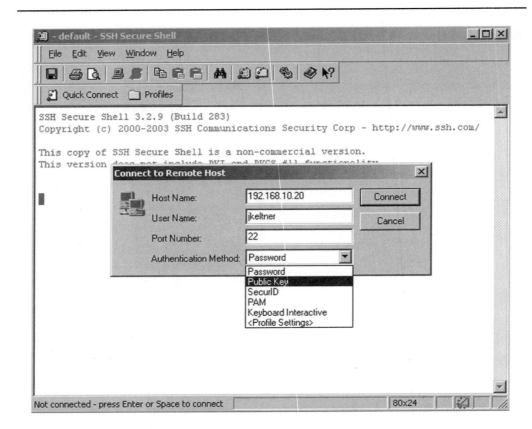

Related Concepts

Networking Protocols—1.1A	Port Numbers—1.2A
SFTP—6.5D	SCP—6.5E

Network+ Objective

6.5—Explain issues that affect device security: Physical security, restricting local and remote access, and secure methods vs. unsecure methods (SSH, HTTPS, SNMPv3, SFTP, SCP, Telnet, HTTP, FTP, RSH, RCP, SNMPv1/2).

Description

The Hypertext Transport Protocol over SSL (HTTPS) is designed for secure communications between a Web browser and a Web server. When a secure connection is used, the protocol in the Web address is identified with "https" rather than "http." The *s* at the end of *http* indicates a secure site. HTTPS uses the Secure Sockets Layer (SSL) security protocol.

Examples

Indicates a secure connection

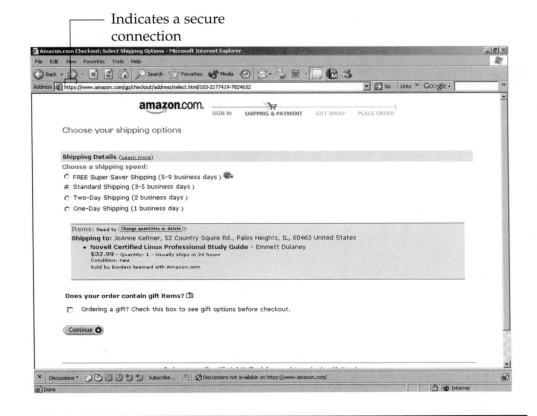

Related Concepts

Networking Protocols—1.1A   Port Numbers—1.2A

SSL—6.3B

Network+ Objective

6.5—Explain issues that affect device security: Physical security, restricting local and remote access, and secure methods vs. unsecure methods (SSH, HTTPS, SNMPv3, SFTP, SCP, Telnet, HTTP, FTP, RSH, RCP, SNMPv1/2).

Description

Simple Network Management Protocol (SNMP) enables an administrator to manage and monitor network devices and services from a single location. SNMP can monitor network devices such as servers, workstations, hubs, and routers, and services such as DHCP and WINS. An SNMP service consists of an SNMP management system and SNMP agents. The SNMP management system queries SNMP agents for information, such as the status and configuration of network devices and services. The SNMP agents gather this information and store it in a management information base (MIB).

Examples

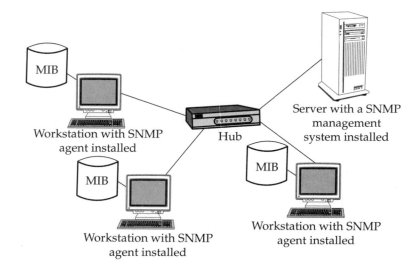

Related Concepts

Networking Protocols—1.1A	Port Numbers—1.2A

Network+ Objective

6.5—Explain issues that affect device security: Physical security, restricting local and remote access, and secure methods vs. unsecure methods (SSH, HTTPS, SNMPv3, SFTP, SCP, Telnet, HTTP, FTP, RSH, RCP, SNMPv1/2).

Description

Secure File Transfer Protocol (SFTP) is a secure version of FTP that encrypts the user name, password, and data to provide the highest level of security compared to FTP and TFTP. SFTP should be used when transferring sensitive data and when security is required.

Examples

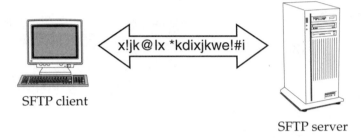

User name, password, and data are encrypted.

x!jk@lx *kdixjkwe!#i

SFTP client

SFTP server

Related Concepts

Networking Protocols—1.1A   Port Numbers—1.2A

FTP—6.5G

Network+ Objective

6.5—Explain issues that affect device security: Physical security, restricting local and remote access, and secure methods vs. unsecure methods (SSH, HTTPS, SNMPv3, SFTP, SCP, Telnet, HTTP, FTP, RSH, RCP, SNMPv1/2).

Description

Secure Copy Protocol (SCP) provides a secure way of transferring files between computers. It is the replacement for **rcp**.

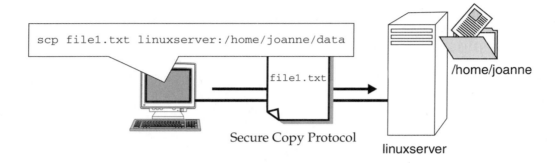

```
scp file1.txt linuxserver:/home/joanne/data
```

file1.txt

/home/joanne

Secure Copy Protocol

linuxserver

Related Concepts

Networking Protocols—1.1A	Port Numbers—1.2A
SSH—6.5A	SFTP—6.5D

Network+ Objective

6.5—Explain issues that affect device security: Physical security, restricting local and remote access, and secure methods vs. unsecure methods (SSH, HTTPS, SNMPv3, SFTP, SCP, Telnet, HTTP, FTP, RSH, RCP, SNMPv1/2).

Description

The Hypertext Transfer Protocol (HTTP) is a protocol designed for communication between a Web browser and a Web Server.

Examples

Web browser

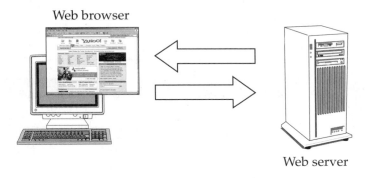

Web server

Related Concepts

Networking Protocols—1.1A	Port Numbers—1.2A
HTTPS—6.5B	

Network+ Objective

6.5—Explain issues that affect device security: Physical security, restricting local and remote access, and secure methods vs. unsecure methods (SSH, HTTPS, SNMPv3, SFTP, SCP, Telnet, HTTP, FTP, RSH, RCP, SNMPv1/2).

Description

File Transfer Protocol (FTP) is a service that can be incorporated into a Web server to support file transfers between a client and server. It is often used to upload Web pages to Web hosting servers. FTP is accessed using an FTP client that is either text-based or GUI-based. When using a text-based FTP client, a series of commands are issued at an FTP prompt similar to the way commands are issued at a DOS prompt.

Examples

FTP Command	Description
bye	Exit the FTP program.
cd/directory	Change the directory on the FTP site.
get	Transfer a file from the FTP site to the client.
help	Display FTP commands.
lcd	Change the directory on the client.
open	Open a connection to an FTP site.
put	Transfer a file from the client to the FTP site.
pwd	Display the current directory of the FTP site.
quit	Close the FTP session.

Related Concepts

Networking Protocols—1.1A   Port Numbers—1.2A

SFTP—6.5D

Network+ Objective

6.5—Explain issues that affect device security: Physical security, restricting local and remote access, and secure methods vs. unsecure methods (SSH, HTTPS, SNMPv3, SFTP, SCP, Telnet, HTTP, FTP, RSH, RCP, SNMPv1/2).